Body
Mind
Spirit

Body
Mind
Spirit

Exploring the Parapsychology of Spirituality

Edited by
Charles T. Tart

Cover design by Jonah Tobias

Chapters 1, 3, 4, 7, 8, and 9 originally appeared in a special
Summer 1995 issue of *ReVision*, a publication of the
Heldref Foundation, devoted to parapsychology and spirituality,
and reproduced here by permission of the Heldref Foundation.

For information write:

Hampton Roads Publishing Company, Inc.
134 Burgess Lane
Charlottesville, VA 22902

Or call: (804)296-2772
FAX: (804)296-5096
e-mail: hrpc@hrpub.com
Web site: http://www.hrpub.com

If you are unable to order this book from your local
bookseller, you may order directly from the publisher.
Quantity discounts for organizations are available.
Call 1-800-766-8009, toll-free.

ISBN 1-57174-073-2

10 9 8 7 6 5 4 3 2 1

Printed on acid-free paper in the United States of America

This volume has been made possible
by the help of many people,
especially my wife Judy
and the Heldref Foundation.

Contents

Contributors

William Braud, Ph.D., absorbed natural science methods and viewpoints as an undergraduate physics major (one of his mentors was a student of the discoverer of cosmic rays). In his doctoral work in experimental psychology at the University of Iowa, he was trained in the behavioral and hypothetico-deductive approaches of learning theory, and studied philosophy of science, epistemology, and ontology with Gustav Bergmann, a member of the Vienna Circle of logical positivists. With colleagues at the University of Houston, the Psychiatric and Psychosomatic Research Laboratory of the VA Hospital (Houston, Texas), and Baylor University College of Medicine, he supplemented his behavioral approaches to learning, memory, and motivation with clinical, psychophysiological, and pharmacological methods. In 1975, he left his tenured university position to pursue studies at a private research laboratory (Mind Science Foundation, San Antonio, Texas), where he developed new methods for exploring topics in biofeedback, physiological self-regulation, altered states of consciousness, and parapsychology. With collaborators at the Stehlin Cancer Research Foundation (Houston) and at the University of Texas Health Science Center (San Antonio), he conducted studies in the then-new field of psychoneuroimmunology. These studies demonstrated the power of mental processes of relaxation and quietude, attention, intention, imagery, and self-evoked positive emotions in directly influencing one's mind and body and in influencing remote animate and inanimate systems.

Within parapsychology, Braud is known internationally for his experimental work on physiological and psychological conditions favorable to psychic functioning. He presented the first paper on using the ganzfeld (sensory restriction) procedure to facilitate telepathy (at the First International Congress of Parapsychology and Psychotronics, Prague, Czechoslovakia, 1973), and his early studies of relaxation, lability, and other psi-conducive states and conditions are well-known and frequently cited. He conducted extensive research programs in direct mental interactions with living systems in which mental processes of intention, attention, and imagery are used to influence activities of distant living organisms such as behaviors, physiological activities, rate of breakdown of human red blood cells, and mental processes in other persons (mental imagery, attention, concentration). He views these latter studies as laboratory analogs of distant healing, and he is especially interested in possible practical applications of psychic functioning and the implication that inner mental "work" on the part of one person may directly facilitate related functioning on the part of someone else in educational, counseling, therapeutic, health-related, and training contexts. The spiritual traditions that speak most strongly to Braud are early Taoism, esoteric Eastern Christianity, and the perennial wisdom found in all mystical traditions.

In 1992, Braud joined the Institute of Transpersonal Psychology (Palo Alto, California) as Professor, Research Director, and Co-Director of the Institute's William James Center for Consciousness Studies. Here, he teaches research courses, supervises doctoral dissertation work, and conducts his own research in three major areas: studies of time-displaced direct mental influences of remote living systems; the impacts of exceptional human experiences (especially mystical/unitive and psychic) upon physical, psychological, and spiritual health, well-being, development, and transformation; and research on innovative and more transpersonally-relevant research approaches.

Braud has published his methods and findings in nearly 200 articles in professional journals and book chapters (including papers in *Science*) and has made nearly 200 presentations of his work at national and international meetings and conferences. He belongs to numerous professional organizations and serves on the editorial advisory boards of several scientific journals. With colleagues at the Institute of Transpersonal Psychology, he is presently preparing a book describing novel research methods for the social sciences.

Stephen E. Braude, Ph.D., is Professor of Philosophy at the University of Maryland Baltimore County. He began his career in philosophy writing in the areas of philosophy of language, temporal logic, and the philosophy of time. After that, he turned his attention to the evidence of parapsychology and the philosophy of science, writing two books and numerous articles on those topics. Since 1986, Braude has also been studying dissociation and multiple personality, and their connection to classic philosophical problems as well as to central problems in parapsychology (such as the relationship between multiple personality and mediumship or channeling). He is currently writing a book on postmortem survival, and he is also continuing recent research on dissociation and moral responsibility, as well as the so-called false memory debate.

Braude is a past president of the Parapsychological Association and the recipient of several grants and fellowships, including a Research Fellowship from the National Endowment for the Humanities. He has written three books: *ESP and Psychokinesis: A Philosophical Examination* (1979), *The Limits of Influence: Psychokinesis and the Philosophy of Science* (1996), and *First Person Plural: Multiple Personality and the Philosophy of Mind* (1991).

Braude is actively engaged in parapsychological case investigations and is particularly interested in observable (and large-scale) psychokinesis and poltergeist cases. He is also interested in tracing the connections between psychopathology and psychic functioning. He suspects that these connections are more important and pervasive than most parapsychologists have appreciated, and that attention to them may shed light on long-standing puzzles about the evidence for postmortem survival.

Braude is also a professional pianist and composer, as well as a prize-winning stereo photographer.

Hoyt L. Edge, Ph.D., is Professor of Philosophy at Rollins College in Winter Park, Florida, having taught there since 1970, where he offers courses in the areas of philosophy of mind, extended human capabilities, cognitive anthropology, existentialism, and American pragmatism.

In addition to recently publishing a book, *A Constructive Postmodern Perspective on Self and Community: From Atomism to Holism* (1994), he has co-authored the text *Foundations of Parapsychology* (1986) and has co-edited *Philosophical Dimensions of Parapsychology* (1976).

His numerous articles in parapsychology include both experimental studies and essays in the philosophical implications of parapsychology. Edge is particularly interested in what parapsychology has to say about human nature and about the natural world. Believing that the modern world, including parapsychology, has been too dualistically oriented, he is especially interested in reconceiving these notions.

As part of this study, Edge has recently focused on cross-cultural studies and has engaged in concentrated research on the Australian Aborigines and the natives of Bali, examining their general world-views, and especially their concepts of self. As part of this work, Edge has investigated the place of psi in these cultures and has published on Balinese mediumship and researched traditional Balinese healing.

Edge is a past president of the Parapsychological Association and has served a number of years on the Board of Trustees of the American Society for Psychical Research.

Michael Grosso, Ph.D., studied classics and received his doctorate in philosophy at Columbia University. During his years as a student he had a series of puzzling experiences that later led him to investigate the paranormal. He has taught philosophy and the humanities at City University New York, John Kennedy University, and Marymount Manhattan College, and is currently the Chairman of Philosophy and Religion at Jersey City State College, where he teaches philosophy and the humanities.

Grosso has studied transpersonal psychology, psychical research, art, and the creative process. He traveled to Italy to do research on Padre Pio several times. He has listened attentively to people who have had anomalous experiences of every type for the past twenty-five years. His writings, talks, and workshops center around these topics, especially the parapsychology of religion and, lately, work on mediumship and surrealism. He is the author of *The Final Choice*, *Soulmaker* (his psychic autobiography), *Frontiers of the Soul*, and *The Millennium Myth.* The last book looks at the way mythology and the paranormal have influenced history. He recently won the Alexander Imich Prize for the best essay on the topic Miracles: Illusions, Natural Events, or Divine Interventions?

Grosso is currently working on a monograph for the Institute of Noetic Sciences on the evidence, problems, and paradigms of survival research.

He lives with his wife and extended family in bucolic Warwick, New York. In 1995 he built a studio on an old dog house, where he has resumed a lifelong interest in art, and gives workshops on what he calls creative dissociation. He had his first one-man show at the Unitarian Universalist Society of Orange County, New York.

Michael Grosso has recently written a book with the futurist Barbara Marx Hubbard, entitled *Letters From the Future*.

He is the Host at Large of the Cabaret St. John, a site on the World Wide Web, dedicated to networking information singularities. The site can be accessed at www.uninet.net/steppingstone.

Arthur Hastings, Ph.D., is the author of *With the Tongues of Men and Angels: A Study of Channeling* (1991), said by reviewers to be the standard and classic work on channeling. This book is based on four years of research and interviews of channelers. He presented the Invited Address on Psi and the Phenomena of Channeling at the 1989 conference of the Parapsychological Association.

He is also the author of books and articles on transpersonal psychology, health, hypnosis, parapsychology, and communication, including the award-winning book *Health for the Whole Person*. A Core Faculty Professor at the Institute of Transpersonal Psychology (Palo Alto, California) and former president of the Association for Transpersonal Psychology, Hastings is also a member of the Board of Editors of the *Transpersonal Review*.

Dr. Hastings has a Ph.D. in speech and communication from Northwestern University, where he coached national-champion debating teams. His book *Argumentation and Advocacy* (co-authored with Russell Windes) was a widely used textbook on argument and persuasion.

Hastings has conducted first-hand studies of poltergeist hauntings. He was a consultant to SRI International on parapsychology and consciousness research, where he worked with the remote viewing project as an independent judge. His own research in remote viewing used group formats and computer conferencing. Recently he has conducted a remote viewing study with a sailing ship circumnavigating the globe.

He was on the parapsychology program faculty at John F. Kennedy University and has held appointments at Stanford University and the University of Nevada.

Hastings has studied gestalt therapy with F.S. Perls and hypnosis with Milton H. Erickson. He grew up in the Protestant Christianity tradition and has continued his spiritual studies in yoga with Swami Radha and Shyam Bhatnagar, and in Buddhism with the Rev. Master Kennett, Tarthang Tulku Rinpoche, Sogyal Rinpoche, and Ngakpa Chogyan Rinpoche. He is an accomplished amateur magician and uses his knowledge of magic in evaluating possible psychic events.

Jeffrey Mishlove, Ph.D., is author of *The Roots of Consciousness* (originally published in 1975 and re-published in a new edition in 1993), an encyclopedic overview of consciousness exploration; *Psi Development Systems*, published in 1983, an overview and analysis of methods for training psychic abilities; and *Thinking Allowed*, a book of transcripts from his television interview series. In his capacity as host of the weekly, national public television series *Thinking Allowed,* he conducts interviews with leading figures in science, philosophy, psychology, health, and spirituality. More than 300 of these interviews have been broadcast since 1986. Videotapes from this series are available from Thinking Allowed Productions in Berkeley, California, a corporation of which Dr. Mishlove serves as Chairman. Jeffrey has the distinction of holding a doctoral diploma in Parapsychology which is the only such diploma ever awarded by an accredited American University. He received this degree in 1980 from the University of California at Berkeley. In addition, Dr. Mishlove is licensed as a psychologist in California.

Jeffrey Mishlove currently serves as Director of the Intuition Network, a non-profit organization of thousands of individuals in business, government, health, science, and education who are interested in cultivating and applying intuitive skills. The Intuition Network sponsors a computer conference system as well as seminars, tours, conferences, and publications. For more information, send a brief e-mail message (i.e., "send info") to info@intuition.org.

Karlis Osis, Ph.D., was born in Riga, Latvia, in 1917 and is one of the few psychologists to have obtained a Ph.D. with a thesis dealing with extrasensory perception (University of Munich, 1950).

As research associate of the Parapsychology Laboratory at Duke University from 1951 to 1957, Osis was a colleague of Dr. J.B. Rhine. In his research there, Osis pioneered experiments on ESP in animals and worked with humans to study ESP over the dimensions of space and time. Then, widening the scope of his activities, he served as director of research at the Parapsychology Foundation in New York City, where he conducted novel experiments with mediums and a large-scale survey of deathbed observations by physicians and nurses (1957-62). Cases of apparitions seen by several persons and cases of poltergeist phenomena were also studied.

From 1962 to 1975, Osis was Director of Research at the American Society for Psychical Research in New York, and a Chester F. Carlson Research Fellow 1976-1983 (currently emeritus). During this time, Osis conducted a number of pioneering efforts in parapsychology. He conducted his second survey on deathbed observations by physicians and nurses to collect data suggestive of life after death. In an interview with creative artists, Osis found altered states of consciousness to be related to states conducive to ESP. Altered states of consciousness induced by meditation were studied in a four-year project. Osis also explored the relationship between mediumship and ESP by laboratory work with small, carefully selected groups of experienced meditators. Basic dimensions of the meditation experience were worked out by means of factor analysis.

Osis is well known-for his long-distance ESP experiments—up to ten thousand miles—and for his research on the ESP channel—that is, an unknown energy which transmits ESP.

In the 1970s, Osis conducted extensive laboratory experiments on out-of-body experiences. These involved perceptual, physiological (EEG), and physical measurements. Together with Dr. Erlendur Haraldsson, he conducted a large-scale survey of the experiences of dying patients in India and the United States. They also studied psychic phenomena in selected yogis, particularly Sri Sathya Sai Baba, in southern India.

Osis is a past president of the Parapsychological Association and a member of the American Psychological Association, Eastern Psychological Association, American Association for the Advancement of Science, Society for Scientific Study of Religion, and various organizations concerned with the study of psychic phenomena and human personality.

Koneru Ramakrishna Rao studied at Andhra University and the University of Chicago. He received his M.A.(Hons.) (1955), Ph.D. (1962) and D.Litt. (1976) degrees from Andhra University. He was a Smith-Mundt-Fulbright scholar (1958-1959) and a fellow of the Rockefeller Foundation (1959-1960) at the University of Chicago and a Research Associate (1962-1965) at Duke University.

Dr. Rao previously held various academic and administrative positions in India and the United States. He served as Vice-Chancellor of Andhra University (1984-1987) and Advisor on Higher Education to the government of Andhra Pradesh. His other previous positions include Professor of Psychology and

Head of the Department at Andhra University (1968-1976), Director of the Institute for Parapsychology (1977-1984), and Executive Director of the Foundation for Research on the Nature of Man (1984-1994). More recently he served as the Vice-Chairman, State Planning Board of Andhra Pradesh in the rank of Cabinet Minister.

Dr. K.R. Rao traveled extensively in Asia, Europe, and the U.S.A. and lectured at a number of universities and colleges. He received several honours, including the Best Teacher Award from the government of Andhra Pradesh, honorary degree of Doctor of Science from Nagarjuna University, and honorary degrees of Doctor of Letters from Kakatiya University and Andhra University.

Dr. Rao is a member of the American Psychological Association, Parapsychological Association, Society for Scientific Exploration, American Association for the Advancement of Science, and the Indian Academy of Applied Psychology. He was elected President of the Parapsychological Association in 1965, 1978, and 1990. He also served as President of the Indian Academy of Applied Psychology for two consecutive terms (1987-1988). Currently Dr. Rao is the Honorary Director of the Institute for Yoga & Consciousness at Andhra University.

Dr. Rao edited the *Journal of Parapsychology* (1977-1994) and the *Journal of Indian Psychology*. He is the author of several books, including *Experimental Parapsychology: A Review and Interpretation* (Springfield, Ill.: Charles C. Thomas, 1966); *Gandhi and Pragmatism* (Calcutta: Oxford and IBH, 1968) and *Mystic Awareness* (Mysore: University of Mysore, 1972) and about 200 research publications.

William Roll did his undergraduate work at Holte Gymnasium, Denmark (studentereksamen) and at the University of California, Berkeley (BA). His graduate degrees are from Oxford University, England (M.Litt. and B.Litt.) and from Lund University, Sweden (Ph.D.). Roll was on the staff of the Parapsychology Laboratory at Duke University, 1957-64. During this time, he was a founding member and president of the Parapsychological Association. When the activities of the Duke lab were transferred to the Institute of Parapsychology, Roll remained as project director of the Psychical Research Foundation, which was located on the Duke campus and sponsored by the Department of Electrical Engineering until 1980. His most recent academic affiliation was with West Georgia College (now University), where he taught parapsychology as Professor of Psychology and Psychical Research, 1986-90.

Roll is the originator of the "memory theory of ESP," the view that psychic impressions are composed of the percipient's memory images. He is currently completing a paper, co-authored by Michael Persinger, according to which the hippocampus is part of a sensory system for ESP, and that space-time is the perceptual field for this system. The theory ties in with "the longbody," a term (proposed by Christopher Aanstoos) for the group of closely-knit individuals where psi interactions primarily take place.

The longbody concept has led to a new perspective on life after death. Instead of the continuation of the individual as an autonomous and distinct entity, Roll finds, the facts are more suggestive of survival within the longbody to which the departed belonged.

Roll's empirical research has focused on psychics and on field investigations of hauntings and poltergeists (recurrent spontaneous psychokinesis or *RSPK*). He is the first to have made measurements of the distances and directions of moving objects in RSPK and thereby to show the similarity of RSPK to known forms of energy. His use of magnetometers for haunting investigations has provided support for Persinger's hypothesis that the phenomena are due to the effect of magnetic fields on the brains of those present.

Roll believes that psi research has significant practical uses, particularly for counseling, and he was an early proponent of clinical parapsychology.

Charles T. Tart, Ph.D., is internationally known for his psychological work on altered states of consciousness, parapsychology, and as one of the founders of transpersonal psychology. His two classic books, *Altered States of Consciousness* (1969) and *Transpersonal Psychologies* (1975), became widely used texts that allowed these areas to become part of modern psychology.

Tart studied electrical engineering at the Massachusetts Institute of Technology before electing to become a psychologist. He received his doctoral degree in psychology from the University of North Carolina at Chapel Hill in 1963, and then received postdoctoral training with Professor Ernest R. Hilgard at Stanford University. He is currently a Core Faculty Member at the Institute of Transpersonal Psychology and Senior Research Fellow of the Institute of Noetic Sciences, as well as Professor Emeritus of Psychology at the Davis campus of the University of California, where he taught for twenty-eight years. He has been a Visiting Professor in East-West Psychology at the California Institute of

Integral Studies and a consultant on government-funded parapsychological research at the Stanford Research Institute (now known as SRI International). In addition to *Altered States of Consciousness* (1969) and *Transpersonal Psychologies* (1975), Tart is the author of *On Being Stoned: A Psychological Study of Marijuana Intoxication* (1971), *States of Consciousness* (1975), *Symposium on Consciousness* (1975, with P. Lee, R. Ornstein, D. Galin & A. Deikman), *Learning to Use Extrasensory Perception* (1976), *Psi: Scientific Studies of the Psychic Realm* (1977), *Mind at Large: Institute of Electrical and Electronic Engineers Symposia on the Nature of Extrasensory Perception* (1979, with H. Puthoff & R. Targ), *Waking Up: Overcoming the Obstacles to Human Potential* (1986), and *Open Mind, Discriminating Mind: Reflections on Human Possibilities* (1989), as well as numerous journal articles. His most recent book, *Living the Mindful Life (1994)*, further explores the possibilities of awakening from the mechanical conditioning and habit that dulls ordinary life. As well as a laboratory researcher, he has been a student of Aikido (in which he holds a black belt), of meditation, of Gurdjieff's work, of Buddhism, and of other psychological and spiritual disciplines. His primary goal is to build bridges between the scientific and spiritual communities and to help bring about a refinement and integration of Western and Eastern approaches for knowing the world and for personal and social growth.

Further biographical information, as well as the text of many of Professor Tart's publications, can be obtained via the internet, at http://www.paradigm-sys.com/cttart/.

Rhea A. White had a near-death experience in 1952 when she was a junior in college. It altered her interests completely, from wanting to play professional golf to wondering what the meaning of her experience was when she was out of her body and in touch with a reality she had not previously guessed existed. She decided to pursue it via science rather than religion, and joined the staff of the Duke University Parapsychology Laboratory in 1954.

She is still associated with parapsychology as editor of the *Journal of the American Society for Psychical Research*. She obtained a master's in library science in 1962 and pursued a career as a reference librarian from 1965 until her retirement in 1995. In 1983 she formed the Parapsychology Sources of Information Center, one of the aims of which was to compile reference books on parapsychology. The best known is *Parapsychology: Sources of Information* (with L.A. Dale; Scarecrow Press, 1973). An extension of it was prepared by White and published by Scarecrow in 1994, with the title *Parapsychology: New Sources of Information.* Also in 1983, she initiated and edited a semi-annual journal, *Parapsychology Abstracts International*, and *PsiLine*, a bibliographic database of the literature of parapsychology.

In 1990 she decided to concentrate her energies on all the types of non-ordinary and anomalistic experiences people have, not just the parapsychological ones, and especially those that are life-transforming (eventually, if not initially). She devised a term to cover all of these experiences: exceptional human experience (EHE). Her journal began to publish not only abstracts but also articles and was newly titled *Exceptional Human Experience*. In 1991 she enrolled in the doctoral program in sociology at SUNY Stony Brook in order to look at the problems of parapsychology and exceptional human experience from a different viewpoint. It was a very rewarding experience, but had to be abandoned in 1993 because of the press of other responsibilities. In 1995 she changed the name of her organization to the EHE Network, a membership organization, and began publishing a newsletter, *EHE News*. Also in 1995, Michael Murphy and White co-authored *In the Zone: Transcendent Experience in Sports* (Penguin/Arkana).

White has published more than 100 articles in various journals. She was the founding secretary of the professional society of parapsychology, the Parapsychological Association, and was president in 1984. She received the Association's Outstanding Contribution in 1992 Award as "parapsychology's bibliographer." In 1995 she moved from Long Island to New Bern, North Carolina, where she tends her gardens as much as she can, takes walks by the nearby river, and very much enjoys the amphibians that abound where she lives, as well as the hummingbirds.

Editor's Introduction

We are spiritual beings with incredible potential. No, we are nothing but animals, meaningless electro-chemical machines with grandiose and pathological delusions about being more than that.

Which statement would we *like* to be true? Which statement *is* true?

It is instructive and disturbing to compare the following two columns, one the results of a 1994 *Newsweek* survey of Americans' religious experience, the other a quote from a recent article by chemist Peter Atkins, published in the prestigious British scientific magazine *New Scientist* (1992). Atkins is commenting on an article by well-known British author, Mary Midgley (1992), who was concerned about the way science appears to have undermined religion.

> "In a Newsweek Poll [of Nov. 3-4, 1994], a majority of Americans (58 percent) say they felt the need to experience spiritual growth. And a third of all adults report having had a mystical or religious experience . . . 20% of Americans have had a revelation from God in the last year, 13% have seen or sensed the presence of an angel. . . . Outside church, 45% sense the sacred during meditation, 68% at the birth of a child, 26% during sex. . . . 50% feel a deep sense of the sacred all or most of the time in church or at worship services . . ."

> "Fear. Fear seems to me to be what motivates authors to write . . . about the encroachment of science on the tender patches of the soul. . . . There is indeed room for some people to fear, for those who seek to found their lives on the vaporous precepts so favoured by religion now find themselves teetering on the brink on an abyss wherein lies truth: the truth of our mortality, the truth of the absence of soul and the truth of the ultimate insignificance of all human activity. These truths are so consuming as to inspire subconscious fear and to generate the only resort of the vanquished and the disarmed: the stridency of protestation."

If Atkins is right, our civilization is very sick indeed, with a majority of Americans not only *believing* in God, but a fifth of them so deluded that they think they have had actually had a personal revelation from God in the last year! We must be not only "fearful," "vanquished," and "vaporous"; many of us must be rather psychotic! If Atkins is wrong, this kind of message, preached with fervor from the pulpit of science, attacks and can separate us from our vital and necessary spiritual nature.

Questions about what, if anything, is valid about religion and, more importantly, spirituality (the more pure and powerful experiences underlying the social organizations we call religion) have been important to me (and many others) since I was a child. These are not just intellectual or philosophical questions, either; they strongly affect the way we live our lives. If all spirituality is nonsense, e.g., where do we find a basis for a morality that goes beyond "looking out for number one"? Rather than a blanket acceptance or rejection of spirituality, can we ask what aspects of spirituality might be real and which are indeed nonsensical? Such questions came into especially sharp focus for me when I was invited to give an address on science and religion at the historic Second Parliament of the World's Religions in Chicago in 1993. An update of that address is now the first chapter of this book.

I am convinced, through both my professional work as a scientist and my personal attempts at personal, social, and spiritual growth, that this wholesale undermining of spirituality by orthodox science is not only unhealthy but scientifically, *factually* wrong.

The traditional conflict between science and religion is really of two distinct kinds. One is a question of factuality about the physical world, illustrated, e.g., by the fact that the physical, observable facts of geology and reasonable thinking about them cannot be reconciled with the claim made by some fundamentalist Christians that, according to the Bible, the world was created some 4,000 years ago. Our factual and useful knowledge about the physical world has expanded so enormously since the advent of modern science that we tend to assume that *all* of the world has been explained in terms of material science, but this is far from true.

The other conflict between science and religion, our focus in this book, is very much a conflict between *scientism*—a dogmatic, psychological hardening of materialistic belief systems with emotional attachments, rather than authentic science—and "religion" in the worst sense of the word, rigid and unhealthy belief systems that belie the spirituality they claim to be founded on. When relevant solid, scientific research is studied, rather than *scientistic* dogma, we discover a solid, scientific base for viewing human beings as potentially far more than mere material animals, and we find that humans can occasionally exercise various psychic abilities that give credence to a generally spiritual view of the world. To say that such a shift in view, with its potential for a fundamental reconciliation of spiritual and scientific world views—indeed a potentiation of each other—is important for our times is a gross understatement.

This book presents a detailed exploration of the spiritual implications that can be drawn from modern scientific research in parapsychology. Parapsychology, literally *para*, beside mainstream psychology, is the study of things that shouldn't happen *if* the scientistic attitude that we know everything important about the world and the whole world is nothing but the interplay of physical objects and forces is true. If you separate two people by long distances or shielding materials, for example, you can specify that no sound or sight the one creates can be detected by the other, and so they can't communicate. A parapsychology experiment of the *telepathy* variety then shields two people from each other by distance and/or barriers, presents some randomly selected series of targets to one, the sender or *agent*, and asks that she mentally send it to the distant receiver or *percipient*. An objective record is kept of the percipient's impressions and some objective way of comparing it with the target series is used. Insofar as our materialistic understanding of the world is indeed a *complete* picture, nothing should happen in experiments like this beyond occasional chance correspondences, and the level of such chance correspondences can be precisely specified mathematically so we're not misled by it.

Sometimes our materialistic model is verified: there is no apparent communication between agent and percipient. But far too often for chance to be a reasonable explanation, significant information transfer occurs. Mind, consciousness, spirit, intention, has transcended physical barriers. As detailed in Chapter 1, four basic kinds of *psi* phenomena, as they are now generally called, have been established beyond what I consider any reasonable doubt. The procedure I sketched above would be called *telepathy*, where the agent intends to "send" information to the percipient. With a *clairvoyance* procedure, the percipient must directly get the information from some material objects in a distant or shielded place; they are not currently known to anyone who might act as a sender. For a *precognition* procedure, the percipient would be asked to describe some target material which does not yet exist, but whose order will be determined at some future date as a result of a randomizing process. These three forms of psi are generally called extrasensory perception (ESP).

The fourth form of psi, *psychokinesis* (PK), involves the direct influence of the mind on matter without the normal intervention of our muscles or other physical apparatus. An agent might be told to mentally influence the way dice are thrown in a machine or the output of an electronic randomizer, for example.

I said that this book presents a detailed exploration of the spiritual implications that can be drawn from modern scientific research in parapsychology. I want to stress two words in that sentence. First, it's an exploration, not the final word, because the potential relationships between genuine science and genuine spirituality are so vast that we can only begin here, and because parapsychology is still a young, small field of science. Second, we focus mainly on scientific parapsychology in this book. In the public mind, "parapsychology" has become associated with everything apparently mysterious, from astrology and Atlantis to the ostensible zoological anomalies of Bigfoot and the Abominable Snowman. There might be something useful in astrology, perhaps as a counseling technique, but I have seen little solid scientific evidence of any connection between the heavens at birth and later personality traits. Atlantis might have been real, but the evidence is pretty sparse, etc. Scientific parapsychology, on the other hand, is a discipline over one hundred years old (counting its earlier form, psychical research) that has been much more restricted in scope but very careful in using the best kind of scientific methodology to solidly establish the reality and nature of some basic psi phenomena, discussed in Chapter 1 and other chapters, that are very relevant to questions about spirituality.

The scientists and scholars writing here are leading figures in scientific parapsychology whom I invited to expand and react to the themes of my first chapter outlining the relevance of parapsychology to spirituality. This book is unusual, for scientific parapsychologists usually prefer to stick close to rigorous laboratory findings and say little about the implications for our spiritual lives. This is done for many reasons. For one, the laboratory work is fascinating, challenging, and absorbing, and can easily fill a career.

I understand and accept this fascination, having succumbed to it for two decades in my own laboratory research. A much more important reason, however, is that there is so much emotionally intense opposition to parapsychological findings from the defenders of scientism against what they treat as heresy. I use the religious term *heresy* deliberately, for while these vocal pseudo-critics of parapsychology claim they are defending science, their actual actions more closely resemble those of the Inquisitors defending the True Faith from heresy. Most parapsychologists have tried to avoid this emotionalism by confining their statements to laboratory data and methodological issues. Our contributors have decided the importance of the findings for issues of spirituality is more important than this conservative, defensive strategy that it was hoped (in vain) might lead to wider acceptance of parapsychology in the mainstream scientific community. The result is exciting reading!

Let me give you some idea of what will be discussed.

Chapter 1, my invited address at the 1993 Second World Parliament of Religions, has the deliberately provocative title *World Parliament of Superstition? Scientific Evidence for a Basic Reality to the Spiritual.* Delegates had come from all over the world to dialog on the role of religion in today's world, but I wanted us to directly face the fact that to many modern people this whole Parliament was an exercise in futility: religions were scientifically nonsense, weren't they, in spite of speaking with authority? Knowing that many delegates would be wearing traditional religious garb, I, as a representative of science, wore my "religious vestments": a white lab coat to give my talk in and so establish my "authority." Perhaps I would announce that, from the perspective of science (scientism, really), the best thing the world's religions could do would be to dissolve themselves and convert to some kind of "rational" humanism? Instead, weaving both personal and scientific themes, I outlined how we have strong scientific evidence in parapsychology and why that gives general support to some kind of reality to a spiritual world and a spiritual life. This chapter sets the general theme of this book.

Parapsychologist William Roll's Chapter 2, *My Search for the Soul,* then sensitively explores the theme of personal spiritual experience and longing interacting with the development of scientific parapsychology. "I am sixteen and living in the small town of Birkerod in Denmark when my mother dies. . . . Sometime afterwards, I get up one night and find myself looking at my body which is still on the bed . . ." Alternating back and forth between his personal experiences and the development of parapsychology, Roll finally describes one of his own theories to explain spiritual and paranormal events, that of the "longbody."

Chapter 3, *Some Reflections on Religion and Anomalies of Consciousness*, by psychologist[1] and parapsychologist K. Ramakrishna Rao, is a detailed look at the roles of religion and science in our society, leading to several provocative suggestions toward establishing a parapsychology of religion. This field proposed by Rao could, among other things, give descriptive accounts of religious experiences that are uniformly applicable in all religions, construct empirical tests for validating specific forms of religious experience, and devise methods and procedures for gaining religious experience. As Rao notes, quoting from the most prominent founder of modern parapsychology, the late J.B. Rhine of Duke University, "The conclusion is inescapable that there is something operative in man that transcends the laws of matter and therefore, by definition, a nonphysical or spiritual law is made manifest. The universe, therefore, does not conform to the prevailing materialistic concept. It is one about which it is possible to be religious; possible, at least, if the minimal requirement of religion be a philosophy of man's place in the universe based on the operation of spiritual forces."

Chapter 4, *Exceptional Human Experiences and the Experiential Paradigm*, by editor, reference librarian, and parapsychologist Rhea White, reminds us that while the laboratory is the most convenient setting in which to study reality, psychic and spiritual experiences happen to real people in real life, and the full range of these exceptional experiences must be kept in mind to fully see the interaction of the psychic and the spiritual. Indeed, the category of exceptional human experiences (EHEs) and their transformative power may be more fundamental than divisions such as psychic and spiritual, and may lead to a broader conception of what science is than our current, overly masculinized version. White notes, "I cannot define EHEs outside the context of a broad definition of human nature, or as I prefer to say, human being. I think that the most viable aspect of humans is that both as a species and as individuals, no matter when, where, or how long we live, we are unfinished creatures. Moreover, that is not our curse but our glory. I think Keats was correct in saying that earth is 'a vale for soul-making.' Because we are transitional creatures, there will always be more for us to grow into and become—more to learn, more to know, more to be, more to share. Everyone's life aim, then, should be not simply to maintain the status quo, but to expand both inner and outer boundaries. The question each of us must ask, and that only we can answer, is: What is the best way for me to grow? What directions should I take that will enable me to express what I am in the fullest way, given my native talents and my life circumstances?" White enriches these questions by surveying the hidden assumptions of our Western world view that are highlighted and brought into question by exceptional experiences.

Philosopher and parapsychologist Michael Grosso notes in Chapter 5, provocatively titled *The Parapsychology of God*, that "In spite of the onward march of science and the propaganda of disbelief, people persist in attitudes of fear, petition, worship, propitiation, and even of love toward supernatural entities." "Why," he asks, "do so many insist on peopling the universe with gods and goddesses, angels and demons, and other supernatural beings?" After examining the roots of belief and parapsychology's contribution toward showing how some of this may be real, he goes on to argue, "Parapsychology, insofar as it confirms the existence of a transcendent psi factor, thus opens up the world of human experience. It does so by remythologizing and reenchanting experience with magical and spiritual potencies; at the same time, it gives substantial hints on how even an adventurous skeptic might, in harmony with the free spirit of science, explore the mysteries of godmaking and spirituality. . . . The parapsychology of god, as I conceive it, is not a religion, nor is it a branch of science, although it draws upon, and aims in part to synthesize, these traditionally opposed forms of thought. It borrows from religion—from magic, mysticism, and shamanism—its raw, transcendent data and poetic power while shedding its dogmas, superstitions, tribalism, and absurdities. It borrows from science its detached love of truth, its methods where appropriate, and its evolutionary cosmology, while shedding its conceit and doctrinaire materialism."

Chapter 6, *Some Thoughts on Parapsychology and Religion*, by Stephen Braude, another philosopher/parapsychologist, discusses the implications of the existence of psi in everyday life. Since we use our ordinary faculties semi- and unconsciously in the services of our needs, how might psi function in a like way? He notes a theme from the world's religions that could be expressed in the adage, "You can't fool God," and explores how psi abilities imply a link between people who might think they are totally separated, a link with important consequences. Braude also touches on what I think is an important factor behind the irrational resistance to psi shown in scientism: "Ironically, once we grant the possibility (in fact, the likelihood) that psi occurs outside the lab or seance room and plays a role in everyday life, we must concede that it might also be an unrecognized causal factor in ordinary scientific experiments. And if so, it is easy to see how this would complicate the interpretation of normal and apparently straightforward scientific research. . . . for all we know, psi influence might have been biasing the results of centuries of scientific experimentation."

In Chapter 7, *Intuition: A Link between Psi and Spirituality*, parapsychologist Jeffrey Mishlove deals directly with potential practical applications of psi. Under the broader term of intuition, he notes that every discipline recognizes roles for extraordinary ways of understanding, especially in its creative aspects. He suggests, "These converging insights and methodologies from psi research, the testimony of spiritual experience, and the broad field of intuition suggest to me that we have the potential to use intuitive consensus in a disciplined fashion as a tool for exploring realms of consciousness that have previously been relegated to philosophy, mythology and theology."

Parapsychology and Spirituality: Implications and Intimations, Chapter 8, by psychologist and parapsychologist William Braud, not only looks at our over-masculinized science from another angle but, drawing on his extensive laboratory research on influencing people's mental and bodily functioning by psi, finds: "Some years ago, I was amazed and delighted to find that a large number of factors known to facilitate psychic functioning sorted themselves into three clusters that closely matched the three familiar virtues of faith, hope, and love—virtues emphasized in virtually all spiritual traditions." After analyzing these in more detail, Braud concludes, "Parapsychological findings can be useful to those on a spiritual path as they can provide a certain degree of confidence and trust that at least some of the processes and concepts encountered are 'real' in a more traditional sense and are not delusions, projections, or misinterpretations. They also can serve to remind us that we are not alone in having exceptional experiences; such experiences are normal, natural, and remarkably widespread." He is concerned not just with the scientific aspects of psi, though, but with the growth aspects. "But these scientific reassurances, though of value, are only partial. A great deal of what is encountered along the spiritual path is quite beyond the reach of current science. Here, one must be armed with trust, faith, hope, love, discernment, and a tolerance for ambiguity and for contraries, rather than with the feelings of safety, certainty, familiarity, and understanding that science can provide."

Hoyt Edge, another philosopher and parapsychologist, in *Spirituality in the Natural and Social Worlds,* Chapter 9, draws out the consequences of the deliberate split between science and religion we have inherited from old battles. "I will argue that parapsychology suggests a more relational world view, denying the interior, privatized view of self and spirituality developed in the modern world; in turn, this approach to self implies a more natural and social spirituality.

"My argument in the first part of the paper is presented in two stages: (1) Modern science was intentionally defined as an approach that was the antithesis of religion; this analysis incorporated dualism and atomism. (2) Atomism rejects the possibility of parapsychology; in fact, it attempts to define parapsychology *a priori* out of existence. In turn, atomism suggests an epistemology which undercuts a major function of spirituality, i.e. the experience of the connectedness of life."

One of the most important, and so emotionally controversial, areas of life is the question of whether our consciousness survives death in some form. This arouses such strong hopes and fears, as well as being an exceptionally difficult area to research, that most parapsychologists avoid it. Yet belief in some form of survival is central to many religions. Parapsychologist Karlis Osis in Chapter 10, *Phenomena Suggestive of Life After Death: A Spiritual Existence*, examines the evidence that there is some kind of survival of consciousness, either as some kind of existence in a nonmaterial realm and/or as reincarnation. Noting the controversial nature of this area, Osis remarks, "The neurosciences have lately been admirably successful and useful—except in seeing the limitations of their reach: that part of us which transcends physiological functioning. Nothing stands so clearly in the way of the neurosciences' overclaims than parapsychological findings on phenomena suggestive of life after death. No wonder it releases passionate debates, even by scholars who are otherwise clear and rational!" And summarizing his review of the evidence for various possibilities of survival, he notes that "Most Americans, regardless of their age or level of education, say they believe in life after death. When death approaches us or our dear ones, the research findings mentioned above might be useful to these believers and, possibly, to some others, especially if they themselves have experienced phenomena suggestive of afterlife. . . . The spiritual and the psychic have often been pictured as enemies. The animosity between them stems from aberrations in both fields and from not knowing much of each other. At the heart of the matter, they are neighbors and friends, able to help each other."

I further explore the possibility of survival of death in Chapter 11, *Who or What Might Survive Death*, taking a more detailed psychological look at what aspect of self might survive, given how much of our ordinary personality is based on bodily habits and a relatively unchanging physical/social environment. I sometimes express my evaluation of the evidence by saying that after a period of confusion, fear, and unconsciousness as I die, I won't really be too surprised if I regain consciousness. On the other hand, I'll be very surprised if *I* regain consciousness.

One of the claims of religion is revelation: communications from nonmaterial, spiritual beings about the nature of the world and how to live. Inspirational or nonsensical? Transpersonal psychologist and parapsychologist Arthur Hastings, in Chapter 12, *Channeling and Spiritual Teachings*, examines the nature of such ostensible entities and their communications, and how we can use them. "The same mixture is true of contemporary channeled messages. In these messages can be found teachings and inspiration that speak to the spiritual needs of our time and its challenges. In the best of the messages there is an intelligence and perspective that can contribute to social values and personal guidance. But channeling also can express the trivial, fallacious, and pretentious, and be given credence that diverts attention from authentic transpersonal communication. As with many other sources of spiritual teaching, there is a place here for discernment along with open minded consideration."

Finally, in Chapter 13, *On the Scientific Study of Nonphysical Worlds*, I briefly propose a method for going beyond purely subjective belief and disbelief in supposedly nonmaterial realms. This is intended to be provocative: I think we might be able to produce scientific evidence that, on balance, favors or argues against the independent existence of particular spiritual realms, even if we can't conclusively settle the issue.

To start this introduction, I said, "We are spiritual beings with incredible potential. No, we are nothing but animals, electro-chemical machines with grandiose and pathological delusions about being more than that." I then asked which statement we would like to be true, and which is true. The other contributors to this book and I have our preferences and likings, our biases, but our discipline as scientists and scholars is to try to separate what we can conclude as reasonably and probably true from our desires. My best understanding, after a lifetime of studying these issues both personally and scientifically, is that we are spiritual beings and we are animals, electro-chemical machines. We certainly have a high capacity to believe nonsense, but that capacity applies in all areas of life, including the idea that we are *nothing but* electrochemical machines.

I am proud to call myself both a scientist and a "spiritual seeker," and *I am not being unscientific in doing so*. Given the intense, irrational feelings that so often dominate the advocates and debunkers of both science and the spiritual, this is not an easy position to come to or find social support for, but it is a sound, scientific one. I hope that you will share this feeling after reading these contributions, and that unnecessary conflict will be eliminated in your personal and professional interest in the spiritual!

Notes:

1. Most parapsychologists were originally trained in some other field of science or scholarship, and I mention those fields here as part of introducing authors.

Chapter 1
World Parliament of Superstition? Scientific Evidence for a Basic Reality to the Spiritual

Charles T. Tart

[This chapter is based on an address to the Second Parliament of the World's Religions in Chicago in 1993.]

Are all of us here today, you and especially me, a bunch of fools? Wasting our time attending a meeting on religion, when everybody "knows" that science long ago showed religion was all nonsense, the refuge of the superstitious and weak-minded who can't face harsh reality? The opiate of the masses?

We usually prefer to ignore that question, but we can't do it very well in today's world, so I'm going to make it the central issue in this talk. Not simply because it's impolitic to ignore such a politically powerful area as science, but for a basically spiritual reason. That reason is well expressed in a saying, attributed to a mystical group, that I take as a personal credo, viz.:

> There is no God but Reality.
> To seek Him elsewhere
> Is the action of the Fall.

The relevant interpretation of this is that even if you have high spiritual goals, if you ignore *any* aspects of what reality is in your search, it is bound to become distorted and fail.

To address the question, then, of whether religion is all nonsense, I'm not going to give you a typical scholarly presentation on relationships between science and religion, with lots of detailed data and references as to who said what about what. I've written about many aspects of that in a formal way in other places (Tart, 1972; 1975; 1979; 1981; 1986; 1988). Rather, I'm going to tell you a story as the central framework of the facts and ideas I want to present. It is a personal story, my story in some ways, but it's also the story of Western man and woman in our times. I am not uncomfortable adding this personal element, as most scientists have been conditioned to be (if I speak and write in an impersonal style I must be really objective, yes?), for some of my own psychological research has been on the ways our personal biases play important roles in distorting the scientific process—as well as the process of living in general. I aspire to objectivity as any scholar or scientist does, but I've found that the best way to deal with biases is to face them, not pretend that they aren't there.

Preview

At this historic Parliament, many participants are wearing dress—turbans, robes, etc.—appropriate to their faiths. So I stand before you wearing, as it were, one of my robes of office, a symbol of purity, my "religious" vestments—a white lab coat. With these vestments I invoke the authority of one of the most powerful "religions" of our times: Scientism, a powerful and dogmatic religion, that always pretends it is real science.

I could also describe my wearing of this lab coat as a cheap trick to get your attention or, more accurately, I could say I am using the cultural conditioning we moderns have all had in order to draw your attention and so more effectively emphasize some central points of my message today, such as (a) the fact that science, in the form of scien*tism*, has degenerated into a rather deadly but powerful religion in many ways, and (b) that it is a religion that too frequently captures our attention and feelings in a mindless way, just as this lab coat affects your perception of me in ways that are largely automatic and conditioned. I shall go on to show, as a scientist, how genuine science, as opposed to scien*tism*, can both help and be inspired by genuine spirituality.

Personally, I wear this lab coat, my identity as a scientist, proudly. I love doing science and I'm good at it. I also spend a lot of my time doing spiritual practices—I have just returned from a month-long meditation retreat, for example—which, I hope, will make me a wiser and more loving person, and I have little conflict between my spiritual aspirations and my role as a scientist rigorously pursuing knowledge. Indeed, I believe genuine science and genuine spirituality need each other desperately if our planet is to survive!

Now for the first thread of our story.

The First Thread: Childhood Religion

The religious part of my story began around 1940, when I was three, and so old enough to begin absorbing the deep faith of my grandmother, a Lutheran. She eventually took me to Sunday school and church and I was a devout Lutheran until my mid-teens.

As an orthodox psychologist, I know of many studies that show what deep and usually permanent impressions our early childhood experiences have on us. To illustrate, when my grandmother suddenly died of a heart attack, when I was seven years old, I was heartbroken. Although my parents did what they could, I developed rheumatic fever about a year later. My adult psychological understanding tells me that I wanted to die and go to heaven to be with my grandmother. If I had "succeeded" with the rheumatic fever, I would have literally—and poetically—died of a broken heart. Good things happened in my life then and I'm still here, but I share this to illustrate the intensity of my religious feeling as a child. The love for and from my grandmother permeated my understanding of religion.

As an unorthodox psychologist, a transpersonal psychologist, I would add that I am not stating that there is nothing to early religious feelings but reflections of relationships to parents and other loved ones. They are important, but hardly the whole story. As young children we usually have not had too much of a dose of cultural repression and conditioning, and so are closer in some ways to our *trans*personal, our spiritual core.

This beginning religious story, with many twists, is what many of us have lived. Our parents' or other relatives' religion is given to us wholesale when we are open, impressionable, naive children. The "twists," of course, are enormous. At its worst, the early religious story is one of fear-based indoctrination into a pathological, dysfunctional belief system, incorporating the shortcomings and neuroses of the parents, the community and the religion, and producing a lifetime of stupid and useless suffering for ourselves and others. At its best, you at least stay somewhat in touch with your spiritual core and, hopefully, develop a mature, loving spirituality that brings happiness and meaning into your own and others' lives.

The Second Thread: Developing Intelligence, Developing Conflict

The second thread of the story is about the development of intelligence and knowledge. As young children, our relationship to our parents, other adults, and society are rather like the way the ancient Greeks pictured the relations of humans and gods. We are weak to the point of total dependence for our very lives on our parents, we know little of the world around us, and our thinking is simplistic and frequently erroneous. Our parents, by contrast, seem and are god-like, knowing so much and being so powerful!

But we grow. Our knowledge of the world and people, our ability to think and reason, our ability to see below the surface of things, develops enormously. We develop skill in using our bodies and, hopefully, skill and intelligence in using and understanding our emotions. Orthodox psychology has studied and understood this process in great detail. Few people reach their full potentials in these areas, unfortunately, but most adults have grown enormously compared to themselves as children.

As my mind, body, and feelings grew, I became more devout in some ways but also began to question what I had been taught about religion in other ways. I vividly remember my confirmation class when I was about twelve, for example. We had been memorizing and studying the Ten Commandments. I took them very seriously and did not want to do anything wrong, but I didn't understand the one about adultery. How could I avoid committing this sin if I didn't know what it was? I asked my pastor during a class. To my puzzlement and embarrassment, he blushed and looked uncomfortable and then told me not to think or worry about it, that commandment was only of concern to adults! Young as I was, I had grown enough to know I was not being given an honest answer and I had done something wrong to even ask. This kind of evasion and use of authority to inhibit inquiry sowed doubts about the religion I had been taught. I was also puzzled and angered by the amount of hypocrisy I began to recognize in church members, and by knowing more adults who were non-religious or anti-religious.

Conflicts with religion as it was taught to us are a part of the story of practically every person who has had a formal religious upbringing. How they are handled and the resulting outcomes, relatively healthy or pathological, show great variation. Many people give in to authority in order to fit in and receive approval, crippling a part of their natural intelligence, for example. I will come back to this issue after introducing the theme of science.

The Third Thread: Science "Disproves" Religion

The third thread of the story is relatively unique to recent human history: it is the wide-ranging conflict between science and religion.

I loved science, even as a young child. I was naturally curious as to how things worked, as well as attracted to the glamour and *power* of science. Getting a chemistry set for Christmas, for example, was one of the highlights of my life! We had not become sophisticated enough to begin to think about the ecological and psychological costs of technological progress yet, and science was our glowing hope for continually improving the lot of the human race. I wanted to be a scientist when I grew up!

With my teenage years I became an avid reader of books on various areas of science, spending an amount of time in the library that would probably be considered unhealthy. But I was doing just as much reading in religious, occult, and metaphysical books, as I wanted to know how to make religion actually *work*, not just be some ideals I and others couldn't seem to live up to very well.

For a long time I felt little conflict between my growing knowledge of religion and science. I, as I learned many early scientists had done, accepted God as Creator and saw science as an exciting opportunity to reveal the wonders of creation. Indeed, science was (and still is to me) a noble quest, based on a dedicated, disciplined, and basically spiritual commitment to discover and serve Truth at all costs and on a humility where you admit to and refine your wrong opinions and failed experiments.

As I became older and more knowledgeable, and could think more clearly, the conflict became clear. Science, especially the material sciences such as physics and chemistry, had no need of God or anything supernatural. Indeed, the scientific community seemed to regard religion as not only useless but pathological, and my later studies of clinical psychology, as well as my increasing understanding of my own neurotic shortcomings, showed innumerable examples of Western religious beliefs cutting people off from reality and acting as the seeds and causes of all kinds of psychopathology.

The second and third threads of our story converge here: how do people deal with the conflict between traditional religious upbringings and modern secular society as they begin to think for themselves? Especially as they become scientifically knowledgeable?

As with all human stories, there are many variations on the way the story continues. Here I will focus on two common paths and a third, less common, path that is my own and is a path for reconciliation and mutual benefit between genuine science and genuine spirituality in our times.

Trying to Resolve Conflict: 1—Compartmentalization

The first common path of conflict resolution is what I have called the "way of compartmentalization": the conflict between science and religion is not really faced or resolved, but is covered over by the common human ability to dissociate, to hold conflicting beliefs in, as it were, different compartments in one's mind and to try to never open both compartments at once. So you have one compartment which opens for an hour or so on the holy day of your religion and then closes, then the main compartment, the beliefs for dealing with the "real world" for the rest of the week, reopens. Many people are thus conventionally religious, going to church on Sunday, e.g., but living pretty secular lives the rest of the time.

Psychologically speaking, compartmentalization often seems to work. It usually avoids overt psychological conflict as long as there are no crises in life that call for a deeper response than a secular one. On the other hand, compartmentalization in one area can easily lead to more widespread use of this defense, and *there is always a price to be paid*: a loss of wholeness, a loss of depth and authenticity.

Trying to Resolve Conflict: 2—Extreme Belief or Disbelief

The second common path of conflict resolution is one of psychological extremism. For many people this means an active rejection of their childhood religion and an active embrace of a secular, ostensibly scientific approach to life. If their religion was associated with denials of self-worth and massive guilt (far too common a story, unfortunately), this may involve the psychological defense of reaction formation, so their childhood religion, often all religion, is violently attacked. On the other hand, some people go to the extreme of a forced, brittle faith in their religion and see science and the secular world as irrelevant or evil. As with compartmentalization, both these extremes are psychologically unhealthy, involving a loss of wholeness and more specific psychological defenses that distort perception and behavior.

As a psychologist interested in personal growth, I have always been fascinated (and discouraged) by the ways in which we restrict ourselves, in which we lose our vital energy and higher possibilities to automatized psychological strictures and defenses. The sad thing is that we usually don't consciously know we're doing this, it just becomes an automatic, habitual way to live.

I sometimes give workshops to help people become more mindful of who they really are and what their psychological and spiritual possibilities might be. But you must *personally* discover what holds *you* back. If you *know* you believe something, for example, you can observe the consequences of your beliefs and try to alter or refine them and so keep in better touch with reality. When your beliefs become automatic habits of perception, thinking, feeling, and action, though, they are a set of shackles chaining your mind. In a while I will describe an experiential exercise I devised some years ago to help people become more conscious about some of the beliefs and restrictions that had become so automatized among us Westerners, specifically the beliefs that constitute the "religion" that sociologists call scientism.

Genuine science was (and still is) a quite noble and spiritual process, having arisen from beliefs that a search for better knowledge about the world, for Truth, could reduce the suffering and increase the happiness of humanity. Absolute honesty and dedication were necessary qualities to be a scientist, and you accepted what the universe, Reality, taught you through the factual results of your experiments, even if they weren't what you had hoped to find. You tried to be always open to new information, new data, new ways of making sense of data, so you needed to be rather humble about your own ideas. They were *always* subject to empirical test.

This noble quest, vastly successful in so many areas, especially the physical sciences, is practiced by real human beings, though, and we don't always measure up to the requirements of absolute honesty, humility, and open-mindedness. We get attached to our theories and explanations; we don't like to or refuse to look at data that looks like it would contradict our beloved theories and "laws." We forget to be open-minded about *everything;* we accept the general beliefs of our culture outside our special area of research, possibly even within it. The need for social approval, or to keep a job or get a promotion, can make many sloppy about looking at contradictory information, or even overtly dishonest.

We all know what happened historically. The physical sciences became more and more successful. Since everyone wants to be successful, even the social and psychological sciences started to emulate the physical sciences. I have no real need to wear a white lab coat, for example: there are no chemicals in my lab that I have to keep from spilling on my clothing. But doesn't it make me look like a *real* scientist?

So all the sciences copied the physical sciences to various degrees, and that meant a working philosophy of materialism. If something can't be sensed by our bodily senses or measured by a physical instrument, it isn't real! Coupled with some of the obvious excesses and pathologies of religion as grounds to reject it, materialism became a dominant force in Western culture.

Scientism

If someone wants to consciously adopt a materialistic philosophy of life, or any particular set of religious beliefs, that's all right with me. I firmly believe that people should be able to choose their beliefs, as long as they are willing to be responsible for the consequences and treat everyone else decently. Unfortunately, my psychological studies have shown me that most of us were pressured and conditioned, seduced and brainwashed, into particular belief systems when we were children, with little knowledge, consciousness, and choice involved. This brings us back to the experiential exercise I mentioned earlier, which I call the Western Creed exercise.

To make people more aware of the scientistic, materialistic beliefs that are largely implicit in them, even if they think they are deeply spiritual people, I ask them to participate in a "belief experiment." They are asked to deliberately give as much energy and belief as possible, "play the game," to entertaining a particular set of beliefs for about fifteen minutes. While doing so, they are to observe the emotional feelings generated. They are asked to wait to *intellectually* analyze the exercise until it's over. Afterwards they can go back to their usual beliefs and evaluate what they've learned from the experiment.

To increase the emotional impact of the experiment, I make use of our common American cultural conditioning and our natural instinct to be social creatures, just as I am deliberately making use of this white lab coat. I have my students stand at attention in neat, orderly rows, with their right hands over their hearts, the way we learned to pledge allegiance to the American flag in school. In unison we then recite aloud the Western Creed.

I'm going to read the Creed to you but not ask you to recite it with me, as the full-scale exercise usually generates strong emotions that I have people work out afterwards. We don't have time for that, but just listening will give you some emotional feeling for the effects of the Creed.

Note that the formal structure of the Western Creed is a deliberate parallel to the Apostles' Creed[1] of Christianity. This is not an attack on Christian beliefs—I deeply admire anyone who uses his Christian faith to behave as Jesus asked us to and so become a more loving human being—but a way of making the consequences of our automatized scientistic beliefs clearer by contrasting it to a well-known set of religious beliefs. Here is the Western Creed:

> I BELIEVE . . . in the material universe . . . as the only and ultimate reality . . . a universe controlled by fixed physical laws . . . and blind chance.
>
> I AFFIRM . . . that the universe has no creator . . . no objective purpose . . . and no objective meaning or destiny.
>
> I MAINTAIN . . . that all ideas about God or gods . . . enlightened beings . . . prophets and saviors . . . or other nonphysical beings or forces . . . are superstitions and delusions. . . . Life and consciousness are totally identical to physical processes . . . and arose from chance interactions of blind physical forces. . . . Like the rest of life . . . *my* life . . . and *my* consciousness . . . have no objective purpose . . . meaning . . . or destiny.
>
> I BELIEVE . . . that all judgments, values, and moralities . . . whether my own or others . . . are subjective . . . arising solely from biological determinants . . . personal history . . . and chance. . . . Free will is an illusion. . . . Therefore the most rational values I can personally live by must be based on the knowledge that for *me* . . . what pleases me is Good . . . what pains me is Bad. . . . Those who please me or help me avoid pain are my friends . . . those who pain me or keep me from my pleasure are my

> enemies. . . . Rationality requires that friends and enemies be used in ways that maximize my pleasure . . . and minimize my pain.
>
> I AFFIRM . . . that churches have no real use other than social support . . . that there are no objective sins to commit or be forgiven for . . . that there is no divine or supernatural retribution for sin or reward for virtue . . . although there may be social consequences of actions. . . . Virtue for *me* is getting what *I* want . . . without being caught and punished by others.
>
> I MAINTAIN . . . that the death of the body . . . is the death of the mind. . . . There is no afterlife . . . and all hope of such is nonsense.

You will seldom find the beliefs of scientism expressed this blatantly. But you will find them expressed more indirectly, as if they were scientific "facts," in millions of places, such as college textbooks in the various sciences. They are not simple facts, of course; they are theories, interpretations. The automatic, mindless acceptance of them is not good science: yet they are very widespread in our culture.

You can probably see why I tend to call this a "sadder but wiser" exercise. Scientism provides a pretty dismal and depressing view of life for most people. But what makes it really sad is that the large majority of people who participate in this Western Creed exercise discover that parts of them believe much of this depressing philosophy and it adversely affects their lives, even though these same people have consciously thought of themselves as "spiritual seekers," as being far more spiritual than most people in our culture. They realize how deeply these kinds of beliefs have been conditioned in them just by their being alive in these times, and how these beliefs are constantly being reiterated, reinforced, and rewarded, directly and indirectly, in contemporary culture.

We could discuss the psychological and spiritual ramifications of this exercise at length, but time restrictions do not allow it. But there is one vitally important point to make: just because we don't feel good about this scientistic belief system is *not* a sufficient reason to reject it!

Recall the spiritual maxim I quoted at the beginning of this talk:

There is no God but Reality.
To seek Him elsewhere
Is the action of the Fall.

Now let's come back to considering the ways people have of dealing with conflicts between science and religion. We looked at compartmentalization, and we looked at extreme reaction formations, such as scientism. Let's look at a third way.

Trying to Resolve Conflict: 3—Psychical Research and Parapsychology

I, and a very few others, were lucky in finding a third path. As part of my voracious reading as a teenager, I discovered the early scientific literature on psychical research and its modern descendant, parapsychology.

In the latter part of the nineteenth century the conflict between science and religion was, if anything, more intense and overt than it is now. Scientific progress had indeed shown that many religious ideas, especially ones pertaining to the nature of the physical world, were just plain wrong. Furthermore, understanding of abnormal extremes of psychological functioning had shown how even apparently normal people could have trance-like states in which unusual hallucinations occurred, often of a religious flavor. Thus it became increasingly easy—and fashionable—for intellectuals to dismiss religion *totally*, seeing it as a product of primitive superstition, pre-scientific and outmoded attempts to understand the world, and psychological aberrations and delusions.

A number of brilliant intellectuals and scholars, however, realized that the fashionable dismissal of *all* religion in the name of science, materialism, and modernity was too extreme. There seemed to be some human experiences that, on the face of it, would not yield to physical explanation and suggested that there was more to humans than, as it used to be phrased, ninety-eight cents worth of chemicals.

A reliable, educated gentleman, for example, might suddenly have had a dream that his son, currently stationed in India, had tragically been killed by an elephant. The gentleman would not be the type to worry excessively and might normally never recall *any* dreams. Yet when a sailing ship arrived from India a few months later, the sad letter would confirm that the son had indeed been killed at that time by a runaway elephant. This was hardly proof of a really major idea such as the existence of God, but it was (and still is) totally unexplainable in terms of physics or any reasonable extensions of physics, and suggested that the human mind—or soul, whatever you want to call it—is something importantly more than ninety-eight cents worth of chemicals, is perhaps something "spiritual."

Thus in 1882 the Society for Psychical Research was formed in London. Its purpose was to use the methods of science and scholarship that were working so well in so many areas of life and apply them specifically to studying the kinds of unusual human experiences that seemed to imply a spiritual dimension to humans. The Society's founders knew that much that went under the name of religion was superstition or error, but was there a core of truth? Were we throwing out the baby with the bath water? They conducted detailed surveys of such experiences, for instance, filtering out rumors and third-hand stories and collecting testimony only from reliable witnesses, preferably those who had independent corroboration of their stories.

There is a fascinating history of psychical research that I could talk about, as well as the evolution of laboratory-based parapsychology, leading to well over a thousand published, high-quality, scientific experiments which show the existence of several psychic abilities and tell us a little about their nature, but there is no time for that here. Instead I will outline the main point, namely the existence *beyond any reasonable scientific doubt* of four psychic abilities, abilities of *mind* that provide a solid, scientific basis for seeing humans as far more than the old ninety-eight cents worth of chemicals. I need hardly point out that this change in perspective has important moral implications in the long run also, for the ninety-eight cents worth of chemicals has become $50,000 for a transplantable eye, $10,000 to $40,000 for a single, transplantable kidney, $2,000 for an ovum, plus other increasingly marketable body parts (Kimbrell, 1993): when humans are seen as nothing but biological preparations, the have-nots and the powerless become more and more desirable commodities for the haves and powerful.

The four major kinds of psychic functioning, *psi* abilities as they are generally called now, are three kinds of extrasensory perception (ESP), viz. *telepathy, clairvoyance,* and *precognition,* and a kind of direct motor effect on the world, *psychokinesis* (PK). There are other kinds of psi effects also, but I focus on these four as there are dozens to hundreds of experiments establishing each one, whereas the others haven't been investigated so thoroughly.

The controlled laboratory procedures that have demonstrated these psi abilities involve setting up a situation in which, given our scientific knowledge of the physical world and reasonable extensions of it, *nothing can happen.* You then have people try to mentally gather information that is at a distance or shielded from them, or materially affect some target that is similarly distant or shielded from them. According to the materialistic approach, you are wasting your time.

I won't go into details for lack of time, but describe just one of the more interesting methods to give you a flavor of parapsychological experimentation. This is the *ganzfeld* method. *Ganzfeld* is German for a uniform, featureless visual field. You tape halved ping pong balls (acetate hemispheres, if you want to talk fancy!) over a receiver's eyes and shine a light on them. The receiver sees a featureless field, but soon begins to project his or her own visual imagery on this field and describes it aloud. Meanwhile a "sender" in a distant room looks at a randomly selected picture and tries to telepathically send it to the receiver. An outside judge is given the pictures and transcripts of a series of such sessions, without being told which target picture was intended to go with which ganzfeld imagery session.

If telepathy were something which worked reliably all the time, we wouldn't need formal experiments, of course. If there were no such thing as telepathy, on the other hand, all we would see in a ganzfeld experiment would be occasional, random correspondences between a receiver's imagery and the correct target picture. But if telepathy occasionally manifests, even with just partial flashes of information transfer, the outside judge should find consistently higher correspondences between the transcripts of imagery intended for a particular target than between that target and imagery from other sessions. And that is exactly what has been found. Thorough analyses and meta-analyses (see Bem and Honorton, 1994, for a review) have shown that some form of psi occurs with fair regularity in ganzfeld studies.

Occasionally the "hits" are spectacular, as when the target series was a set of Viewmaster clips on Las Vegas and the receiver described her imagery as looking like a scene from Las Vegas. Much of the time psi effects are small, and sometimes they don't show up at all in particular laboratory studies. Psi would not form a very reliable communications system at this time, but its implications are more important than its applications.

The primary implication is that, *using the best kind of scientific methodology, the human mind has occasional abilities to transcend space and time that are totally inexplicable in terms of the material world.* That is, materialism, while it may be a useful working hypothesis in many areas, especially the physical sciences, is totally unable to explain important aspects of human nature. Thus *scientism is a factually mistaken "religion" insofar as it purports to be based on scientific fact and a total view of reality.*

Let's look at some aspects of this a little more specifically. Consider telepathy. The human mind can occasionally have some sort of direct information transfer, factual information or emotional tone, "contact" if you prefer, with other human minds. Nothing about brains or bodies can explain this. The electrical radiation from our brains is enormously weak and could not carry information over any useful distance.

Consider clairvoyance. Occasionally a mind can directly know the state of affairs of the distant physical world, without using the senses of the body. This can be gross characteristics of the physical world, such as the ink marking on a concealed card, or more subtle characteristics, such as the internal electrical state of a computer-like device.

Consider precognition. Occasionally a person can correctly predict a future event which is, in terms of widely accepted physical principles, inherently unpredictable, such as the order of a deck of cards which will be thoroughly shuffled at some future time and repeatedly cut according to future conditions such as the temperature in a distant city and the barometric pressure in another city. Precognitively and clairvoyantly detected events have also included the outcomes of events based on quantum mechanical random event generators.

Consider psychokinesis. Occasionally just wishing for a certain physical outcome has some detectable influence on that outcome. A striking example is biasing the outcome of an electronic, computer-like device that randomly produces a binary outcome. The person causing the biasing, the agent, usually has no idea how the device works, and usually doesn't have sufficient technical education to understand an explanation even if he or she were given one.

These sound like the characteristics of *minds*—or perhaps souls—that may be quite enmeshed in the characteristics of matter most of the time but can somehow operate and (at least partially) exist independently of matter, minds that occasionally have access to nonphysical sources of information we cannot begin to adequately conceptualize; that perhaps may be capable of surviving physical death. And if these are characteristics of people, may there not be minds or a Mind much greater than our own? God?

These are big jumps, of course, and eventually involve some leap of faith as to what one ultimately concludes. But it will be a faith based on high quality, scientific evidence of what is possible in reality.

Resistance to the Findings of Parapsychology

As you know, the scientific establishment in general pays no attention to the findings of parapsychology. They are almost never taught as part of a scientific or even a general education. Most scientists (and laymen and religious professionals) can honestly say they have seen no evidence to make them take the field seriously, which illustrates the degree to which scientism has permeated the scientific enterprise. Since scientism functions as a dogmatic, closed religion, part of the *implicit* education of scientists is the occasional disparaging remark about what nonsense parapsychology is. We want social acceptance, to belong, so we don't look at the evidence and then can indeed honestly say that we have never seen anything to convince us! Many of the most outspoken pseudo-critics of parapsychology are insulted if you ask them to read the literature: why should they waste their time on what they know is nonsense?

This kind of obstinate closed-mindedness is often found in religion—although formal religion has no monopoly on it—and the rest of us look down on it. It is too bad this kind of scientism is so common in science. What is needed is not mindless resistance and orthodoxy in any area of knowledge, but open-minded investigation.

Transpersonal Psychology

Parapsychology is still a very small field, even though its roots go back more than a century. A much larger and faster growing field of investigation, though, is *trans*personal psychology, a twenty-five-year old branch of psychology that actively investigates mystical experiences and the like, experiences that are *trans*, beyond our ordinary personal and biological self. It is primarily interested in understanding and helping to facilitate such experiences. We moderns are desperate for genuine spirituality based on deep experience, not simply ideas, and there is great hope that transpersonal psychology can bring into our culture a nonsectarian spiritual vitality that can help us.

Transpersonal psychology rests on an understanding that a "successful" spiritual life needs a solid basis in deep experience. Words and doctrines, emotions based simply on hope and fear, produce a shallow and frequently neurotic religion that does not stand up well to the stresses and strains of contemporary secular life. To exaggerate somewhat in order to underscore the point, it is not enough to hear about what God said to someone long since dead and be told what to do by someone who heard it from someone who heard it from someone, etc.; you need to directly hear from God yourself in an experience that transcends your ordinary self, that shakes you to your foundations.

There is little time for me to really go into what this developing field of transpersonal psychology is all about, but let me just give you the titles of a few recent articles from the *Journal of Transpersonal Psychology* to give you the flavor:

"Death and Near-Death: A Comparison of Tibetan and Euro-American Experiences" (Carr, 1993)
"The Art of Transcendence: an Introduction to Common Elements of Transpersonal Practice" (Walsh & Vaughan, 1993)
"Transpersonal Psychology Research Review: Psychospiritual Dimensions of Healing" (Lukoff, Turner & Lu, 1993)
"Separating from a Spiritual Teacher" (Bogart, 1992)
"A Preliminary Study of Long-Term Meditators: Goals, Effects, Religious Orientation, Cognitions" (Shapiro, 1992)
"Spiritual Issues in Psychotherapy" (Vaughan, 1991)
"Guru and Psychotherapist: Comparisons from the Hindu Tradition" (Vigne, 1991)
"Looking into Mind: an Undergraduate Course" (Mansfield, 1991)
"Mindfulness, Spiritual Seeking and Psychotherapy" (Tart & Deikman, 1991)
"Adapting Eastern Spiritual Teachings to Western Culture" (Tart, 1990)
"Psychodynamics of Meditation: Pitfalls on the Spiritual Path" (Epstein, 1990)
"Intimate Relationship as Path" (Welwood, 1990)
"The Technology of the Praeternatural: An Empirically Based Model of Transpersonal Experiences" (Nelson, 1990)

This third way of trying to resolve the conflict between science and religion, using the best of science to try to separate the wheat from the chaff in religion, has been my path, and I hope that my sharing of it has shown its usefulness.

Conclusion

I started my talk by asking,

Are all of us here today, you and especially me, a bunch of fools? Wasting our time attending a meeting on religion, when everybody "knows" that science long ago showed religion was all nonsense, the refuge of the superstitious and weak-minded who can't face harsh reality? The opiate of the masses?

My answer, as a scientist and as a psychologist, is that yes, we are all certainly foolish at times, but that is a general human characteristic in all areas of life; we are not fools simply because we believe that there is something more to religion. The data of first-class scientific research shows that there is something very important going on under the classification of "religion," and we would be fools not to use the resources of science to clarify what that is. And we would also be fools not to let the potential and power of genuine spirituality inspire our scientific efforts, lest the world expire in that slough of despondency known as scientism.

Notes:

1. I believe in the Holy Ghost; The Holy Catholic Church; the Communion of Saints; The forgiveness of sins; The Resurrection of the body; and the Life Everlasting. Amen.

Chapter 2
My Search for the Soul

William G. Roll

I am sixteen and living in the small town of Birkerød in Denmark, when my mother dies and my feet are knocked from under me. It is December 1942, and we are occupied by Nazi Germany. My father is in California, out of reach.

Sometime afterwards, I get up one night and find myself looking at my body, which is still on the bed. It's more strange than frightening. I discover I can repeat the experience if I wake up with a peculiar tingly sensation in my chest and face. My consciousness, when I find myself out of the body, is otherwise the same as my ordinary, waking self. There is nothing numinous about these episodes, and I never venture into distant places. The farthest I get is the front yard. But the experience is as real as getting up in the morning and going to school. I think this must be what survival is like, a permanently detached soul wandering around the house and yard.

My dictionary says that the soul is the same as spirit. *Spirit* comes from *spiritus*, Latin for *breath*, which animates body and mind. In Danish, *spiritus* means alcoholic drinks, which animate many Nordic bodies. The word for spirit is *ånd*, and to breathe is *at ånde*.

Another word for *soul*, I learn, is *psyche*, which also means *mind* and *self. Mind* comes from *menos*, Greek for *remember*, and shows that the psyche has a past. *Self* goes back to the Sanskrit *swa*, *one's own*, *oneself.*

I discover something else about the psyche. Psyche is a Greek princess loved by Eros, and Joy is their offspring. The inscription "Know Thyself" at the Oracle of Delphi is an invitation to a joyful encounter.

I have been confirmed in the Lutheran church and heard a similar story from our priest. Eros is now the Father, Psyche is the Virgin, and Christ is "Joy to the World." Birkerød has a fine old village church, red brick with stepped gables, but I feel little joy within its walls. Being confirmed has it rewards, though: a big party, special gifts, and a near-adult experience. My grandfather gives me *Tertium Organum* by P.D. Ouspensky, and I learn how things that seem separate may be connected in the fourth dimension.

The only self I know is my bodily self and its out-of-body shadow. Like Peter Pan's, my shadow is detachable but no more exciting than the original. It is nonmaterial, though. As an experiment I try to poke my hand through a wall and get it partway in, but the sensation is unpleasant and I pull it out. Another time, I think of being in the front yard, and am there without considering the closed window I have to pass through.

There is a dark obstruction, the Lutheran priest says, that hides the light of love; it is hate. Where love joins, hate breaks apart. Like love, hate is a principle in its own right and originates beyond the self: one divine, the other demonic. Hate too is vibrantly alive and brings an immortality of its own; a hateful deed spawns another. Like love, the principle of hate is personified. Two principles and two princes, the Prince of Love and Light and the Prince of Hate and Darkness. Two principalities, too, heaven and hell, and between them a third, earth, where angelic hosts battle hellish demons for human souls. Good and evil originate beyond, but humans possess the free will to choose. Supporting this scenario are the Greco-Judaic ethics and cosmology.

When the Bible is written, earth is populated by perilous spirits and mythic creatures, but is also familiar, flat, with the dome of heaven above and the pit of hell below. Then Ptolemy, the Egyptian astronomer, discovers what the seafarers know: the earth is round, not flat, and it is circled by the sun and planets. Though this goes beyond Genesis, there is no contradiction; earth, God's central work, remains at the core. But the thin edge of the chisel of science is in. There it remains until, 1500 years later, Galileo gives it a decisive blow. God's world goes flying, one planet among many around a small star. Galileo is brought to court by the Inquisition and forced to recant. "But it does move!" he whispers.

I learn how the sun of science ascends with Galileo, and the world of the sacred is cast in shadow. Into this darkness rides René Descartes, philosopher knight of the Church, to carve a realm for God. His banner, *Cogito Ergo Sum*, proclaims the individual mind a basic reality and logic its defining feature. From this he argues that there is a thinking substance beyond the material essence of objects extended in space: humans have an immortal soul separate from the physical body.

I don't know about my soul's immortality, but my out-of-body experiences match Descartes' description. My OBE self is clearly separate from the body, it seems to be nonmaterial, and I am as capable of rational thought out of the body as in.

The outcome of Descartes' mission is not what he intends. Instead of a mouthpiece for God, he becomes a minion of science. Since Descartes has shown matter to be devoid of spirit, divine or demonic, nothing now prevents the probing of things and bending them to mundane purposes. The Biblical compass, which points to certain Truth, is replaced by the vacillating compass of science; today's truth could be tomorrow's falsehood. Morality is devalued, the good act is not to serve your immortal soul but your mortal needs, and that can mean selling others out.

Toward the end of the 19th century, a strange event occurs in England. The Cartesian mission is revived as an offshoot of science, the bastion of materialism. A group of scholars at Cambridge University, from Christian homes (Gauld, 1982), establish the Society for Psychical Research (SPR). Their goal: to find scientific evidence for the survival of the soul after the death of the body. Apparitions of the departed, mediumistic communications, and out-of-body experiences may provide the evidence. The work, though out in the open, has an underground ambiance; the armor of materialism is being turned against its adherents.

I discover the SPR work when Jacob Paludan, who lives in an old farmhouse next door, befriends me. Paludan is a well-known writer of fiction in Denmark and also reviews books about parapsychology and Eastern religion for the newspapers. Through his books, I discover that many others have had OBEs. Unlike mine, the journeys include visits to distant family or friends and exploring other-worldly realms. I once hear voices in the distance but this is the closest I come to meeting anyone during an OBE. There is a similarity between my OBEs and those I read about. Both are preceded by sensations of mild electric-like shocks in the body and both are as vivid as everyday life, if not more so. There is another similarity. The traveler seems no wiser at the end of the journey than before.

The books on Eastern religion hold out a different promise. I read the Danish translations of the *Bhagavad-Gita* and the *Tao Te Ching,* and I follow Paul Brunton's odyssey to Indian yogis.

The roads lead to the same mountain. The universe in all its diversity is permeated by a Big Mind, a universal consciousness of which everyone is part and which everyone may experience. Travelers are distinctly transformed, the books say. Anger and confusion are replaced by love and understanding. The way is usually by meditation while seated in the lotus position, right foot on left thigh and left foot on right. After some effort, I get my legs into the right arrangement and try to meditate. Big Mind ignores the effort.

The idea that people are connected below surface separations to a universal consciousness appeals to me, and not only because of the promised joy of the union. If people could only reach an understanding of their deeper connections, conflict and war would surely end. Stitching the war-torn world together is for the future. The present is overshadowed by the ogre that has settled over Denmark and that can only be dislodged by force. I buy a handgun from a friend so I can join the struggle. Instead of an entry to the resistance movement, the gun lands me in jail. Someone takes a shot at a Nazi in town, our house is searched, the gun found, and I am sent to prison in Elsinore. My misfortune is double; the ten-day sentence overlaps with Easter vacation from school.

It is spring 1944, the allies are advancing and the Germans digging in for the expected onslaught. The resistance is blowing up factories and trains that serve the fortress; when the Nazis cannot catch the saboteurs, they shoot innocent citizens on the streets instead. In Copenhagen, my mother's sister hides a member of the Holger Danske group in her apartment. My uncle in Elsinore helps the Jews escape to Sweden. In September, what I hope for finally happens; I am included in the resistance. Isak Tegner, a former captain in the Danish navy, asks me to join. Tegner, a neighbor, is the leader of the Birkerød district.

My out-of-body experiences continue, perhaps because I don't sleep well. The Germans pick up suspects at night, and my ears are alert for cars on the road. I go underground and sleep peacefully. Papa is with SHAEF, the U.S. intelligence service. At the Battle of the Bulge, he is racing with a friend for the top of a hill when the other is stopped by a bullet through the head. Papa's brother, Sigurd, is executed in Oslo. He remains in Norway when the family immigrates. There he helps resistance people escape to Sweden. He is arrested, set free, and then shot dead on the street.

May 5, 1945, the fortress falls without a fight. The tables turned, we herd the Germans to prison camps. A phone call from

Norway announces that Papa has landed with the Allied forces. I am away on guard duty; he is relieved I'm on the right side. He makes his way to Denmark in a convertible Mercedes he has acquired from a group of German officers, now forced to walk. We have a joyful reunion, and I learn to drive in Papa's plunder.

His home is in Oakland, not far from the Berkeley campus of the University of California. I move into International House in 1947, and sign up for psychology and philosophy courses to learn about out-of-body experiences and Big Mind.

One afternoon, I wake up from a nap and go over to turn on the light by the door when I see my finger go through the switch, and then my body on the bed. Am I dreaming or really standing by the door, out-of-body? If a dream, should I not also have dreamt that I turned on the light? A strange charade, or perhaps my OBE self is actually by the door. If so, is this my immortal soul? I learn nothing at Berkeley to answer this question, nor anything else about the self, out-of-the-body or in. The psychologists have their noses buried in cages of white rats and the philosophers have theirs pointed at an empty sky.

My readings in parapsychology tell of connections between people and their social and physical environment that remind me of Big Mind. If a universal soul exists and can be experienced, this could be a basis for a new world order. Sociology should throw light on the matter. A year's post-graduate work finds this field as barren as the others.

I discover the parapsychological writings of H.H. Price, a philosophy professor at Oxford University. Price agrees to take me on as his student and my wife Muriel and I go to Oxford. I become a member of St. Catherine's Society and Muriel joins the Department of Anthropology. St. Cath, new and unbound by tradition, suits me. When it takes its place among the colleges, it is with a fresh look. The lofty and light buildings, designed by the Danish architect Arne Jacobsen, stand in lively contrast to the dark hues of the medieval town.

Price introduces me to Eric Dodds, professor of classics and author of a book on psychic practices in ancient Greece (Dodds, 1980). Dodds offers to hypnotize me and send me out-of-body to an unfamiliar place to see if I can observe things there. I am a poor hypnotic subject and remain, body and soul, in Dodds' easy chair. Instead I try the procedure on my fellow students. They are easily hypnotized, depart readily, but do not arrive. I lower my sights to ESP tests, and get better results (Roll, 1976). Dr. J.B.

Rhine, at Duke, sends me ESP cards and encouragement and visits with his wife Louisa. Our daughter Lise has just been born; I have a photo of Rhine holding her in his arms.

I join Muriel in seminars at the Department of Anthropology and we become friends of Professor E.E. Evans-Pritchard. He did his field work in Africa, and I learn how psychic practices are woven into tribal life. I also learn how psychic powers can be part of the arsenal that one tribe uses against another. My dream fades of psychic connections as a basis for brotherhood.

Support from St. Cath, the Society for Psychical Research (SPR), and the Parapsychology Foundation enable me to spend nearly eight years reading, researching, and writing parapsychology. I receive a B. Litt. and an M. Litt. and, in 1957, an invitation from Rhine to come to Duke.

Rhine is interested in the psychic abilities of the living, not in exploring life after death. But he doesn't object when one of his financial supporters, Charles Ozanne, wants to aid survival research. In 1960-61, the Psychical Research Foundation (PRF) is set up to seek scientific evidence for survival. Gaither Pratt, Rhine's assistant and my good friend, becomes president and I project director.

My OBE self explores in its own way. One night I wake up in one of the clearest OBEs I have had. I step out of bed in my OBE body and walk down the hallway to the living room, which I find bathed in moonlight. As I stand in the doorway, I marvel at the clarity of the view—and regret I cannot verify I am actually there. I notice that a shadow from a circular side table covers a corner of the rug. I have no way of knowing, I tell myself, that the shadow will fall exactly this way this night; finally, I can test my OBE vision. I go down on hands and knees on the rug to measure how far beyond its corner the shadow extends. Using my right hand as a measuring stick, I find the shadow overlaps the rug by one hand's length on either side. The experience is not only visual; as I press my hand against the floor, I feel the grain of the wood against my palm. With this precious measurement in mind, I hurry back to the bedroom, arouse my body and return corporeally to the living room to check the shadow. The room is black as soot. There is no moonlight or shadow. Could I have slipped into another time and seen a shadow of another night? I experiment but cannot bring the shadow back by either natural or artificial light. I conclude that the scene is a mixture of my memory of the room and my imagination of shadows on a moonlit night. I have been the victim of a hallucinatory hoax of my own making.

I recall that when I returned from the living room, my OBE body was not vertical, but walking at an angle of about 30 degrees from the floor. It was as if my legs were on a different plane than the visible one. I wonder if the inconsistency holds a clue to the experience. In any case my OBEs cease, perhaps because I have seen through them.

I go to the SPR reports for inspiration. The British explorers, in the footsteps of Descartes, seek a nonmaterial world for the minds of the departed. The data point in the opposite direction. Eleanor Sidgwick (1885) examines haunting apparitions and finds evidence, "which I can hardly expect to appear plausible . . . that there is something in the actual building itself—some subtle physical influence—which produces in the brain that effect which, in its turn, becomes the cause of the hallucination" (p. 148). Edmund Gurney (Gurney, Myers and Podmore, 1886, vol. 2) wonders about "this perplexing problem of the relation of psychical operations to space" (p. 302). He considers that a mental link may be established between the deceased and the percipient of the apparition when the percipient visits the home of the deceased. This link, Gurney speculates, may provide a connection between their minds which then results in the apparitional experience,[1] an explanation that would be consistent with dualism. But, ". . . this is not enough wholly to explain our cases of local attraction. . . . [W]e ought, I think, to have some cases where a phantom has appeared to [a person] without previous acquaintance, on the ground of some community of ideas and interest between the two, unconnected with any special locality. Now, so far as I know, there is not, among our cases recognized as telepathic, a single incident of this kind." (p. 302). He (Gurney and Myers, 1888-89) is confronted with "the survival of a mere image, impressed, we cannot guess how, on we cannot guess what, by that person's physical organism, and perceptible at times to those endowed with some cognate form of sensitiveness" (pp. 417-418).

Myers (1903, II) believes that apparitions, especially "collective apparitions" which are seen by two or more people, occupy physical space, but are not material in the usual sense. An apparition is ". . . not optically or acoustically perceived . . . but an unknown form of supernormal perception, not necessarily acting through sensory end-organs, comes into play" (p. 75). The space occupied by apparitions, he calls "metetherial space." It is ". . . a world where life and thought are carried on apart from matter . . ." (1903, I, p. 264). Gurney (Gurney and Myers, 1888-89) distinguishes "local" apparitions, which are seen in the place the person occupied when living, from "personal" apparitions, which are seen by people who knew the departed. There is a subclass of personal apparitions, which Louisa Rhine (1957b) calls "bystander" cases, where a third person sees the apparition near someone who knew the deceased. Personal apparitions may be a form of local apparitions, according to Rhine (1957a): "[T]hese cases are suggestive of the haunting cases [for "haunting" substitute "local"], the main difference . . . being that [in the bystander cases] the link is a person rather than a geographical location" (p. 39).

I have had to conclude that my OBEs are home-fashioned fabrications, but this does not mean that the OBEs of others are unreal. The case reports (Muldoon and Carrington, 1951, 1956; Crookall, 1961a, b, 1964a, b, 1972; Fox, 1962; Green, 1968) are nearly all veridical and convey the message that if you have an out-of-body experience, you occupy a location in the real world. Some of the research says the same. A young woman in Charlottesville, Virginia, is lying on a couch, her head in a nest of wires from a brain wave recorder, when she experiences herself floating to the ceiling. She turns around and sees a five-digit number researcher Charles Tart (1968) has placed on a shelf high above the bed. Ingo Swann "flies in" from his home in New York to the PRF in North Carolina and recounts a sequence of sounds Keith Harary and Jerry Solfvin (1977) are playing in an empty room. At the American Society for Psychical Research, Swann identifies objects on a platform that can be seen only from the ceiling (Mitchell, 1978). Harary's pet kitten at the PRF is calmer when he reports visiting it out-of-body (Morris, et. al., 1978). Osis and Donna McCormick (1980) place strain gauges near the target pictures. When psychic Alex Tanous "sees" the targets, the strain gauges are triggered, perhaps by his "extra-somatic" body, as Osis suggests, or perhaps by a non-OBE form of PK. The tests seem to support the anecdotal accounts: the OBE takes place in the material environment (except for visits to spirit worlds). It seems that my vision of the moonlit room is an anomalous OBE.

I examine the reports of another project launched by the SPR to discover life after death. Attempts to reach another world with the aid of mediums appear to succeed; information is obtained about the deceased that the mediums apparently could not have known; the story of a new life in a realm of spirits becomes plausible. Then clouds obscure the picture. The researchers realize that the mediums might have learnt the facts not telepathically from the minds of the departed but telepathically from the minds of their survivors, the family members or friends who are present at the tests. To prevent telepathic cues from those present, "absent sitter" tests are instituted. These have the further advantage of preventing sensory cues from the participants from contaminating the results. Instead of personal links to the deceased, "psychometric" objects are substituted. If the medium is handed a piece of jewelry or an article of clothing that the departed has handled, images may be evoked from the person's life.

Psychometry makes little sense to the psychic researchers. Inanimate articles do not have mental qualities. The word *psychometry* is itself a contradiction, joining as it does the non-material *psyche* with *meter*, measurement, the defining feature of matter, according to Descartes. The scholars pass lightly over the practice; the mediums, less educated, use it freely (Hodgson, 1892, 1898; Verrall, 1901-03; Saltmarsh, 1929; Thomas, 1928-29). Eleanor Sidgwick (1915) quotes a supposed spirit communicator speaking through Piper: "Objects carry with them a light as distinct to us as the sunlight is to you. The instant you hand us an object, that instant we get an impression of its owner, whether the present or the past owner and often both" (p. 624).

Sidgwick is as puzzled by psychometry as she was by apparitions. "One's first impression naturally is that all this must be nonsense, but the evidence on the whole seems to show that some effect is produced by [psychometric objects] . . ." (1915, p. 306). Frederick Myers (1903), comments poetically, ". . . objects which have been in contact with organisms preserve their trace; and it sometimes seems as though even inorganic nature could still be made so to say luminescent with the age-old history of its past." Oliver Lodge (1909) speaks of "traces" too, and William James (1909), in his paper on the medium Lenora Piper, compares them to memories.

G.N.M. Tyrrell (1938) suggests that object-reading, his term for psychometry, ". . . points strongly towards the view that there must be a vast amount of *something behind* the physical object as it appears to our senses. In fact, the sense-presentation of the physical world must be the thinnest and most conventionalized abstract if we accept the evidence for clairvoyance and object-reading" (p. 55). The reports agree that a physical object placed in the hands of a psychic may lead to people who have handled it and, because their lives intersect with others, to these as well. The people seen may be near or distant, living or dead.

H.H. Price (1939, 1940) bridges mind and matter by "place memories." It's not just minds that hold memories, according to Price; inanimate objects may do so too. In this way, he accounts for local apparitions as well as psychometry. Place memories may be recalled by the psychically sensitive person in the same way we remember our personal past.

In a different enterprise, departed members of the SPR beam down to earth to assist their colleagues, or so it seems. Through the SPR mediums they announce a method to prove that life goes on in another realm. In the procedure known as the "cross correspondences," one part of a message is received by one medium, another part by another medium (Piddington, 1908, 1918). The theme may be a recondite topic from Greek literature, shrouded in symbols, which can be understood only by experts when the two messages are juxtaposed. But are the senders the departed SPR researchers or their living colleagues, also classical scholars? The latter explanation is preferred by most researchers who consider ESP between the living a demonstrated fact.

Psychical research is exported to the U.S. and becomes parapsychology under J.B. Rhine. Soviet Communism has replaced Nazi Germany as the global threat, and Rhine sees psychic phenomena as scientific refutation of materialism, and therefore of Soviet Communism. Work with mediums is abandoned in favor of volunteer subjects who know nothing about psychometry, local apparitions, or other occurrences where mind seems to merge with matter.

Psychic powers enter the cold war more directly, when psychics seek Soviet submarines in the Pacific. The Russians also employ psychics but neither party seem to reap much benefit. The research has an interesting spin-off when Ingo Swann (1993), the leader of the U.S. team, is given a set of longitude and latitude coordinates. He accurately describes buildings and people on an antarctic island that is thought to be uninhabited. When Mariner 10 is dispatched toward Jupiter, Swann overtakes it and discovers an unknown ring around the planet. This and other of Swann's discoveries are later verified. His depiction of Mercury is less accurate but includes the shape of its magnetic field. Swann does not occupy an OBE body. He uses "remote perception," and needs to know only the spatial coordinates of the target.

The evidence for out-of-body travel is clouded by inaccuracies. When Charles Tart (1967) works with Robert Monroe, the famed OBEer gives erroneous accounts of the places he supposedly visits. Seventeen subjects do little better than chance in describing the targets in OBE tests by John Palmer and R. Lieberman (1975). At the PRF (Roll and Harary, 1976), Harary projects himself to a room where we have posted large letters of the alphabet, but sees the wrong letters as often as the right. Osis (1978) builds an optical device with two images of the target, one that can be seen if the OBEer is located in front of the device, and one that is concealed inside and presumably perceptible only to a non-OBE form of ESP. The subjects, instructed to stand out-of-body in front of the box, sometimes describe one image, sometimes the other, and sometimes they see neither. At times the subjects score below chance expectancy, thereby showing evidence of psi-missing, a hallmark of ESP. OBEs, it seems, are not perceptions of physical reality, but mental constructs that may or may not reflect actual events.

Rhine's position that mind is unlimited by physical space and time implies life after death but at the same time makes it impossible to verify. If ESP has no limits, evidence for contact with the dead can equally well be due to the psychic abilities of the living subjects.

Dead men may tell no tales, but people who have nearly died have a lot to say. Raymond Moody (1976), a psychiatry intern at the University of Virginia, listens as patients who almost died describe OBEs and transcendent experiences. I hear similar stories from people who are in good health but deep despair. Like Moody's patients, they have given up hope when they find themselves out-of-body and moving to a world of love and light. Kenneth Ring (1984) brings us down to earth with the discovery that even near-death OBEs may give erroneous information. The experience of being out of the body is unmistakable, but OBEers are often wrong about where they went.

Ian Stevenson (1974b, 1975, 1977, 1980) finds evidence in the "rebirth memories" of some young children that they have lived before. An examination of the cases (Roll, 1984) reveals a familiar feature; the images of a previous life tend to emerge in the environment where it was lived. As Price points out, past events may persist in the places and among the people where the events occurred. There they may take the form of apparitional images, mediumistic communications, psychometric impressions, or memories from another life. The past events often concern people who suffer sudden illness, attack, or accident. When this results in death, the apparitions may be interpreted as the return of the dead, and the remembered events as their souls reborn in another body, or in the case of trance mediums more briefly in the medium's body. But the apparitions and memories associated with the departed seem no different from those representing people who are still living. There is a further similarity. Apparitions are often spun from whole cloth, with no relation to real persons; likewise, "false rebirth memories" are generously interspersed among those that reflect actual lives.

The finding that children seem more sensitive than adults in responding to past lives may be due to children's greater psychic sensitivity (Drewes and Drucker, 1991; Shields, 1976; Rhine, 1961). The question why a particular child should pick up a particular string of past events and not others remains unanswered. A rebirth case involving an adult woman shows the remembered life to be related to her present needs (Roll and Lagle, 1987).

The best experiential evidence for a soul that can exist apart from the body, out-of-body experiences, dissolves in the light of systematic examination. This does not mean that OBEs are fly-by-nights. They have a significant purpose, not as vehicles for survival in the next world but as aids to survival in this (Noyes, 1972; Ehrenwald, 1974). When a person is in the depth of despair and life is at risk physically or mentally, an ejection seat seems to be activated in the mind that lets the conscious self escape or seem to escape, like the pilot from a damaged plane. The OBE self, feeling free from the damaged vehicle, allows its automatic pilot to take over. Anxiety is reduced, the autonomic nervous system switches from sympathetic to parasympathetic, heart action is lowered, and bloodflow is diverted from the extremities to vital organs. If the body has been damaged by accident or attack, bleeding may slow down. At the same time, the relaxed state is conducive to psychic sensing, with the result that the out-of-body experience is sometimes illuminated by awareness of actual events.

Gaither Pratt often tells me he will die before old age. One November day in 1979, he stands by the fridge in his kitchen, when he falls over without warning. He is sixty-nine and leaves well prepared. Gaither has set the combination of a padlock and promises to return, if he can, with the numbers that will open it. As an aid to memory, he encodes the numbers in a sentence he can easily recall. We arrange for a medium to try for the key. Psychic communication often flows best between close relatives, so I ask Gaither's daughter and one of his sons to join the project (Berger et al., 1981; Roll, 1981). Gaither is a persistent, even dogged researcher before death; if his determination endures afterwards, and if the means are there, he will fulfill the mission. We have no success. Ian Stevenson (1980), who invented the method, records thirty attempts for lock combinations from the recently deceased, and thirty failures. Previous trials for posthumous messages have the same outcome (Gay et al., 1955; Salter, 1958; Berger, 1987). The single message to come through is prepared by SPR researcher J.G. Piddington (1918). It is received by the cross-correspondence mediums, unfortunately well before Piddington has passed on.

Four exhaustive searches have been made for a soul existing apart from its body, studies of apparitions of the departed, rebirth memories, out-of-body experiences, and mediumistic communications, including posthumous messages. Explorations for the departed have been made also in supposed phone calls from the other side (Rogo and Bayless, 1979), in tape recordings (Raudive, 1971; Roll, 1989), and in dreams. None have provided evidence for the existence of the departed beyond their places and people.

Does the soul then dissolve at death? I don't think so, but the evidence is not where we have looked.

The search for the soul has been obscured by the long shadow of Rene Descartes. Psychic researchers have assumed that the soul, if it endures, must be separate from the material world; they have assumed that the soul must be distinct from other souls; and they have assumed that it must be engaged in conceptual thought.

We have been like Nasrudin, the mythical Muslim sage, when he is trying to find his lost key. A passerby sees him searching under a street light and asks where he lost it. Nasrudin points down a dark road, and the passerby asks why he isn't looking there. Nasrudin replies, "Why, there's no light there!" The Cartesian *cogito ergo sum* casts a circle of light, but not where the key to life after death can be found.

Searching elsewhere, we see a different soul. The memories and semblages of the deceased do not persist in a nonmaterial realm, but among their places and objects. Nor can the identities of the departed always be distinguished. In one mediumistic study (Hyslop, 1905) a father's memories are mixed with his daughter's, in another (Hyslop, 1908) the names of sister and mother are transposed, and in a third, the departed ". . . lost completely the sense of personal identity" (1908, p. 347). It is primarily people whose lives overlap before death that seem to be entwined afterwards. A medium describes the lives of two brothers as one, and another medium adds events to the life of the primary communicator from the person's father-in-law (Stevenson, 1973b). Overlapping identities are found as well in rebirth cases (Stevenson, 1974, pp. 67-91 and pp. 274-320).

The Cartesian credo has deep religious and sociological roots, and it conforms to contemporary concepts of mind. The human brain has two compartments, of which the left is usually the seat of language and thereby of the sense of self as an entity cut off from others (Persinger, 1993). There is another perspective, the view from the right hemisphere, with its wider vista and sense of self (Roll and Persinger, 1996).

The limited vision restricts the full expression of human nature. The isolated soul, subject to the logic of its left mind, finds itself in a race of conquest and compiling. The only lane in life becomes the fast lane. When time is short, space contracts and the landscape loses its luster. Piles of possessions replace love and compassion. Possessions possess, and life becomes an addiction to addition. The right mind, less vocal and less enamored of number, opens to a wider and more kindly view.

To get the right answer, you must ask the right question. When you ask if the mind persists after death, you must have a valid idea of mind before death. The mind of the living, we know to be formed by inheritance and by circumstance of person and place. Should we not expect the strands of mind seen after death to show the pattern of the loom where they were woven?

The Cartesian features are shown by the mind neither before death nor after. With one striking exception: the belief in an incorporeal soul, separate from others and characterized by thinking, seems supported by out-of-body experiences. The OBE self, on first acquaintance, seems a validation of the Cartesian soul. Closer up, the OBE self turns into a mirage cast up by the brain to protect itself. This is true of my OBEs, and it seems to be true of others'.

The body's soul, apparently confined to the body or apparently outside in OBEs, is not unimportant. It is the body's caretaker. The body's soul makes us look after the body, defend it or, in OBEs, seemingly leave it. But the body's soul is not our most important soul. It is subservient to a higher authority. If required by family or group, we sacrifice body and well-being for the benefit of the larger corpus. This larger body is no more righteous than the smaller, only larger. I call it the longbody (following Aanstoos, 1986). The longbody soul is our psychic self; it includes significant others as well as our lands and possessions. It stretches back in space-time, farther than the body's life.

Like the stones in a riverbed, which are found to be the bones of ancient creatures, the objects that surround us are the limbs of beings with memories and intentions that persist through time. A person's longbody includes the small body and its places as well as significant others, living and apparently departed. In the same way as the physical body persists though its cells die, a longbody persists though the selves that make it may seem to perish. ESP, PK, psychometry, and precognition connect and coordinate the limbs of the longbody across space and time (Roll, 1989).

What seems inanimate to the body's soul may be part of the longbody, notably the people and things within the person's circle of psychic interaction, such as family and friends, land and possessions. These are permeated with meaning and memory; they are as mental as they are material. The dualistic view is the view from the small body. Matter feels different from mind to the small body, heavy, recalcitrant, immune to command, and so we place it in another part of nature.

With the new perspective, the data of psychical research fall into place like so many pieces of a jigsaw puzzle. Apparitions of the dead, rebirth memories, mediumistic communications, or the scenes of the past from a psychometric object reveal a space behind the familiar space, "a vast amount of *something behind* the physical object as it appears to our senses," as Tyrrell saw.

Physicists tell us that time and space extend beyond the visible and touchable four-dimensional objects that make up the world for the body. From the longbody perspective, four-dimensional space-time is not restricted to the fraction of a second that confines the classical senses, but extends into the past of person and place. This realm may be measured by meter and minute but is ruled by meaning.

Meaning can contract space-time. An emotionally charged event in the distant past can fold up time to loom over the present. This is not only evidenced by the findings of psychology and psychical research but is seen wherever the human drama unfolds, in Bosnia, Ireland, Palestine, Sri Lanka, Rwanda. The material world is alive with mind, sometimes deadly mind. When this is understood, the danger may be deflected.

As we step back for the wide view, space-time may contract, but family increases. Black and white are parent and child, Jew and Arab are brothers. Another step, and we have four legs, then fins. When we move forward again, and do not forget, kinship and kindness remain.

If clouds from the past threaten the future, a vision may appear on the mind's screen that goes beyond its knowing. Precognition is not future-seeing but prediction drawn from meaning-space-time. We know the future insofar as we know the past. The wider and deeper we are present in the past, the better we may see and shape the future. If we do not know our roots, we cannot know the future or mold it. Forecasting may be the most important form of psychic sensing and may guide behavior whether it enters awareness or not. Depending on intention, accident may be avoided or evoked; the positive or negative psi of everyday life.

The longbody is restricted by other longbodies and their places and must often fight for life or expansion. Like the body, the longbody is subject to disease and dissolution. Poltergeist disturbances are not visitations by demons but can be symptoms of longbodies in distress. The soul of our longbody may be sensed as angelic, longbodies as demonic. Good and evil depend on position.

What we have found is not a mind that may survive apart from its body, but rather groups, or longbodies, that we know persist beyond the lives of their members. The question is not if your longbody survives your death; it does if your group does. The question is whether you will be aware of your longbody after death. Rosalind Heywood (1976), the SPR writer and researcher, describes two longbody experiences, one where she seems to merge with a being at the Houses of Parliament. The body of this being, she feels, consists of its members, past and present, and persists after their goings. At Eton, her son's school, she is similarly absorbed. These embodied beings, persisting into the future and interwoven with other parts of her longbody, become her vehicle for survival.

We are a triple helix of body and body's soul, longbody and psyche, and universe and Big Mind. Three interlaced lineages, genetic/biological, social/psychic and religious/spiritual. Or simply body, mind, and spirit. To be well is to express our triune nature by intention and action. To be moral is to be selfish in the larger sense. You are your brother's keeper because his self is part of your self.

Near-death experiences give supporting experiential evidence. They often begin with the experience of the body's self detaching from the body and occupying another, mental one. The OBE body, itself a mental image, moves about within the mental sphere that has been formed by its bodily life. Sometimes there is a bleedthrough to the psychic realm, and the OBEer may catch glimpses of the larger landscape, but the little self cannot land without letting go of its littleness, without dying. In terms of experienced time, this could be ages because of the slowing of the brain's clock. The second phase of the NDE may occur after a transformation pictured as moving through a tunnel into a vibrant realm where the OBE soul expands into a new and larger self, the psychic soul of the longbody. This is often experienced as an ecstatic union with loved ones, living and departed. The mythical marriage of Eros and Psyche is consumated.

There is a dark side. The union with others includes those whom the person has hurt in life, now with the tables turned. Hurtful deeds are painfully felt, the way the receiver experienced them. The balance restored, night becomes day, and the NDEer is freed for the final phase, union with the being of love and light, with Big Mind.

Another way opens up to explore longbodies. It begins at Duke. Rhine has an impressive crystal ball on his desk that I admire. I'll have more use for it than he, he says, and gives it me. I don't see any images, but it's a good conversation piece. When Raymond Moody visits, he asks about it. I explain, and Moody sees an image almost at once. Later on, he questions me about apparitions. I don't see any myself, but work with people who do; they cause no harm, I say, and often point to problems that need solving. Moody, a lover of Greek antiquity, digs deeper and discovers the temples of the dead where the ancients went to see their departed. The centerpiece was a cauldron of oil or water, a liquid crystal ball. Others use reflective surfaces such as shiny metals or mirrors. Moody installs one in his home and invites visitors to see what they can. Many see their loved ones (Moody & Perry, 1992). When he asks me to try, I see no person but have a peculiar vision. At the center of the field, somewhat to the right, I see a shape of intertwined images that I interpret as knowledge attained and applied. To the left there is floating form, unattached to the former but with feelers stretched out in its direction. It represents, I know, poltergeists and haunts and the people caught in their web. The image is not mysterious but reflects my preoccupation with these disturbances and how to bring them to healing light.

Moody cannot respond to all the requests for reunion sessions and asks others to help. In this way, I set up a mirror room in my home where people come to seek their departed (Roll and Braun, 1995). The method makes good sense to me. You use a mirror to see yourself; Moody's mirror is for seeing your longbody, especially members you seem to have lost.

This is how it all adds up, at least for me. I find myself as a soul separate from the body. I look closely and find this soul is within and supports my body. Then parapsychology shows me a larger soul, a psychic soul, and I see this soul nourish a larger body. Beyond this I observe the planet and the Milky Way and I sense a larger sustenance still. Guided from before, I reason that this is the soul of the universe that surrounds me.

For each soul there is a time and a place, and an end of time and place. When the body dies, the borders of its soul subside into the psyche, the soul of the longbody, and its larger space. When the longbody dies, the psyche is absorbed in Big Mind. Each body and soul is emplaced in its own realm of time and place, the larger encompassing the small, the small usually unaware of the larger. Nothing disappears; only the vision expands or contracts.

The larger states of awareness can best be understood by explorers who are able to go there, or are willing to be guided by those who can. You cannot draw a reliable map without knowing the land. Charles Tart's (1972) manual of "state-specific" sciences has guidelines.

> "Guess now who holds thee?" "Death," I said.
> But there the silver answer rang, "Not Death, but Love."
> — Elizabeth Barrett Browning
> *Sonnets from the Portuguese*

Notes:

1. Whately Carington (1944, 1945) incorporated the same concept into his "association theory of telepathy." According to this, a telepathic link may be established between people solely by their having ideas or thoughts in common. The proposal is one of the few testable theories of telepathy and I attempt, unsuccessfully, to verify it at Oxford (Roll, 1975, pp. 87-94).

Thanks to the Bigelow Foundation for support in the writing of this paper, and to Lisa Sheehan for editorial assistance.

Chapter 3
Some Reflections on Religion and Anomalies of Consciousness

K. Ramakrishna Rao

Introduction

In Western societies, religion and science have managed somehow to accommodate each other and coexist. The divinity school and the medical school, for example, situated as they are side by side in the same campus, teach different and often contradictory things about who we are, where we come from, and what happens when we die. The chaplain and the physician in the hospital setting have functions that are based on conflicting assumptions concerning human nature. The same person can be a scientist in the lab, wholly working within a materialistic and rationalistic framework, and a man of faith, devotedly attending church on Sundays and offering prayers to the almighty God.

Parapsychology began as an endeavor to test the assumptions of both science and religion with the hope of finding the common basis in fact. Many of the pioneers in the field of parapsychology were motivated by the expectation that the phenomena they were investigating would have a scientific bearing on their religious beliefs. J.B. Rhine, for example, was drawn to psychical research, as it was then called, after a double disappointment—first with religion and then with science.

Rhine strongly felt that parapsychology would eventually provide a scientific basis for religion and that parapsychology would be to religion what biology is to medicine, or physics to engineering (Rhine, 1947). Originally he planned to become a preacher, but he dropped out of the course because he "saw no logical ground for the role of the minister." He told his psychology professor before leaving the school:

In my course on religion we talked about man's soul as if it were the most real thing in the world, and over here in psychology we talked about brain reactions as if that is all we know about human beings. The word "soul" doesn't appear in any of the textbooks we have read. You don't even use it in the classroom. Thus in one classroom I am a living soul; in the other, a brain machine. Now these two do not parallel; they are divergent. I had to choose between them; and since I get a feeling of certainty in all my science classes that I can't get anywhere else, the more scientific I get, the less I find there is for me to go out and preach about. I just do not know what to think about these questions in religion. I do not know if there is any spiritual world (Rhine, 1951).

Abandoning the goal of becoming a minister, Rhine, along with his wife Louisa, pursued graduate study in biology at the University of Chicago with "devotedly single-minded . . . acceptance of mechanism in biology" (Rhine & Rhine, 1978). The Rhines respected thoroughly the "hard science approach" and felt strongly that science is the ultimate answer for all the questions of fact. They had little sympathy with those like their departmental head in botany, who defended "evolution at the famous Scopes trial in Tennessee, but at the same time . . . was the national lay leader of the Presbyterian Church" (p. 185). "What was science worth," they asked themselves, "if it could not quite as logically apply to questions in one department of science as in others? If we were fascinated by the baffling scientific story of man's evolutionary origin, why should we not give all the other questions of fact over to research instead of leaving them to speculative philosophies and authoritarian theologies?" (p. 185).

Rhine clearly underestimated the limiting power of the epistemological assumptions of science on the one hand and the extent of reluctance on the part of religious traditions to come under scientific scrutiny on the other. We see now why neither science nor religion is comfortable in the company of scientific parapsychology. Most mainstream scientists have simply ignored the data the Rhines and their colleagues have so carefully gathered; and some have even expressed their unconcealed hostility to the field of parapsychology. At the same time, very few religious leaders have come out in support of the study of parapsychological phenomena. Some doggedly condemned the field as the devil's workshop. Whereas scientists have ruled out the case for psi on *a priori* grounds of its logical impossibility, religionists have repudiated it on moral grounds.

Every religion, to the extent it is institutionalized, tends to perpetuate orthodoxy and fundamentalism beyond the essentials of religious experience. Brian Inglis (1977), for example, suggests that as Christianity spread and had to deal with pagan rituals there arose a need to specify authority and endorse orthodoxy. The practice of divination which was quite prevalent then became a suspect because one could propagate heresy as something inspired by the holy spirit. Consequently, the institution of oracles was suppressed by the politically powerful Christian orthodoxy. Mediumistic practices and inspirational utterances tended to be regarded as the work of demons which acquired the connotation of evil spirits.

Brian and Lynne MacKenzie (1980) have called our attention in a very pointed way to the inherent incompatibility of science and psychical research. They have argued that "the incompatibility of parapsychology with modern science is neither accidental nor recent, but is built into the assumptive base of modern science itself. It is because the aims and claims of parapsychology clash so strongly with this assumptive base that the field attracts such hostility" (p. 135).

The spectacular achievements of physical scientists have had such a powerful impact that reality has come to be equated with its physical dimensions. A mathematico-physical view of nature has been all that seems warranted on rational grounds, and anything that has stood in opposition to this view is suspect and to be rejected in scholarly and scientific circles. To be sure, many religious convictions have come into sharp conflict with the scientific world view. Theologians have dealt with these conflicts mostly by avoiding confrontation and by seeking accommodation with science by practicing "great circumspection" in explaining scriptures. They either have retreated from asserting specific statements of fact that conflicted with scientific views or have attempted, where possible, to join science for a common demonstration of certain tenets (MacKenzie & MacKenzie, 1980). There is thus no denial of the manifest opposition between the so-called scientific world view and parapsychology on the one hand and between religion and psi research on the other. At the same time it is not difficult to see that parapsychology in its essentials is not incompatible with religion or science in their true senses. I shall argue in what follows that parapsychological phenomena provide the essential grounds for believing in and validating religious experience and in so doing we find in parapsychology the necessary interface between science and religion.

On Religion

According to Arnold Toynbee (1956), religions as practiced contain both essential truths and nonessential practices and propositions. This is true, according to him, of all the seven "higher religions." The essential truths, he goes on to suggest, are valid without regard to time and place. In a sense, these essential truths or counsels are indispensable to human life. Without them humanity would not be human. In order that these essential truths be communicated to people living in a certain temporal and social context, they become institutionalized, and the local and temporary circumstances influence religion, and thus the religions accumulate accidental accretions. While these are useful and necessary, one is often prone to mistake means for ends and consider the accidental accretions as no less sacrosanct than the essential truths themselves. This, according to Toynbee, is what makes the "higher religions" degenerate into taboo. Hence we are faced with the "task of disengaging the essence from the non-essentials in mankind's religious heritage." As he puts it: "What is permanent and universal has always and everywhere to be translated into something temporary and local in order to make it accessible to particular human beings here and now. But we ought never to allow ourselves to forget that every translation of this kind is bound to be a mistranslation to some extent and that it is therefore also bound to be contingent and provisional. The penalty for neglecting the perpetually urgent task of discarding the current mistranslation is to allow the light radiated by the essence of a religion to be shut off from human souls by an opaque film of accretions" (Toynbee, 1956, pp. 271-272).

True religion, then, is not necessarily what goes on in the name of religion. Institutionalized religion is often a mistranslation of higher truths experienced by the truly religious, the founders of various religions. Religion in its basic connotation is a means of experiencing a higher level of consciousness. Religion therefore may not be considered as a body of sacred truths, but rather a method or a set of practices believed to achieve a state of awareness and feeling that takes us beyond the normal states of awareness and being, and to stand in a special relationship to something considered divine.

William James (1914), in a similar vein, defends "experience" as being more fundamental to religious life than any philosophy. He argues that the efforts to construct religious objects out of reason alone resulted in dogmatic theologies. It is James's conviction that the religious truths should be treated on a par with scientific truths. He says that "the attempt to demonstrate by purely intellectual processes the truth of the deliverances of direct religious experience is absolutely hopeless" (p. 455). All religions unanimously hold that their truths are facts of experience. And if facts cannot establish their own truth, no abstract reasoning could hope to prove it. According to James, *"immediate luminousness . . . philosophical reasonableness,* and *moral helpfulness* are the only criteria" (p. 18) by which true religious experiences are identified.

James believes that personal religious experiences are the outcome of mystical states of consciousness and that these states provide the factual evidence for the religious hypothesis. James mentions four marks by which we can justifiably distinguish a mystic experience from a non-mystic experience. First, mystic experiences are ineffable in that they defy any adequate expression in words. They are more like the experiences of feeling than of intellect. Second, they possess a noetic quality. Unlike the experiences of feeling, they are experiences of knowledge. They carry with them a kind of conviction. "They are illuminations, revelations, full of significance and importance" (p. 380). Transiency and passivity are the other two less sharply marked criteria of a mystic state.

In the Eastern traditions, the goal of religious endeavor is to achieve a state of transcendence. The Buddha sought to identify the source of all suffering and to overcome it by attaining the state of transcendence called *nirvana.* It is a state of fulfillment, of equanimity, of calm contentment and of supreme insight. He believed that the transformation to a state of transcendence from *samsara,* the ego-serving mundane existence, can be brought about by a system of practical training, self-discipline, and effort. As Radhakrishnan points out, the Buddha sought "to start a religion independent of dogma and priesthood, sacrifice and sacrament, which would insist on an inward change of heart and a system of self-culture" (1992, Vol. 1, p. 357).

In the Advaita tradition of the Hindus, the ultimate reality is the pure being of consciousness as such. The empirical being or the individual consciousness is a phenomenal manifestation of the supreme conscious being, limited by the mind, intellect, senses, and body. The supreme consciousness not only provides the necessary support to the individual but also acts as the witnessing consciousness throughout the life history of the individual. It is possible to transcend the limitations of our bodily conditions and achieve understanding of the supreme, this understanding consisting of the realization of the identity of the individual consciousness with the supreme consciousness.

Advaita distinguishes between four states of consciousness: (1) the waking state, (2) the dream state, (3) the state of deep sleep, and (4) the transcendental state. In the waking state the content of our consciousness is largely determined by external objects. It is the state where consciousness is processed by the whole set of our psychophysical system. Dream consciousness is made up of the same stuff as waking consciousness, except that its content is not empirically real. It is illusory in the sense that on waking one realizes the unreality of what is experienced in the dream. The deep sleep state is characterized by the abeyance of all distinctions including the distinction of the subject from the object. The fourth state of consciousness, the transcendental state, as described in the *Mandukya Upanishad,* is "beyond empirical determination, beyond the grasp (of the mind), undemonstrable, unthinkable, indescribable, of the nature of the consciousness alone wherein all phenomena cease, unchanging, peaceful and nondual."

When one attains the fourth state of consciousness, there is a realization of the identity of the individual and the supreme consciousness. Just as on waking one recognizes the illusoriness of dreams, so does the one who realizes the highest state of consciousness understand the illusoriness of waking experience. What seems to be unique to transcendental or pure consciousness is that it is, unlike any phenomenal awareness, nonintentional. There is no object that one is conscious of, except consciousness itself. Pure consciousness is nonintentional and objectless and contains no ego sense. Phenomenal awareness of objects as manifested in our ordinary consciousness belongs to conscious *states* but not to consciousness as *such.*

Partaking in pure consciousness gives one the experience of transcendence. In a state of transcendence one loses such distinctions as *I* and the *other,* the *subject* and the *object.* The experiences themselves go beyond our normal categories of understanding, time, space, and causation. For that reason it is considered an ineffable state. It is suggested that the experience of transcendence is accompanied, not only by a conviction of its transcendental character, but also by remarkable behavioral and attitudinal changes such as those attributed to saints. It appears likely that the experience of transcendence involves *realization* that goes beyond mere understanding. It is a state where there is no dissociation between knowing and being as exemplified in the Upanishadic statement "knowing Brahman is becoming Brahman." The transcendental state of pure consciousness is not a rational presupposition or a logical abstraction. It is claimed to be a fact of mystical experience. In Eastern traditions, specific procedures are suggested for experiencing transcendental states. Even in the Western religious traditions, prayer and ascetic practices may serve similar roles.

In summary, then, a distinction may be made between religion as subjective transcendental experience and institutionalized religion, a body of practices and beliefs. The latter at its best is a means of obtaining religious experience, a transcendental state of consciousness.

On Parapsychology

Over the years, parapsychology has acquired a variety of connotations, some restrictive and some broad and sweeping. I believe, however, that a general consensus definition of parapsychology would be that it is the study of anomalies of consciousness. In the Western scientific tradition, consciousness is considered to be localized and bound to individual cortical structures and therefore cannot exist independently of the brain. It is assumed to be self-evident that it is impossible to have awareness of a physical event or a material object without being in a sensory contact with that event or object and that it is impossible for consciousness to cause any changes in the material world other than changes in one's own brain (Broad, 1953). These presumptions rule out the possibility of (a) consciousness surviving bodily death, (b) one having information about objects and events that are shielded from his/her senses, and (c) consciousness directly influencing external objects or events.

Since the beginning of the recorded history of human kind there have been reports suggestive of paranormal communication (Inglis, 1977). There is growing scientific evidence to suggest the possibility of acquiring information that is apparently received independently of our sensory process as in extrasensory perception (ESP) and of direct action of mind over matter independent of our motor system as in psychokinesis (PK) (Rao and Palmer, 1987). Also, there are a number of cases of a person claiming to remember events in a previous life (Stevenson, 1974, 1977).

Clearly, all these phenomena are inconsistent with the Western scientific world view. Therefore, they are regarded as anomalies in need of explanation.

From the time of J.B. Rhine's monograph *Extra-Sensory Perception,* first published in 1934, literally hundreds of carefully carried out experimental studies have accumulated a massive data base that not only makes a strong case for the existence of psi (a term that includes ESP and PK) but also offers interesting insights into the nature of psi. For example, the results of psi research show that the physical aspects of the target, such as size, shape, color, and form do not seem to have any intrinsic effect on psi. Neither do space and time or the causative complexity of the psi task. Any hypothetical relationship of distance to ESP must assume that there is some energy transmission between the subject and targets that is inhibited by the distance factor. But if precognition is a fact, and we have strong evidence to believe that it is, what is the nature of this transmission that occurs between the subject and the not-yet-existing target? Thus, the evidence for precognition and the success of ESP experiments over long distances lead one to believe that space and time are not constraining variables as far as psi is concerned. Another significant aspect of psi is the relative ineffectiveness of task complexity in constraining psi. Stanford (1977) has reviewed the relevant literature and concluded that "the efficiency of PK function is not reduced by increases in the complexity of the target system" (p. 375).

If psi is unconstrained by space and time and the complexity of the task, and if the psi situation is such that distinctions between thought and matter, cognition and action, subject and object become less than meaningful, it would seem that psi may function beyond the familiar categories of understanding and may point to a state of being that cannot be properly classed as mind or matter. Psi phenomena raise the question whether there exists a realm of reality beyond the phenomenal world of appearance, which is primarily a product of our information-processing capabilities and mechanisms. One may rightly wonder whether we are not dealing here with the Kantian "thing in itself." What is interesting, however, is that the thing in itself which, according to Kant, must remain forever beyond the human reach may in fact be the reality to which psi has direct access, a reality assumed by most religions.

Another characteristic of psi phenomena is the apparent lack of any discernible connection between a psi event and its assumed cause. This led C.G. Jung to postulate that psi belongs to a class of synchronistic acausal events (Jung & Pauli, 1955). To make any sense of synchronicity as an explanatory hypothesis, we have to assume a kind of omniscience on our part and regard archetypes as being nonlocal in the sense that they can function independently of space-time constraints (Rao, 1977). Yet the problem of communication between the individual and the archetypes remains unresolved. We need to explain the dirigibility aspect of psi, that is, the synchronization of archetypal activity with the wishes of the subject or the experimenter in a successful psi test.

Unlike spontaneous psi, laboratory effects involve a connection between someone's intention and the subsequent observation of an effect. Without such an intention or expectation, observed effects would be no more than improbable coincidences. It is this characteristic, often stated in terms of expectations and experimental hypotheses, that gives *meaning* to coincidences. But the volition itself, it seems to me, is not the cause of the observed effect in the sense of a formal or efficient cause. Only in a teleological sense can it be considered a cause of a psi effect. This point is becoming increasingly apparent in the theoretical attempts to regard psi as goal-oriented.

Thus there is a primary role for volition in the psi process. The attempts to explain psi by the postulates of quantum physics also find the connection between physical events and psi in the realm of human will. In Walker's quantum mechanical theory of psi (Walker, 1975), for example, the hidden variables that are postulated to reconcile the demands of the deterministic and stochastic conceptions of the development of the state vectors are equated with "will." Walker argues that will can effect changes, not only within one's brain, but also in the world outside. In PK the will of the subject or the experimenter determines the collapse of the state vector for a physical system at the quantum level with macroscopically diverse potential states.

It is interesting to note that Walker's theory, which is said to be an extension of the Copenhagen interpretation of quantum physics, sounds clearly dualistic. The will and the so-called hidden variables seem to have the same ontological primacy as energy, which accounts for the events in the material world. That the will influences only the microlevel quantum systems, which rarely manifest in macroscopic physical systems, is beside the point. What is important is that even "physical" theories of psi do seem to assume principles or processes that are not a mere extension of what is ordinarily understood as physical, but things that are commonly regarded as mental on a Cartesian model. In an important sense, Walker's theory is a significant reversal of the physicalistic model. One could even characterize it as essentially vitalistic because the central principle that accounts for psi is located in the will of the subject. This shift to a response-centered approach from the stimulus-centered physical model is what gives Walker's theory a vitalistic look. Note that Walker in his explanation of psi is not looking at the process by which the energy patterns emanating from the stimulus objects reach the subject, but rather at the object itself and the will variables. The development of a "dualistic" physics—and this is what this theory attempts to develop—would indeed constitute a paradigmatic change, and its acceptance would have revolutionary consequences for physics.

Whether consciousness and will or volition are themselves physical is not the question. The essential point here is that they are nonlocal and are unconstrained by time and space, which makes it reasonable to assume that at some level all the things in the universe are somehow interconnected or even bound together. This may be the universal oneness to which most religions refer. It may be the basis for belief in the survival of bodily death. I can speak as a Hindu and as someone familiar with Buddhism that these religions must presume a reality, in whatever form they may attempt to describe it, that seems to be an indispensable condition for parapsychological phenomena to occur, a universe in which psi would not be an anomaly. So, then, if parapsychology establishes the genuineness of psi and the nonlocal aspect of psychic phenomena, we may see the connection between the religious world view and the scientific world view.

On the Parapsychology of Religion

J.B. Rhine, the founder of experimental parapsychology, who helped to narrow the focus of the field to empirically researchable areas, felt that the parapsychology of religion is an important area to pursue. Some fifty years ago he discussed the relevance of parapsychology to religion in an editorial in the *Journal of Parapsychology*. "If parapsychology finds answers to the questions for which religious doctrines have been developed in the past," he wrote, "there is no reason why these should not replace the earlier conceptions in much the same way that chemistry has replaced alchemy and scientific medicine has taken the place of the practices of pre-scientific days" (Rhine, 1945, p. 1).

Rhine proposed to the FRNM Board of Directors in 1968 that they consider establishing a separate branch of the FRNM devoted to the parapsychology of religion. Recognizing that "organized religion is not yet ready for a deliberate step on this firmer pavement of scholarly testing," Rhine felt that "the time has come when a quiet research program could be undertaken by a branch of the FRNM which we might call the Institute for the Parapsychology of Religion."

Dr. Rhine's interest in the parapsychology of religion is of course a continuation of such interest among a long line of psychical researchers. The prominent among them are F.W.H. Myers and William James. Myers' hunch that the subliminal consciousness is the spiritual component of our personality, which is not only the source of paranormal awareness but is also the one that survives bodily death, adds a distinctive new dimension to the Western approaches to the study of consciousness. Similarly, the studies of religious experience by William James and his understanding of mystic states are a lasting contribution to the parapsychology of religion.

But Rhine was on firmer ground than his predecessors. Rhine saw in his results the scientific basis for believing that there is "an extra-physical element in man," and for rejecting the philosophy of materialism, "the chief enemy of religion." He wrote in *The New World of the Mind* (1953):

> The conclusion is inescapable that there is something operative in man that transcends the laws of matter and, therefore, by definition, a nonphysical or spiritual law is made manifest. The universe, therefore, does not conform to the prevailing materialistic concept. It is one about which it is possible to be religious; possible, at least, if the minimal requirement of religion be a philosophy of man's place in the universe based on the operation of spiritual forces (p. 227).

The basis for Rhine's belief that parapsychological phenomena point to "extra-physical" or "nonphysical" reality is the finding that psi is unconstrained by space-time barriers. Once the physical barrier is broken, Rhine thought, new possibilities open up for understanding the spiritual powers of man and the possibility that the spirit survives bodily death. Rhine also was impressed by the similarity between religious forms, such as prophecy and prayer, and types of psi, such as precognition and telepathy (Rhine, 1975).

The echo of Rhine's statement did not go unheard. In fact, a few theologians and church leaders who felt that "the corrosive acids of a materialistic science ate away at the doctrinal basis" of religious faith saw in Rhine's results a vindication. "All faiths," wrote the Rev. Alson Smith (1951), "are based on the ultimate reality of the extra-sensory, the supernormal, the supernatural" (p. 160). For Rev. Smith, ESP meant evidence (a) for the existence of the soul and of a supreme spirit, (b) for "The Kingdom of God," (c) for free will, (d) for the reality of prayer, and (e) for a basis for more effective morality.

Referring to Rhine's research, the Dean of St. Paul's, the Very Rev. W.B. Matthews (n.d.), said, "The results of these investigations are likely to confirm our faith and to undermine the 'physicalist' view of man and his mind. . . . I do not for one moment suggest that psychical research can prove the truth of religion, still less be a substitute for it. I say that I think it can help us, and for Christians simply to ignore it is foolish and faint-hearted" (p. 8).

The Eastern traditions, especially the Hindu and the Buddhist, recognize that psychic (paranormal) abilities are a natural outcome as one progresses on the path to achieve states of transcendence and has religious experience. They warn, however, that these should not become ends in themselves, but be taken as guideposts to recognize one's success in the pursuit of transcendence. Therefore we read in *Visuddhimagga:* "Psychic powers are those of an average man. Like a child lying on its back and like tender corn it is difficult to manage. It is broken by the slightest thing. It is an impediment to insight, but not to concentration because it ought to be obtained when concentration is obtained" (Buddhaghosa 1923, p. 113).

Parapsychology has substantial implications for religion, constituting a new area of study, the parapsychology of religion. The parapsychology of religion can (1) provide descriptive accounts of religious experience that would apply universally, independent of individual religions; (2) construct empirical tests for validating specific forms of religious experience; (3) discover significant correlations between religious beliefs and practices on the one hand and psychic abilities on the other; (4) formulate instructional aids for those desiring to have religious experience; (5) give training in therapeutic and counseling skills to clergy so that they can responsibly deal with those having religious or pseudo-religious experiences; and (6) help bridge the chasm between religion and science.

All major religions are based on the teachings of a few, described variously as prophets, saints, *rishis,* and so on. All these teachings are claimed to be based on their intense personal experiences. What is the nature of these experiences qua experiences? I am persuaded that a systematic and descriptive study of such experiences would reveal something more basic to religious experience than do the content of these experiences translated to us in common language forms. Religious experience, we are told, is essentially ineffable. The differences in the statement of the content of religious experience as described in various religions may be due to the difficulties of translating the ineffable experience into cognitive content. Religious experience, the mystic experience, the peak experience, and all paranormal experiences may have one thing in common. They are the encounters with consciousness *as such,* pure consciousness in which there is no subject-object distinction, no content but a transformational process that often results in remarkable behavioral changes and beliefs and sometimes translates itself into informational content.

If phenomenological studies of those who have religious and paranormal experiences give us an appropriate description of the essential aspects of such experience, it should be possible to construct empirical tests for validating those experiences as involving genuine access to consciousness as such. For example, criteria for identifying religious experience and measuring its depth and intensity may be developed. Such criteria would be useful in distinguishing genuine religious experience from pseudo-religious experience in a manner similar to the one of distinguishing the fake psychic experiences from the genuine. Several religious forms such as prophesies, prayer, and spiritual healing practices have their counterparts in parapsychological phenomena—precognition, telepathy and bio-PK. Parapsychological results provide a measure of scientific justification for believing that the future can be predicted, that extrasensory mind-to-mind communication is possible, and that it is possible to influence external systems directly by the mind without involving sensory-motor apparatus. An example is the research of Bernard Grad (1965) with Estebany, who was able to influence the growth of plants and healing of wounds in mice. What is of special interest is that Estebany used prayer as a vehicle to channel his abilities. Larry Dossey (1993) discusses the power of prayer in his recent book and makes explicit the connection between prayer, healing, and parapsychology.

> *Prayer says something incalculably important about who we are and what our destiny may be.* As we shall see, prayer is a genuinely *nonlocal* event—that is, it is not confined to a specific place in space or to a specific moment in time. Prayer reaches outside the here-and-now; it operates at a distance and outside the present moment. Since prayer is initiated by a mental action, this implies that there is some aspect of our psyche that also is genuinely nonlocal (p. 6).

If genuine religious and paranormal experiences are grounded in the same source (Clark, 1977), then they must manifest correlations of various sorts. Rhea White (1982) points out numerous instances of psi in the lives of saints. These should be studied in depth. C.B. Nash (1958) found a significant correlation between ESP scores and religious values. Religious and mystical experiences seem to induce important and sometimes instant positive transformations in one's life. Similar transformations appear to accompany near-death experiences. Surveys indicate also that those experiencing psychic experiences also report religious or transcendent experiences, and the former like the latter have a valuable effect on the lives of the experiencers (Kennedy, Kanthamani and Palmer, 1994).

If, as William James states, "the mother sea and fountain-head of all religions lie in the mystical experiences of the individual" (Allen, 1967, p. 425), and if mystical experiences may be had by following certain procedures such as meditation, it should be possible by a systematic study of these procedures and practices as well as other psychic development strategies to develop instructional aids for those aspiring to have religious experience. In the Eastern traditions, as in Patanjali yoga, there exist elaborate descriptive accounts of recommended practices that are believed to lead one to experience higher levels of consciousness, including religious experience. These deserve to be studied carefully and systematized appropriately based on empirical fact.

The parapsychology of religion so pursued could be invaluable to clergy in their training not only for their own pursuit of personal religious growth but also for providing counseling to the clients in their congregations. As in the realm of psychic phenomena, there are pseudo-religious phenomena that mimic the genuine. It is therefore necessary to understand genuine religious experiences as distinct from pseudo, religious-like experiences. The latter may indicate maladjustment and mental illness. The emphasis on the importance of teacher, the *guru,* in the Eastern religious traditions is relevant here. The *guru* is the guide who at every stage of religious development is able to counsel the disciple to proceed in the right direction, avoiding the pitfalls (Rao, 1988).

We need no longer base the validity of our religious beliefs and practices on doctrinal philosophies and theologies inasmuch as they are born out of actual experience and their veridicality can be attested by observation. All religions claim that their "truths" are received as revelations, which are essentially extrasensory forms of knowledge. That knowledge can be obtained independently of rational discourse and sensory experience is a fact that parapsychology has sought to establish. The parapsychology of religion may thus provide the empirical ground for dealing with religious beliefs and practices and thus bridge the chasm between religion and science.

Research has already revealed several commonalities between religious experience and psi phenomena. They point to the possibility of some of our experiences being nonlocal and transpersonal. Factors such as belief and motivation seem necessary for manifesting psi as well as religious experience. Internal attention states such as meditation and conditions of sensory deprivation are known to facilitate the occurrence of religions experience as well as psychic phenomena. Finally, religious experience has important transformational consequences for the one who has the experience. Paranormal phenomena also seem to have similar effects. People with near-death experiences report significant life style changes after the NDE. Abraham Maslow (1968) also reports such transformations when people have what he calls peak experiences. Therefore, one wonders whether in all these cases people are not accessing consciousness as such.

Inasmuch as the characteristics of psi are inconsistent with the materialistic conception of the universe and point to a reality closer to the one that underlies major religious traditions, we may expect parapsychology to provide the necessary interface between science and religion. To be sure, science shall remain science (i.e., rational inquiry into reality), and religion religion (i.e., revelatory experience of reality). But they do not have to contradict or negate each other.

Chapter 4
Exceptional Human Experiences and the Experiential Paradigm

Rhea A. White

In a review essay on Jerome Bruner's *Acts of Meaning*, I contrasted seven negative and seven positive story lines that can be applied to exceptional human experiences (EHEs) (White, 1993c, p. 10). *Exceptional human experience* is a global term for what have been called mystical, psychic, peak, and flow experiences. Although I have isolated more than eighty types of EHEs, for purposes of this article, it is not necessary to list them all. Instead, I will list the five main classes with two examples of each: I. Mystical experience (conversion, unitive experience); II. Psychic experience (out-of-body experience [OBE], precognition); III. Encounter-type experience (angel encounter, UFOs); IV. Death-related experience (mediumistic experience, near-death experience [NDE]); and V. Exceptional normal experience (aesthetic experience, empathy).

By "story lines" I mean folk explanations that are used in daily life to affirm or deny the reality of exceptional human experience. I feel these story lines, or narrative themes, play a very important role. Not only do they influence the lives of the experiencers, who must live with one or more of these labels, but the more socially sanctioned narratives may partly determine the spiritual quality (or lack thereof) of a culture by allowing (or preventing) the expression of spirituality in daily life. The recognition or rejection of exceptional experiences is influenced less by academic theories than by the story lines about them that are in active use at any given time in specific societies and even entire cultures. Although scientists may well say these so-called explanations are completely unfounded and very likely illusory, "mere folk psychology," nonetheless they are more powerful than scientific data or theories when it comes to how people respond to exceptional experiences, whether their own or those of others. They also can influence or even change the "reality" science studies, because that reality at least partially is socially constructed.

Before going further, I will summarize my philosophy of exceptional human experience. I cannot define EHEs outside the context of a broad definition of human nature or, as I prefer to say, human being. I think that the most viable aspect of humans is that both as a species and as individuals, no matter when, where, or how long we live, we are unfinished creatures. Moreover, that is not our curse but our glory. I think Keats was correct in saying that earth is "a vale for soul-making." Because we are transitional creatures, there will always be more for us to grow into and become—more to learn, more to know, more to be, more to share. Everyone's life aim, then, should be not simply to maintain the status quo, but to expand both inner and outer boundaries. The question each of us must ask, and that only we can answer, is: What is the best way for me to grow? What directions should I take that will enable me to express what I am in the fullest way, given my native talents and my life circumstances?

I don't think this question can be answered solely by reason and logic. We need to become aware of what Jung called the gradient of our beings. I think the best way to sense that drift is via the exceptional human experiences that life gives us. By definition, we cannot make them happen. They are as spontaneous as moments of grace, which indeed they may be.

I also need to explain why I am dealing, in this book devoted to parapsychology and religion, with exceptional human experiences in general, not just psychic experiences. I can no longer think of psychic experiences in a vacuum without relating them to other exceptional experiences and to life itself. I now treat psychic experiences as one type of exceptional human experience for several reasons that are outgrowths of either Western postmodern ideas or folk views concerning these experiences. For too long academics, especially in psychology and parapsychology, have ignored the folk wisdom of the general populace, a point which is also argued by Bruner (1990). I am trying to learn about psychic and other EHEs from fellow humans regardless of how they make their livings, their social situations, or their educational backgrounds. I think intellectually untrained minds may have more to teach academics about psychic and other exceptional human experiences than academics can currently teach them.

But even academically, a growing number of surveys conducted over the past twenty-five years by social psychologists, sociologists, and national opinion pollsters, such as Gallup and the National Opinion Research Center, do not deal simply with parapsychological experiences. They cover a broad range of experiences that are lumped together under the rubric of "the paranormal," including mystical and psychical experiences, UFOs, witchcraft, NDEs, magic, OBEs, Loch Ness monster, Bigfoot, Bermuda triangle, astrology, etc. At first I was simply annoyed by this grouping. I read the parts relevant to psychic experiences and ignored the rest. Then some people began theorizing across whole groups of experiences. Some, like Neher (1980) and Reed (1988), attempted to explain away the experiences. Others, notably Hilary Evans (1984, 1987), tried to develop a theory that would include and connect many of them. Others, such as Grosso (1985), Rojcewicz (1986), and Stillings (1989a, 1989b) connected three or more types of exceptional experience. Other investigators who set out to study only one type of EHE, such as NDEs or UFOs or mystical experiences, found that at some stage psychic experiences were associated with the experience they were studying. I regret that space does not permit me to do justice to all the people involved in this highly important connective work.

Finally, at the folk level, people in general apparently do not separate psychic and mystical experiences as sharply as scholars studying individual types of EHEs, especially parapsychologists. For example, for years *Fate* magazine has had a column based on letters from readers called "True Mystic Experiences," but most of the experiences published are psychic experiences. The Religious Experiences Research Unit at Oxford University, now the Alister Hardy Research Centre, on the other hand, has been collecting spiritual experiences for many years, but a goodly number of them are what parapsychologists would label spontaneous psi experiences (e.g., see Hardy, 1979).

All of these straws in the wind encouraged me to let go of the hard and fast boundaries I had assumed existed between these different types of experience and to dive into a murky sea where differentiation was decidedly blurred and sometimes, perhaps the best of times, practically nonexistent. Currently I think of this sea as the matrix of the new worldview we need so desperately, a view that connects individuals, regardless of their stations in life, with the sacred.

I also think of the new worldview as a picture puzzle, with all the different kinds of exceptional experiences that the old worldview considered "paranormal" or "anomalous" or "unusual" as pieces of the puzzle. In order to complete the puzzle we need to do two things. We need to gather all the pieces—that is, recognize all the different forms of exceptional human experience—and we need to keep in mind the overall picture that is emerging as we connect the pieces with one another. No single experience (i.e., puzzle piece) can possibly reveal the entire picture. Only through the connective work of fitting more and more pieces together will the general worldview emerge. Ken Ring (1989a, 1992) is now relating his work with NDEs to UFO encounters. Raymond Moody (Moody & Perry, 1993) is now relating his work with NDEs to mirror visions. Gabbard and Twemlow (1984), in their pioneer research on out-of-body experiences, found that their OBEers were also having mystical and psychic experiences. UFO investigators also are noting that mystical and psychic experiences are associated with UFO encounters (Cassirer, 1988; Mack, 1994; Ring, 1992).

Other writers, taking note that certain people have a tendency to have several types of EHEs, have attributed this to the fact that they may be fantasy-prone individuals, and fantasy may take several different forms. I suggest that in actuality they may be more in touch than other people with spiritual reality, or perhaps with what Ring (1989b, 1992), Stillings (1989a), and others are calling the imaginal. If one does not view individual EHEs as beads on a string but as seeds of spiritual growth, I have observed that in time, and by heeding the message inherent in each exceptional experience, experiencers tend to have additional experiences of the same and/or other types, depending on their situations at the time, not because they are prone to illusory experience but because when one takes EHEs seriously and attends to them one becomes involved in a process that is conducive to further EHEs. It is not so much a personality trait as a process in which experiencers become engaged, depending on how they respond to their exceptional experiences. (Undoubtedly imagination and even storytelling are part of the process, just as they are in scientific theorizing.)

This is why in my current work I am attempting both to further particularize the puzzle pieces and to draw generalizations based on treating all the different types of exceptional experiences as a class. I have called the latter (White, 1994) the generic approach to EHEs, including psychic experiences.

I purposely devised the secular term *exceptional human experience* rather than using *spiritual experience* because, based on the old paradigm, most people consider only mystical and other religious experiences to be spiritual. The point I want to make is that many experiences that have been considered not only as not spiritual but as illusory can provide spiritual orientation. The secularization of society has played an important role in detaching humans from specific traditional religious pursuits, thus laying the groundwork for the inherent spiritualization of the world. Cohen and Phipps (1992), in a study based largely on experiences collected by the Alister Hardy Research Centre, present examples of exceptional experience that occur at the various stages of the spiritual path, but they emphasize the commonness of the experiences. They write that they hope to show that the way to enlightenment "starts not in some distant monastery, but at our own door" (p. vii). They used the experiences of "contemporary people living very much in the everyday world" (p. vii). This is all brought home by a statement of Thomas Merton's that represents a life-changing insight he had during a moment of exceptional experience: "The whole illusion of a separate holy existence is a dream" (Shannon, 1992, p. 191).

Humans have been reporting exceptional human experiences since the beginnings of recorded history, and although many individuals have changed because of them, world conditions have worsened, until now we face planet-wide devastation from a variety of sources. My hypothesis is that EHEs have yet to come into their own. Their main application is in self-transformation, but this means working with one's experiences over a lifetime and weaving them into one's life story. How we compose our stories depends on the paradigm we unconsciously adopt. If it is the mechanistic or physicalist paradigm, there is no place for EHEs. I suggest that it is EHEs themselves that allow us to view a spiritual paradigm as reality. Once one begins to do that, one is embarked on a lifetime process of increased positive relationship between oneself and other people, other forms of life, and the planet itself; one also sees increased meaning in one's own life and in life in general, and experiences of awe, wonder, and delight become more frequent. From a rational perspective, an exceptional human experience can be responded to in a neutral, positive, or negative way. Only the positive response will lead to transformation, first of the individual, and then of the society in which the individual lives.

The response people make depends on the type of story or theory of EHEs they believe in. Charles Tart (1975) has presented some of the intellectual and theoretical underpinnings for EHEs, especially psychic and spiritual experiences. For this article I went over his observations point by point, relating them, wherever possible, to observations based on the content of exceptional human experiences (EHEs). I examine Tart's (1975) contrasting paradigms—that of Western academic culture in general and the science of psychology in particular, which he calls the physicalist view—and the viewpoint of what Tart calls "the spiritual psychologies" (p. 4), or "psychologies that are integral parts of various spiritual disciplines" (p. 5). Note that as Tart presents it, the spiritual psychologies set forth a dynamic view of human nature and of life that the traditional paradigm denies. (For a dynamic view of human nature and its relevance to EHEs, see White, 1993a.)

Tart lists and describes the assumptions (or story lines) in sixteen main categories, each with a number of subcategories. The main categories he treats, followed by the number of subcategories in each, are: the nature of the universe (5), the nature of [hu]man nature (9), the function of [hu]man[s] in the universe (6), the nature of human consciousness (3), altered states of consciousness (4), the mind-body relationship (2), death (2), personality (6), cognitive processes (13), emotion (7), learning (4), memory (3), motivation (2), perception (3), social relationships (3), and miscellaneous (5).

I will present, in Tart's words or paraphrases of them, his view of each of the traditional physicalist assumptions, followed by his view of each of the assumptions from the viewpoint of the spiritual psychologies, followed by what I have learned concerning that aspect from my study of EHEs. (Where Tart uses "he," "his," or "man," I have changed the text to "human," "he or she," etc.)

It is my view, expressed more fully elsewhere (White, 1992, 1993b), that although the world's religions have been the major carriers and promoters of the spiritual psychologies in the past, in the future each person must live this psychology in ordinary life so that the entire earth can become sacred ground. We now have access to all the spiritual psychologies of the world, as well as various forms of psychotherapy and other self-help approaches. What we need is to become aware of how we are drawn to a particular one or ones and to begin the development of our spirituality from that base, which most likely will change as the process continues, yet it will be part of the same process. We will find the right one for us by heeding our EHEs, not by rationally drawing up a list of pluses and minuses. Moreover, one cannot talk oneself into spiritual development. One has to be moved, one has to become a person who needs and wants to develop spiritually. Here again, our EHEs provide the impetus. In exceptional human experiences the world "out there" and/or one's larger Self within grip the individual as he or she is uniquely situated in time, place, and personality and moves that person to begin, providing sufficient indication of how that person can continue that long conscious journey back to the Self that is everything, always demanding a large measure of faith at every new step, of course (part of the process). The most important characteristic of EHEs is that they are not dependent on either rationality or the physical senses, although both may play subsidiary roles.

In presenting the material, the assumptions are numbered in the order in which they are listed by Tart. A ***P*** denotes the physicalist assumptions, an ***S*** denotes the spiritual assumptions, and an ***E*** indicates generalizations based on EHEs. (All page references are to Tart, 1975.) Because there is insufficient space here to treat all of Tart's categories, I present only the first four, which are the more general ones, which include twenty-five assumptions.

I. ASSUMPTIONS ABOUT THE NATURE OF THE UNIVERSE

P1. No purpose is behind the creation of the universe (p. 66).

S1. The creation of the universe is assumed to be purposeful in the sense of having been created by the divine or self-created (p. 66).

E1. In several EHEs the experiencer feels part of a meaningful process that is inherently purposeful. Although this purpose is often implicit, in some the experiencer is led to a vocation in which the purpose becomes explicit and can include every aspect of the person's life and being. (I consider a strong sense of vocation as a type of EHE in itself.) As Cohen and Phipps (1992) observe, "the beginning of the path is marked for many by sporadic glimpses of states of being that will become permanent, perhaps after many years, if the path is seriously pursued" (p. 2). I think those who reject these experiences do so largely for social reasons—because they are associated with negative story lines. This is confirmed by Cohen and Phipps (1992), who note: "To some these moments have acted as pointers along a way that they will henceforth follow with greater confidence. But others have found them embarrassing, even alarming, and have devised various means of explaining them away" (p. 2).

P2. Life is an infinitesimal and insignificant part of the universe, which in itself is dead (p. 66).

S2. The universe is partly or entirely alive, purposeful, and evolving. A human's "relationship to a living, interconnected, and evolving universe is quite different than if he [or she] assumes the universe is dead and purposeless" (p. 67).

E2. Many EHEers experience the earth, and sometimes what they can only call the "universe," as living and pulsating with meaning. I count the "Gaia experience" or Frank White's (1987) "overview effect" as a type of exceptional experience. Several astronauts have experienced it while looking at earth from outer space. Edgar Mitchell (1974), who was one of the first, writes of his peak experience during the Apollo 14 flight: "The presence of divinity became almost palpable and I knew that life in the universe was not just an accident based on random processes. This knowledge came to me directly—noetically. It was not a matter of discursive reasoning or logical abstraction. It was an experiential cognition" (p. 29).

P3. Only physics studies the real world, and so it is the ultimate science, and all other sciences must reduce [their] data to physical data (p. 67).

S3. "The spiritual psychologies may or may not accept the 'reality' of the physical world, but they postulate a psychological or psychical reality as just as real or even more real than physical reality" (p. 67).

E3. Exceptional human experiences are exceptional because sooner or later in their development they will be experienced as both inside and outside, both objective and subjective. They are experiences of a self that is both within and without, and that is alive and growing toward an increased sense of unity.

P4. Reality is limited to what can be perceived by our senses or by a physical instrument that serves as an extension of those senses (p. 68).

S4. The nonphysical can be just as real as the physical and their reality cannot be judged by their physical registration.

E4. Some exceptional human experiences can be physically observed, especially those involving psychokinesis, but most of them cannot be detected directly, yet they are consciously experienced, even though they cannot be physically registered. Although they usually cannot be verified physically, their personal, social, and cultural effects can be documented at length.

P5. Time is linear and only the present moment actually exists (p. 68).

S5. The past and future exist in the present or are accessible in the present. In a sense every moment is eternal, not simply temporal (p. 68).

E5. The special quality of many EHEs is their timelessness, or their independence of the present moment, not only in mystical moments when time seems to stop, but also in verifiable moments in which people see the future (precognition), the past (retrocognition), and possibly past lives (reincarnation).

P6. It is possible to understand the way the physical world works without understanding ourselves. "Physicists . . . are studying the 'outside' physical world, using their instruments and their intellects, and their own personalities and spiritual natures are not taken into consideration" (p. 69).

S6. "One's nature, one's personality, or one's level of spiritual being will have a profound effect on his [or her] understanding of the universe" (p. 69).

E6. In order to view data or think about them globally, scientists are best equipped if they have had and worked with one or more EHEs. Keller (1983) has documented how Barbara McClintock, while doing the research that would win her the Nobel prize, had to retreat and do work on herself before she could return to her microscope and properly view and integrate what she saw. How one views one's EHEs is directly dependent on one's spiritual growth, and one's spiritual growth is dependent on how one views one's EHEs.

II. ASSUMPTIONS ABOUT THE NATURE OF HUMANS

P7. Humans are their bodies and nothing more (p. 70).

S7. Humans potentially or in actuality are "something else in addition to a physical body." Humans essentially are mental beings and the body is "only one component of the total nature" of humans (p. 70).

E7. Exceptional human experiences alter one's sense of self, either by revealing heretofore unexperienced inner heights and depths or extending outer boundaries to include other humans, organisms, and even the universe. The apex of EHEs is the experience of the universe as one's own body and of one's self as its center, which results, not in egomania, but in reverence for all life.

P8. Humans exist "in relative isolation from [their] surrounding environment. [They] are essentially independent creatures" (p. 70).

S8. A human "has some kind of psychic or spiritual connection to all other forms of life, is both influenced by them and influences them" (pp. 70-71).

E8. Almost all exceptional human experiences serve as a means of connecting previously separated organisms, persons, and places, usually by transcending boundaries. Psychic experiences transcend time and space, and some even appear to make connections beyond the boundary of death. These connections are far from intellectual. They are experienced as being as real or "more real" than the experience of physical objects. Hoffman (1992) presents the case of a young girl, Renee, who had a unitive experience while riding in a car (to be described later). After that, she came back feeling as though she were a soul trapped inside her body in an unreality from which she could not get out. Then, she says, "I knew that my soul could never die. It was the part of me that was God, and I immediately wanted to find my way back to oneness again" (p. 94). As an adult she found her way back through Taoism and Zen. Her words echo those of the medium, Mrs. Willett, who complained that to come back to her ordinary consciousness after serving as a channel was "just like waking up in prison from a dream that one has been at home" (Balfour, 1935, p. 218).

P9. "A human being's life starts at birth, is determined almost totally by physical factors . . . and ends in death" (p. 71).

S9. Some spiritual psychologies view the present life as based on previous lives and that it extends "on in some form after death. Thus an individual may come into life with a mission or purpose" (p. 71).

E9. The experience of previous lives or of life after death are specific EHEs. They provide awareness of such states not by discursive knowledge about them but as if one were recalling a time and place one had been.

P10. A human being "is completely determined by his [or her] genetic inheritance and environment" (p. 71).

S10. Humans have some "responsibility and free will" in connection with their lives, "even though doing something about it may be difficult" (p. 72).

E10. EHEs provide the vision to know what one should do with one's life and the strength and energy to carry it out. A stage can be reached where even obstacles are viewed as integral parts of the process because one has touched a source that one knows will unfailingly bring what one requires.

P11. Even though we intellectually believe that humans are completely determined, in practice we act as if we have free will (p. 72).

S11. "If we do not have some kind of psychological and spiritual awakening, which must start by recognizing our limitations, we will be trapped in recurring psychological patterns throughout our lives, and perhaps through an afterlife or other lives to come" (p. 72).

E11. EHEs initiate a process of working on oneself in which one can view one's own shortcomings and limitations and how to change them through various spiritual exercises. In addition, our limitations can be used as the source of the energy needed to turn them to service on behalf of the whole organism. There is that at the heart of the universe that can transmute any human failing into a positive attribute, though thus far this has been accomplished infrequently. For example, Dannion Brinkley (Brinkley with Perry, 1994) recounts in detail how his two NDEs transformed him into a force for good. Until he underwent life review experiences in which he relived his past acts from the viewpoint of those he had hurt, maimed, or killed, he says he had been entirely selfish and violent. For example, he estimates that from the fifth through the twelfth grades he had a minimum of 6,000 fistfights. After being a seventh grader for three days, he had earned 154 demerits (thirty meant suspension). In the army in Viet Nam, when he was unable to carry out a mission of killing a certain government official staying at a small hotel because he was always surrounded by guards and others, he simply blew up the hotel itself, eliminating fifty or so other people along with the official. What halted his destructive course was not a precept but an exceptional experience.

P12. "We have a rather good understanding of the history of" humans (p. 72), which is accessible through written records.

S12. "Many theories about human psychology are based on the generally accepted views of human history preserved in books, but many of the spiritual psychologies have quite different views" (p. 72) of the human past and often depend on oral traditions. Whereas the written words hold that humans have made progress, "some of the spiritual psychologies believe we have been going downhill" (p. 73) when compared to more spiritually advanced past civilizations.

E12. Although some psychic, mediumistic, and shamanistic teachings, which originate in EHEs, may reproduce elements of the oral tradition, the more important role played by EHEs regarding progress lies in the circumstance that those who are steeped in exceptional experience have become jarred loose from the deterministic forms of philosophy and history in their very experience of self. From the sense of self that EHEs provide, experiencers see quite clearly—even without dependence on the oral tradition—not only that the human species in the twentieth century is not the apex of evolution but that it is in a seriously regressed state. EHEers therefore look outside the modern paradigm for answers, turning to native peoples, to pre-Enlightenment ideas, to oral traditions, and, perhaps most importantly, to the knowledge inherent in their own EHEs and those of others.

P13. It is assumed that today "we understand the origin and evolution of [hu]man[s]" (p. 73). In short, humans are the result of a series of accidents or the result of physical circumstances.

S13. The spiritual psychologies theorize that human evolution is guided by nonphysical forces, and some even hold that humans are not a product of the earth at all.

E13. Certain EHE puzzle pieces corroborate the spiritual psychologies, especially NDEs, stories of UFO abductions, and encounters with angels. Various mediumistic communications relay a similar message, perhaps the best known today being *A Course in Miracles*, which was communicated through a woman who had no previous mediumistic experience and who wanted very much to reject the role. Some words of British medium Ena Twigg are relevant: "People try to tie sensitives to a wheel of continual evidence. . . . The purpose of communication is to give people an idea of their true identity and the true purpose of living" (Twigg, 1972, p. 191). Parapsychologists have concentrated on the evidential aspect of psychic experiences as well, either by trying to substantiate them or by belittling experiences because they cannot be verified. Hardly anyone has asked about the potential meaning of psychic experiences, but this is changing (see Kennedy, Kanthamani, & Palmer, 1994).

P14. Either not much can be expected of human beings, or human ability is unlimited (p. 73).

S14. Both of the above views can blind us to our true nature. Humans are capable of evolving, but this does not refer to technological growth. We need "an actual experiential understanding of our limits and our insignificance in relation to the whole cosmos" (p. 74).

E14. EHEers have an experiential knowledge of their place in the universe. They know that no one is insignificant and no one is poorly placed because each person is rooted in the same underlying unity. Humans can develop spiritually whoever and wherever they are. Although it is a growth that is not necessarily recognizable to others, its influence can be profound.

P15. "Each [hu]man is isolated from all others, locked within his [or her] nervous system" (p. 7). Because our consciousness has a physical force, we are cut off from everyone and everything else.

S15. Because spiritual psychologies do not accept humans as being strictly physical, they are "open to the possibility of direct contact between one human being and another, contact between the spiritual essence of each that is not limited by the physical properties of the nervous system" (p. 74).

E15. Many types of exceptional experience, especially psychic and mystical experiences, consist of the experience not only of not being separate from others but of actually being one with them. One of the world's most famous mediums, Mrs. Willett, on one occasion exclaimed: "It's so heavenly to be out of myself—when I'm everything, you know, and everything else is me" (Balfour, 1935, p. 218). Astronaut Russell Schweickert, while looking down on earth from outer space, felt that "all those people down there" were himself and that he represented them. He noted that when he returned he had a different relationship between himself and the planet and "all those other forms of life on that planet, because [he] had that kind of experience" (White, 1987, pp. 12, 13).

The life-changing experience of Renee, mentioned earlier, occurred when she was five years old and riding in a car with her family. While gazing out the window, she says, "Suddenly, as if a slide had changed in a theater, the scenery somehow became different. . . . I felt instantly at home in the universe, and knew—I can't emphasize this enough—God's essence. I became the trees that I saw, the birds, the blades of grass, the sky, the hills, even the car. Everything was everything. It was the total cosmos and all of it was me. . . . everything was absolutely necessary to the whole, or none of it could be at all" (pp. 93-94).

P16. Psychological energy is a derivative of physical energy. Thus, the upper limits of what humans can do are "not too far above the ordinary" (p. 74).

S16. There are nonphysical energy sources, and it is these that "make us alive and human" (p. 75).

E16. Some EHEs testify to types of energy and the ability to perform exceptional feats that seem well beyond the normal limits, such as incorruptibility, levitation, materialization, psychokinesis, being "in the zone" in sports, stigmata, unorthodox forms of healing, and other seemingly "paranormal" and "miraculous" feats. Many examples are given in Murphy (1992).

III. ASSUMPTIONS ABOUT [THE] FUNCTION [OF HUMANS] IN THE UNIVERSE

P17. Humans have "no function in a purposeless universe" (p. 75).

S17. Spiritual psychologies include a function for humans in the universe, whether it be to glorify God, evolve in consciousness, "to act as a channel for higher evolution forces to reach our levels, and so on" (p. 75).

E17. If EHEs are viewed, not as static events, but as seeds or initiators of a process, then the process they seem to set going in the life of an individual who is willing to cooperate appears to be one that is either connected to or an outgrowth of the universe. One feels involved in a process that is fed both from within and without and that expands inwardly as well as outwardly. As Tom Berry (1988) puts it so well: a "human is less a being on this earth or in this universe than a dimension of the earth and indeed of the universe itself" (p. 195).

P18. "The only real purpose of life is to maximize pleasure and to minimize pain" (p. 75). Humans invent a function for themselves, choosing those that would give them the most pleasure, whether it be found in pursuing wealth or finding meaning.

S18. The spiritual psychologies stress that we must learn to transcend our attachment to pain and pleasure, and/or that pain must be faced with full conscious awareness because it contains the seeds of important learning and growth" (pp. 75-76).

E18. Several types of exceptional experience demonstrate that pain in the service of a meaningful goal, which might itself be an EHE, can be transcended. Russian weightlifter, Uri Vlasov, states:

"At the peak of tremendous . . . effort while the blood is pounding in your head, all suddenly becomes quiet within you. Everything seems clearer and whiter than ever before, as if great spotlights had been turned on. . . . At that moment you have the conviction that you contain all the power in the world . . . you have wings. There is no more precious moment in life than this, the white moment, and you will work very hard for years just to taste it again" (Lipsyte, 1975, p. 280).

Also, people who have had NDEs often are "sent" or "choose" to come back specifically to share their knowledge that death is not painful, lonely, or meaningless. EHEs assist people in learning to let go of their egos, not because self-abnegation is good, but because the larger self that takes its place is filled with calm, peace, joy, laughter, wonder, and delight.

P19. "The universe is a harsh, uncaring, unresponsive place" (p. 76). Self-preservation and seeking the pleasure principle are the "best human beings can do" (p. 76).

S19. "The universe is harsh, but it is not uncaring" (p. 76). It is just and lawful, and can teach us if we will pay attention. In a sense, "your level of spiritual being attracts your life" (p. 76).

E19. The method by which the universe teaches us usually includes an EHE of some kind. Each one should be heeded for the special lesson inherent in it which, if worked with, will open up as does any seed when watered, fed, and tended. Then one will have participated in creating something new that also benefits others.

P20. "We are here to conquer the universe" (p. 76). To ensure our needs for survival, pleasure, and to minimize pain, "we must take a harsh, uncaring universe and shape it to our needs as we see them" (p. 76).

S20. "We are here to understand our place in the universe," and when we understand it, to "fulfill our function . . . not to try to shape the universe to fit our limited view of what is good for us" (p. 76).

E20. Exceptional human experiences take us inside the process of the universe and the process that is inside us. Having felt/experienced the sense of connection to deeper levels of self, others, other life forms, and the earth that many EHEs provide, one is no longer able to think in terms of "conquering" the universe or exploiting the earth or other life forms any more than one would be inclined to saw off one's own arm or leg or that of a loved one. I know an EHEer who feared spiders and stinging insects as a child. Now she has developed a bond with jumping spiders, and a keen, caring interest in Daddy Longlegs and bumblebees.

P21. "We are by far the supreme life form on earth, and are probably the only intelligent life form in the whole universe" (p. 77).

S21. "There are beings (usually nonphysical, but including possible extraterrestrial beings) that are far more intelligent than we are, and far more evolved in a large variety of ways. . . . we must make enormous efforts, but help is available" (p. 77).

E21. Once a person has had an EHE and has begun the process of adapting his or her life to it and has experienced the dynamics of intra- and interpersonal growth that is part of that process, one knows there is a greater intelligence at work far more powerful than any merely human intelligence. Moreover, EHEs direct our efforts and empower us to go beyond our previous bounds and those of others; they provide us with what can only be described as the experience of being aided and abetted by something beyond our own physical organism, personality, and life circumstances.

P22. "Lower organisms exist for" the benefit of humans (p. 77).

S22. We have "obligations toward lower life forms, as well as . . . higher forms" (p. 77).

E22. EHEs provide a sense of connection to both lower and higher forms of life such that all sense of hierarchy disappears. What is left is a pulsating sense of oneness and of a dynamic in which we are all bound together in the same process.

IV. ASSUMPTIONS ABOUT HUMAN CONSCIOUSNESS

P23. "Only human beings are conscious" (p. 78).

S23. "Higher, nonphysical creature also possess full consciousness" (p. 78). Also, lower organisms are assumed to possess various degrees of consciousness" (p. 78).

E23. EHEs tend to promote the idea that the entire earth and everything in it is sentient, to a greater or lesser extent, and if we are not personally aware of it, it is our lack, not that of the other life forms. Interspecies communication, when it does appear to occur, is an EHE in itself, and a highly valued one. Author Rosamond Lehmann relates that after visiting some Irish monuments purported to have been "centers of spiritual power," while traveling back by car she passed the time by reading aloud Edward Taylor's "Upon a Wasp Chilled by the Cold" to her companions. She considers it "a unique tribute" to the wasp's beauty and "spirited hold on life," because a wasp "is not apt to be celebrated with tender observation and concern." When they arrived at the airport, she got out, and some porters began shouting warnings at her. She "was met—greeted would be the more appropriate word—by a surge of wasps. I can only say that they circled before me as if performing a kind of ceremonial dance. A murmorous swarm, not buzzing but singing; a faintly unearthly sound" (Inglis, 1987/1989, p. 171). Even though we rarely find anecdotes like this in our textbooks, it is certainly part of the oral tradition, and, I suggest, even as it happened to Rosamond Lehmann, it happened to all of us. Each of us speaks to and for every other. This is a key message of EHEs and the basis of interspecies communication.

P24. Humans are conscious (p. 78).

S24. This assumption is questioned by some of the spiritual psychologies. According to Gurdjieff, most humans are automatons, but the spiritual psychologies recognize that "real consciousness is possible" (p. 79).

E24. EHEs help to create a new sense of self that is built on connection, not separation. If EHEs are heeded, the process deepens and expands consciousness, including what appears to be ESP. This still is not "real" consciousness, but it is closer to it than the everyday consciousness of most.

P25. Consciousness is the product of brain activity, and this "is identical with the activity of the brain" (p. 79).

S25. The brain and nervous system are viewed as "an instrument of consciousness," and consciousness is seen "as a factor every bit as real in its own right as physical things. . . . Consciousness may . . . exist independently of the brain" (p. 79).

E25. In certain EHEs, such as OBEs, NDEs, and UFO abductions, the body with its brain is perceived as outside the knowing self, which leaves it behind while the person moves unfettered through physical walls. ESP and PK experiences, including precognition, indicate that there is that in us that can know things that have not entered the mind via sensory pathways.

CONCLUSION

I hope this analysis of Tart's first four categories shows that EHEs, when viewed in a dynamic relationship with a self that is undergoing spiritual growth, provide an experiential component to what the spiritual psychologies have taught through the ages. Both EHEs and the spiritual psychologies go well beyond the physicalist paradigm's limited view of reality and of human beings, other life forms, and consciousness itself. I am calling the worldview that EHEs reveal the experiential paradigm, because its conceptualization rests on the being of the experiencer rather than physical or logical grounds. It is my guess that all spiritual psychologies had their origin in exceptional human experiences, and that these psychologies were fueled by EHEs at all the major stages of their development. EHEs open a person to the existence of a spiritual reality, create a path that one can follow through it, and not only equip experiencers to naturally follow the precepts of the spiritual psychologies, but make it possible to apply these inner forms of knowing and being freshly in each new age. EHEs are the experiential learning and knowing components of the spiritual life.

I close with a passage that Mrs. Willett channeled. Although she was exceptional among mediums because she did not go into a deep trance but remained awake, on this occasion, her observer, Lord Balfour, noted: "She was clearly not her normal self, especially toward the end" (Balfour, 1935, p. 217), when she also broke from her usual pattern in that she spoke instead of writing automatically. She referred to the "golden thread of eternity in the warp and woof of human life," which surely is a metaphor for EHEs. She said that it is these golden "moments that make the true record of a life; and in proportion to the richness of those experiences is the richness of each human life to be measured. It's the escape from the smaller into the larger—separate no longer but one life alone" (Balfour, 1935, p. 218).

Chapter 5
The Parapsychology of God

Michael Grosso

> *I [have] endeavored to trace the operation of natural laws and forces, where others have seen only the agency of supernatural beings.*
>
> — Sir William Crookes

Since the rise of science, religion and spirituality have been under attack. This historic conflict between science and religion has appeared on many fronts. For example, the Copernican revolution revealed the limitations of Biblical geology; the effect was to shatter the Christian conceit of earth-centeredness. Meanwhile, Galileo founded a cosmology that substituted mechanical for final causation; it is inert matter that makes the world go round—not love, purpose, or the beautiful.

Before long the philosophers were concluding that the human mind was a mere epiphenomenon, a thing devoid of substance and autonomy, thus undercutting the prospects of immortality. Renaissance scholars such as Lorenzo Valla started scientific Bible criticism—a practice with wicked potentials. Enlightenment *philosophes*, such as Voltaire and Montesquieu, created more mischief by inventing comparative religion, which shook church dogma. Nineteenth-century evolutionary theory embedded human life firmly within naturalism, seeming to further discredit notions of divinity. Advances in neuroscience made a mockery of the world of spirits. Nietzsche announced the death of God; Marx reduced religion to a drug; Freud, to an illusion.

And so it went.

However, despite all the dizzying advances of modern science and scholarship, religious belief and spiritual quest are alive and kicking. In spite of the progress of science, interest in religious and spiritual matters is stronger than ever. In America, Pentecostal, evangelical, and charismatic Christianity have flourished in the twentieth century, and from the liberal wing grows a grass-roots New Age movement that shows no sign of subsiding. One notes a powerful interest in shamanism, and some people are talking of a renaissance of Buddhism in America. Moreover, reports of channeling (a kind of mediumship), near-death experiences, Marian visions, angelic encounters, and spiritually-tinged tales of flying saucers have been widespread throughout the century.

What happened in the Soviet Union is instructive; for seventy years Communist ideologues tried to wipe out religion, but when the Soviet Union fell to pieces, the Russian Orthodox church was still standing; also, New Age spirituality is quite strong in Russia today.

Not all spirituality is innocent stuff. The case of David Koresh and the recent mass murder-suicides in Switzerland and Quebec demonstrate the seductive power of millenarian spirituality, while survivalists in the American northwest mix apocalyptic phantasies with Neo-Nazism. Indeed, the amount of spiritual ferment, affiliated and non-affiliated, both here and abroad, is immense (Grosso, 1994). Is it all based on one gigantic illusion? If so, we should build shrines to Ate, the Greek Goddess of Illusion.

Parapsychology and the Persistence of Religious Belief

How are we to account for the persistence of religious belief, the endless claims of contact, vision, experience of transcendent, nonphysical, and supernatural agents and entities (Grosso, 1992)? Two sharply contrasted views are possible: (1) that we are witnessing a mass failure of nerve, a dangerous regression to infantile, superstitious, and illusory thought processes; or (2) that we are in the throes of the end of history and that the plethora of supernatural claims and appearances are signs of encroaching apocalypse.

I reject both these views; the first, because it clashes with matters of fact; the second, because it is metaphysical, appealing to a minority of Biblical fundamentalists. I don't believe that behind the mass of religious, God-related phenomena is sheer illusion nor do I believe that any one religious view holds the answer to the persistence of religious claims. How, then, can we explain the enduring life of these claims and these phenomena?

I believe there is an empirical core of truth to at least some of the fundamental claims of spiritual life. In particular, I believe that psychical research and parapsychology provide data and concepts for a new interpretation of religious and spiritual phenomena, and can account for the persistence of beliefs and experiences that bear on supernatural entities, worlds, and dimensions. First, however, some remarks on terminology.

In discussing the parapsychology of god, I use *god* (lower case) in the Greek way; the Greeks talked of *to theon*—gender neuter—meaning "the godlike" or "the divine." *To theon* is power; it exists free from the constraints of time and space, a label for the archetypal powers of the universe. *To theon* embraces a host of divine or spiritual beings: gods, goddesses, angels, demons—an assortment of space-time transients that travel to and fro in the corridors of myth and folklore. In my view, parapsychology throws light on these entities traditionally called "supernatural."

The implications of parapsychology for spiritual life have been discussed by previous writers, but have produced little, if any, impact on public understanding. In the thick atmosphere of dogmatic materialism, most anthropologists, folklorists and psychologists since the nineteenth century have been inclined to view the beliefs of "savages" as either insane (Frazer thought African witch doctors insane), deluded, or given to imposture. Freud extended the application of Frazer's and E.B. Tylor's reductionism from the primitive to the Biblical worldview.

However, at least two writers, Andrew Lang and Caesar de Vesme, acquainted with psychical research, were interested in the parapsychological origins of magic and religion. Lang wondered in *The Making of Religion* (1898) whether the rappings, luminosities, and movement of objects without contact that were reported by remote barbarians, educated neo-Platonists, and Boston mediums all sprang from a common human faculty. If so, Lang felt, magic and religion would have some foundation in reality. Lang believed in certain unexplained "human faculties" that were "inconsistent with popular scientific materialism," and expressed his annoyance in 1898 at anthropologists who dismissed magic and religion without taking into account these demonstrable human faculties.

De Vesme wrote a two-volume history of what he called "experimental spiritualism" in which he sought to "demonstrate that the origin of religions is . . . due to the observation of 'supernormal' facts whose true interpretation is still undecided, and of whose further study may, therefore, well show that the basis of religion is legitimate; and this, be it clearly understood, without touching on questions of revelation, faith, or dogma, but strictly confined to experimental and scientific grounds" (de Vesme, 1931). J.B. Rhine also noted the psychic-religious connection when he wrote: "Religious communication is basically psi communication, pure and simple: it is neither sensory nor motor; it is unequivocally extrasensorimotor. . . . All the physical miracles, whether in the healing of disease, the miraculous movement of objects, or the control of the elements, had to be manifestations of PK" (Rhine, 1973).

Why haven't these empirically-based attempts to re-mythologize religion captured more informed attention? The reasons are not hard to grasp. Conservative religious feeling is bound to recoil from a theory that undermines pretensions to absolute truth-claiming; on the other hand, the parapsychology of religion may seem to concede too much to traditional religion, more than most committed materialists would find easy to digest. The prevailing views fall into two camps: the religious literalists and absolutists at one end of the spectrum and the scientific materialists and reductionists at the other. Parapsychology can help us avoid these two lopsided positions; indeed, I believe it provides a kind of rosetta stone for re-deciphering and re-validating encounters of the godlike kind.

Breaking the Ontological Barrier

One reason for the excitement that revolves around quantum mechanics and certain other ideas in recent science is that they seem to give greater play to the possibilities of human existence in a universe that is less bleakly restrained than the old mechanistic one. The mechanistic worldview seems to crush all soul, magic, and enchantment from the world. Personally, I doubt if post-mechanistic science accomplishes the job of reenchantment directly; it does, however, liberate the imagination by demonstrating that fundamental features of nature are wildly counter-intuitive and counter-commonsensical. Arthur Koestler's *The Roots of Coincidence* illustrates this fact with vivid examples such as massless neutrinos and their ghostlike capacity to pass through solid matter or tachyons that seem, like precognition, to reverse the arrow of time. More recently, physicist Fred Alan Wolf's *The Eagle Quest* and *The Dreaming Universe* show how quantum mechanics is compatible with the shamanic worldview.

Nevertheless, in the quantum world we are still dealing with bits (or smears of probability) of *physical* reality. Something more radical is needed to restore the "enchantment" and to validate the transcendent—something that breaks the ontological barrier of physical reality itself.

The one body of data that bears directly upon transcending the barrier of physicalism belongs to parapsychology. Parapsychology provides the cosmic reenchantment factor *par excellence*. That factor is called *psi*, which refers to extrasensory perception and psychokinesis, the ability to receive information independently of physical sense and the ability to influence the physical world by direct mental agency. In my judgment, parapsychology has produced significant evidence for a transcendent psi factor in nature.

As for those who stubbornly deny the reality of the evidence for the paranormal—the pseudo-skeptics to whom Charles Tart refers—I am sure they do so for deep reasons, reasons so deep and convoluted that they remain impervious to the quality of evidence. I suggest we ignore the pseudo-skeptics, whose attitude toward the paranormal is as boring as it is biased. It's time to move on to more interesting things. Again, I agree with Tart, who says we should quit the "weak," defensive form of claiming the reality of psi, and proceed to a "strong" form. In short, it is time to begin exploring the big implications of the data, and get on with the business of learning how to use what we have learned in a wise and humane way.

The Question of Supernatural Entities

In spite of the onward march of science and the propaganda of disbelief, people persist in attitudes of fear, petition, worship, propitiation, and even of love, toward supernatural entities. Why do so many insist on peopling the universe with gods and goddesses, angels and demons, and other supernatural beings?

The emotional need to believe is undoubtedly great. And where there is no way to falsify a religious claim, the emotional need is apt to prevail. This psychological crutch theory of religion is confirmed by the old saw that states there are no atheists in foxholes. I grant this but deny it is the whole story; the true story is more complex and, I believe, far more interesting.

I believe that one of the reasons religious belief and spiritual experience persist, regardless of intellectual or political climate, is that a psi factor is at work in our experience of the world, a basic human ability to transcend fundamental constraints of physical reality. Once we admit that there is a nonlocal, atemporal[1] factor at large in nature, and that it is symbiotically related to the human psyche, the view of our spiritual potential opens up considerably.

For example, the nonlocal psi factor might manifest in archetypal experiences (C.G. Jung often cited G.B. Rhine's work as providing an ontological underpinning for the theory of archetypes). Or the psi factor may be the agency behind the genius of a Zoroaster, a Christ,[2] or a Joan of Arc. Again, transcendent psi may be the substratum of fact behind angelic intervention and demonic possession, the force enlivening visionary inspiration, shamanic healing, and mystical transport. New dimensions of meaning become possible once we grant the reality of this protean psi factor in nature.

Factors in Psi Studies Conducive to Spirituality

Certain features of psychic life confirm and support some of the grand ideas of spiritual practice. Consider four examples of the interface between the psychic and the spiritual. First, let me note the connection between what researchers call the "goal-directed" nature of psi and how it may relate to the creative power of spiritual vision. Second, and complementary to the first factor, is the importance of learning the art of "effortless intention." Third is the importance of internal attention states to psychic and spiritual life. The fourth factor deals with the role of belief, trust, and receptivity in our psychospiritual life.

Goal-Directed Psi and the Creative Power of Vision

Research indicates that the way to mobilize our psychic power—whose possible range and forms, let us recall, remain unknown—is to think *teleologically*.[3] For example, the physicist Helmut Schmidt describes psychokinesis as a "goal-directed" (or teleological) process. According to Schmidt, ". . . PK may not be properly understood in terms of some mechanism by which the mind interferes with the machine in some cleverly calculated way but it may be more appropriate to see PK as a goal-oriented principle, one that aims successfully at a final event, no matter how intricate the intermediate steps" (Schmidt, 1974). As a goal-oriented process, psi neither calculates nor relies on information processing but comes about by concentrating on goals.

An important practical point follows from this. Goal-oriented mental processes are not linear but imagistic; you focus on the image, the end-state. You don't struggle with the "how" or dwell on the obstacles that must be surmounted; as the Papago Indian do in their song magic, you evoke images of the place where you want to be or the state you desire to embody. You don't worry about the informational steps that separate you from your goal. This, quite frankly, resembles magical thinking—which is perhaps why conservative rationalists are reluctant to admit the reality of PK.

People think teleologically in spiritual practice. The Bible tells us to love God with our whole mind and our whole soul. In Buddhism, right understanding and right intention are essential to the way; the goal, the disposition toward treading the path to enlightenment is the first step toward release from useless suffering. Roberto Assagioli, the inventor of psychosynthesis, spoke of the importance of the transpersonal will. Thus, in the Lord's Prayer, we say, "*Thy* will be done." Centered on the supreme goal, we allow the details of our life to conform thereto.

The image has a special relationship to psychokinesis. Every image, as the philosopher H.H. Price once suggested, is inherently psychokinetic and, apart from competing images, tends somehow to realize itself. "Purity of heart," said Kierkegaard, "is to will one thing." The goal-oriented nature of psi explains the importance of the image in religious and spiritual life; if Price is right, spiritual images are tools for mobilizing goal-oriented psi. As we ardently embrace these spiritual images, they in turn may awaken our paranormal creative powers. Without a vision, says the Bible, the people will perish. This idea is echoed in the trivia of the psi labs; without mustering the right kind of intentionality, the target is missed.

Effortless Intention: Let Go and Let God

In spiritual life, we have goals and visions, but if we pursue them with the wrong kind of egocentric, anxiety-producing effort, we defeat ourselves. The British parapsychologist Robert Thouless has written of "the effortless intention to succeed." Intention without desire—such seems to be the formula for success in the psychic world. This attitude is reminiscent of the *Bhagavad-Gita*, which counsels us to act without obsessing over results. So our goal-orientedness ought not to be rigid. Thouless talks of the "gamelike" attitude of the successful psi experiment; the Eastern mystic talks about *lila*, the playful point of view.

Goal-orientation leads us to a complementary principle in the parapsychology of god: aim—but without strain. Parapsychological and spiritual data agree. Anxious, egocentric striving impedes psychic functioning. Rex Stanford refers to "release of effort" as naming the trick of getting out of the way of the psi-allowing process. William Braud speaks of the need for cognitively "labile" styles. Rhea White has studied the rhythms of focus and relaxation in successful ESP experience. We can slip free from the noose of time and space when we quit trying too hard. Parapsychology seems to ratify the popular saying: Let go and let God.

The great spiritual traditions, along with modern psi findings, agree on the need to let go of egocentric striving. A classic text by the Jesuit Jean-Pierre de Caussade, *Abandonment to Divine Providence*, shows how everyday life offers a sufficient path to enlightenment, providing that one abandon and learn to release oneself from self-defeating effort. The spiritual path is open to us, from moment to moment, in the affairs of daily existence, says Caussade. All that is necessary is to abandon oneself to divine providence, just as Krishna urges Arjuna to enter the battle of life resolute yet divinely indifferent to results.

Meanwhile, the Taoist exalts action through non-action—*wu wei wu*. And Martin Heidegger, in his *Discourse on Thinking*, meditates on the importance of "willing not to will." My favorite master of will-lessness is Chuang Tzu, who, in an ironical piece called "Perfect Joy," wrote, "Contentment and well-being at once become possible the moment you cease to act with them in view, and if you practice non-doing (*wu wei*), you will have both happiness and well-being." From lessons in the psi labs to the wisdom of Taoism one finds a thread of continuity, a call to learn the art of freeing oneself from oneself.

Internal Attention States: the Royal Road to the Superconscious

One of the strongest empirical findings of parapsychological research is that people are more likely to be receptive to the nonlocal universe if they attend to their internal states. External states distract us from awareness of ESP "signals." ESP is a matter of detection, of noticing what is present; internal attention makes us more sensitive, more alert to hidden stimuli. Thus, in dreams, hypnosis, sensory isolation, and meditation, the probability of detecting nonlocal sources of influence increases. The late Charles

Honorton did extensive meta-analyses supporting this link between psi and internal attention states (Honorton, 1977).

One way a psychic focuses on the inner plane is to work in darkness. Skeptics might say this is because darkness makes cheating easy. Although this is plausible, it is not the whole story. The British parapsychologist Kenneth Batcheldor found that darkness relieves the medium of the sense of owning or causing the phenomenon, feelings that apparently interfere with the psi-process. Darkness helps us overcome "ownership inhibition." Rex Stanford speaks of "externalization of responsibility." But this of course is just what religious belief accomplishes. To believe in God, in your guardian angel, or in any other tutelary deity, is like stepping into a comfortable dark room, a space where you no longer feel responsible, and where you feel free to just let things happen and surrender to creative powers beyond your control.[4] Thus, the spiritual stress on inwardness is validated by psychical research. If you desire to know the saving truth, said St. Augustine, "go within." In a similar vein, Patanjali's *Yoga Sutras* make retreat to and control of inner states the basis of the path to spiritual liberation.

The Sheep-Goat Effect and Spiritual Trust

What makes people psychic? Researchers have begun to build a profile of the "psi-conducive" personality. Psychics, for instance, tend to be extraverted and spontaneous in their behavior. Studies also show that people who believe they will perform well at a given psi task do tend to "score significantly." Likewise, nonbelievers tend not to score well and sometimes even deviate from chance in their negative performances! This is known as the "sheep-goat effect" (SGE), where the sheep are the believers; the goats, the disbelievers in psi. The "sheep-goat" effect squares with the traditional emphasis on faith as the right attitude toward the transcendent.

Three comments on this interesting finding: (1) First of all, the expression *sheep-goat* has misleading connotations; sheep are known for their proclivity to follow—one thinks "like sheep going to the slaughter." The idea of *sheep* connotes mindlessness, a caricature of psi ability. In my opinion, it makes more sense to speak of learning a "special skill."

(2) My second point is that we need to probe more closely into what's involved in belief. Kenneth Batcheldor (1984), who studied the psychology of psychokinesis, wrote of "unwavering

conviction," conviction so calm and self-assured that it does not become astonished (or frightened) by success. Oddly enough, in the face of miracles, a certain nonchalance seems the best attitude.

What is meant by saying that one *believes that something is possible*? Several possibilities come to mind. Belief might be about not having cognitive inhibitions—about being disposed to a kind of cognitive emptiness, an attitude some mystics recommend. Saint Paul, who was as pronounced a psychic as he was a mystic, talked of the *kenosis*—the "emptying" of oneself before God. Then again, "I believe that x is possible" might mean "I have an image of x." In that case, one's beliefs would be exercises of the imagination. The parapsychology of god needs to probe the subtleties of belief.

(3) The belief variable is a constant in the literature of spirit. In the New Testament, the word is *pistis*, which means something like Batcheldor's unwavering, nonanalytic "trust or confidence." The Gospels are full of tales of healing and exorcism; Jesus typically says to a healee, "Your faith has made you whole." The importance of "faith" is confirmed by parapsychology. Once again it appears that ancient spiritual teachings are empirically grounded in matters of psychic fact. Healing in the New Testament is a co-operative venture, the result of a special group dynamic, characterized by cognitive disinhibition.

In summary, goal-directedness, release of effort, inward focus, and spontaneous trust and confidence all come into play in parapsychology and spirituality. Evidence from the lab, from spontaneous cases of psi, and from the psychology of religious life all seem to mutually confirm each other. Is this merely coincidental or is there a common empirical substratum? But now consider another link between parapsychology and spirituality.

Christian "Symphonic" Thinking and Batcheldorian Paranormal Group Dynamics

Hints toward what we may call paranormal group dynamics have been cited—for example, the so-called experimenter effect. In the group dynamic of psi experimentation, it is sometimes the experimenter's charisma and enthusiasm that generates the psi.

But this "charisma" also depends on the right group responsiveness. In fact, a delicately balanced group dynamic is needed. When Jesus came to his hometown, scripture says the people "took offense" at what seemed like his lofty pretensions; after all, they knew him as the carpenter's son, not as a prophet; so it comes as no surprise when we hear that "he did not do many miracles (*dynameis*) there because of their unbelief (*apistian*)" (Matt. 13:58).

Another passage in the same gospel gives a clue to the power of paranormal group dynamics. "Again I say to you," runs this strange sentence, "that if two of you agree on earth about anything that they may ask, it shall be done for them by my father in heaven" (Matt. 18:19). The word in Greek for *agree* is *symphonein*, from which we get our word *symphonic*. Literally, "sounding together." Notice what we are told: When the group thinks *symphonically* (a musical, "right-brain" metaphor), it can produce miracles.

This idea is supported by twentieth-century research. Once again I cite Batcheldor, who found from his table-tilting experiments, in which he produced levitational and other effects, that a psi-favorable group dynamic involved a gamelike attitude, marked by good humor, song, spontaneity, and camaraderie.

The Canadian investigators Iris Owen and Margaret Sparrow used Batcheldor's symphonic group dynamic to attempt to create and evoke a paranormal entity they called Philip. In their experiments, observed by many and recorded on television, they "proved that the collective thought of a group of people can produce physical effects" (Owen & Sparrow, 1977, p. 179). Their account of how to conjure up a paranormal entity, in my opinion, provides a model for producing a whole range of supernatural entities. This is not the place to develop this idea, but a few remarks are in order.

The central experimental ploy was inventing a story about an imaginary personage, Philip. It was the creation of this myth, this focal point for the imagination, that served to organize and activate the paranormal group dynamic. It is easy to imagine substituting a story of guardian angels, gods, or other tutelary beings to provide more archetypal and thus more effective foci for mobilizing a group's paranormal psychodynamics. In other words, if an invented entity served as an imaginal focus to produce paranormal effects for a small group of Canadian experimenters, think of the powerful effects likely to be produced by belief in the God of the biblical tradition. The Toronto group produced sounds and movements of physical objects. The group found that personifying Philip, addressing him as if he were a real external agent, facilitated results.

Later, spontaneous poltergeist effects, including apports, occurred unpredictably in the homes of participants in the experiments, thus showing the process acquired an autonomous life of its own. The experimenters found that "even if there was no movement or rapping—the table had a feeling of aliveness, perhaps of vibration, which seemed quite different from its feel under normal circumstances." This observation suggests to me an experimental basis for understanding the ontology of animism. Animism is primal religion. The Toronto group found that by personifying the *table* they were using in their levitation experiments, the table assumed this feeling of aliveness or animation. From this it seems reasonable to suppose that similar evocations of aliveness in objects and facets of the environment were likely to have been produced spontaneously in animistic societies.

One more quote from *Conjuring Up Philip* suggests some further implications for the parapsychology of god. Concerning the experimenters, it is said that "as their interest grew in this imaginary focus of their attention, it seemed to them as if they were gaining some rapport with an unknown entity whose reality became more pronounced as their own interest and imaginations were stimulated." But as interest flagged, so did effects decline. What this suggests is that religions, cults, and myths may rise and fall in creative vitality, in accordance with the rise and fall of belief, interest, and stimulation. If the deities of (for example) ancient Greece no longer elicit the awe and reverence that they once did, that is simply because they have been derogated as inferior and "demonic," and been reduced to the status of literary artifacts. Yet, if the parapsychology of god contains any truth, the Greek pantheon, indeed, all the gods, goddesses, and spirits of old may be thought of as merely asleep in the obscure chambers of the collective unconscious and may, with the requisite paranormal group dynamics, be awakened from oblivion and roused to new life.

Prayer

Prayer is central to religious and spiritual life. For the moment I confine my comments to the notion of petitionary prayer. Scientific materialists are apt to regard petitionary prayer as mainly having psychological value. Prayer may serve as a consoling form of autohypnosis, but that is all.

Parapsychology suggests otherwise. If, for example, ordinary people can by PK bias the behavior of random-event generators, why couldn't they paranormally change the external world through prayer? Or, to ask another question: if we have unconscious psychokinetic abilities, why couldn't we learn to make them conscious, and direct their application?

People seem to do just this when they pray. A person prays to God or her guardian angel; if the research data be our guide, the very act of prayer may activate one's psi powers. In petitioning divine agencies, we forget ourselves, clarify our intentions, and avoid egocentric effort. Parapsychologists, as I said above, refer to this process as involving the "externalization of responsibility." We could say that in psi-mediated prayer we become co-creative partners with a process that is both inside and outside ourselves; whatever the ultimate nature of the transcendent psi factor (the deific factor) it is neither subjective nor objective but transjective, or, to borrow a phrase from science writer Michael Talbot, "omnijective."

Batcheldor discussed the possibility of "ownership inhibition" blocking psychokinetic ability; prayer may be a way of avoiding ownership inhibition (*I'm* not doing it! God or my guardian angel is). The reality of psi enlarges the potential of prayer. Indeed, one could say that every experiment in intentional psi is a kind of prayer. Moreover, as Larry Dossey has recently shown in his book *Healing Words*, there now exists a growing body of empirical evidence (some of it medically important) suggesting that prayer can indeed produce paranormal effects. The effectiveness of prayer is one reason why people continue to believe in supernatural entities. People pray, and they get results. If parapsychological effects are real, it seems *natural* to assume that prayer would be an effective way of influencing the environment.

Survival Evidence and Religious Belief

Psychical research provides evidence—not proof—for one of the main articles of religious hope: the belief in an afterlife. Students familiar with psychical research know there is a significant amount of evidence suggesting that some aspect of human personality survives death. Ghostly apparitions, hauntings, mediumship, reincarnation memories, verifiable out-of-body experiences, and other phenomena occur and give the impression of postmortem survival. Opinion may be divided as to what the evidence really proves; but in any case it is clear that the belief in a postmortem existence is not the product of mere wish-fulfillment. I am convinced experiences suggestive of an afterlife have played a big part in sustaining the spiritual outlook throughout history. Without this body of death-transcending data, religion becomes a less convincing project, and one of its chief hopes is dashed.

Toward the Parapsychology of God

Parapsychology, insofar as it confirms the existence of a transcendent psi factor, thus opens up the world of human experience. It does so by remythologizing and reenchanting experience with magical and spiritual potencies; at the same time, it gives substantial hints on how even an adventurous skeptic might, in harmony with the free spirit of science, explore the mysteries of godmaking and spirituality. So let me conclude with some general remarks on the parapsychology of god.

Against the view that states that when a person believes in, or claims to experience in some way, a supernatural being or enlightened state (such as the Biblical God, the Hindu Brahman, or the Buddhist Nirvana), I think we can say that such a person is not necessarily talking nonsense, suffering from delusion, or indulging in infantile wish-fulfillment; the data of parapsychology suggests that such a person may be in relationship with an objective, transcendent factor of nature. We can call this transcendent factor paranormal, supernatural, or divine; the main thing is that it breaks the ontological barrier of materialism, and thus opens doors to an expanded idea of the self.

This psi factor, according to the present hypothesis, apparently appears in human experience in a variety of forms; it parses two ways, across gender and moral lines. *To theon* may manifest as god or goddess, as helping angel or harming demon; it may assume any of the protean forms of divinity and the daimonic known to comparative religion and mythology. It may also be experienced as formlessness, nonlocal and timeless, as described in Zen satori, Bucke's cosmic consciousness, the mystic light, the presence of God, the nameless Tao, and so on.

Empirical indications suggest that several inner strategies are conducive to encounters with *to theon*, that is, the transcendent psi factor. I have mentioned a few possibilities: release of effort, belief or faith, spontaneity, internal attention states, personification (as a device to externalize responsibility), and active imagination (as in the experiment of conjuring up Philip). These strategies seem learnable, with benefits to subscribers of all religious belief-systems.

The parapsychological model of god is strictly empirical; it is not a theology or a mythology. It may be useful to people in several ways: for example, (a) to non-believers, half-believers, or skeptics (in the Greek sense meaning people who suspend judgment), the present model offers a basis for an experimental approach to that huge domain of human experience we roughly tag with such epithets as divine, deific, supernatural; (b) to the open-minded believer it is way of understanding the universal psychology and parapsychology of spiritual experience. What people make of their personal experimentation here is their own business; their own soulmaking, mythmaking, or practical theologizing. The godmaking model I am describing is pluralistic, democratic, tentative, and revisionary. Based on corrigible empiricism, it makes no claims of absolute truth.

Dogma, then, is alien to the parapsychology of god; if people wish to capitalize their God, that's up to them. But punctuation, from the present perspective, remains a matter of style. A rich imaginer and mystic seer such as William Blake was fond of capitalizing his deific personages. Others will prefer to keep their deities and demi-deities safely positioned in the lower case.

The parapsychology of god, as I conceive it, is not a religion nor is it a branch of science, although it draws upon, and aims in part to synthesize, these traditionally opposed forms of thought. It borrows from religion—from magic, mysticism, and shamanism—its raw transcendent data and poetic power, while shedding its dogmas, superstitions, tribalism, and absurdities. It borrows from science its detached love of truth, its methods where appropriate, and its evolutionary cosmology, while shedding its conceit and doctrinaire materialism.

For everyone, whether believer, half-believer, or skeptic, the pursuit of the parapsychology of god demands a certain sensitivity and sensibility. The idea of a cold-blooded, calculating attempt to "prove" divinity in the laboratory of everyday life would be not only crass but self-defeating. (Probably not all temperaments are conducive to this post-religious type of psychospiritual experiment.) The type of person I imagine exploring the parapsychology of god would have to be open to the mysteries of the universe as well as possess a certain capacity for imaginative empathy.

What I am describing is neither religion nor science, certainly not as we normally understand these branches of human activity. Is there any type of human experience to which we can liken it? What comes to my mind as a possibility is something more akin to art. Consider, for example, the poetic metaphysics of ancient Greece. Greek "religion" was free of dogma, sacred books and fixed theologies; an ongoing collective enterprise, where the divine, the nonlocal factor, appears in many forms and shapes, in epic and lyric poetry, tragedy and comedy, sculpture and vase painting, mystery rites and philosophy. The Eleusinian Mysteries, for example, used psychedelics to induce an encounter with a near-deathlike Being of Light.[5] Neither dogmatic nor compulsively precise, the "truth" of Greek "religion" and spirituality was poetic, experimental, and ever-evolving.

A practical parapsychology of god would require a mentality that differs sharply from that which feeds on the inflexible monotheism of Western science and religion. It would stress the play element in culture (see Jan Huizinga's book on this subject). Or, as in the world of the mythic imagination, one would have to learn the art of suspension of disbelief to explore the parapsychology of god. In any case, it would take the godlike out of the hands of fanatical monotheists of the imagination, whether scientific or religious, and place it back in the democratic world of the poetic imagination. Parapsychology thus offers a basis for the poetics—literally, the making—of the godlike.

My conclusion, then, is that parapsychology is an area of research that, by breaking the ontological barrier of materialism and validating the reality of a transcendent psi factor in nature, vindicates, *in a general way*, the human spiritual quest by grounding it in a dimension of objective experience. In light of parapsychology, those involved in this quest need not shuffle about in embarrassment concerning their basic claims and hopes. Spirituality, even the notion of the "supernatural," of itself need not imply retrograde thinking, neurotic clutching at illusion, or intellectual cowardice. If parapsychology in its central claims is right, then it is the scientific materialists who labor under illusions, and who are in denial of important dimensions of human experience.

Notes:

1. Psi includes retrocognition and precognition.
2. See, for example, the chapter "The Psychic Origins of Christianity" in my *Frontiers of the Soul* (Grosso, 1992).

3. Note that scientific materialism was supposed to have done away with “final” or “teleological” causation.
4. Batcheldor thought it possible to learn to control our psi powers, but felt there is powerful resistance to doing so; hence it is convenient at the present stage of our psychospiritual development to cling to the fiction of tutelary deities.
5. See the relevant chapter in *Frontiers of the Soul.*

Chapter 6

Some Thoughts on Parapsychology and Religion

Stephen E. Braude

One common theme in the world's great religions is, to put it roughly and colloquially: you can't fool God. That is, if you do something reprehensible, you might fool others into thinking that your behavior was acceptable, and you might even fool yourself (at least on a superficial level) into thinking the same thing. But, according to this view, there is a sense in which you're really not getting away with it. The major religions all have something to say about the price we ultimately pay for our earthly transgressions. It may have to do with the place in which we are eventually forced to reside (and I don't mean New Jersey), or it may concern the number of times we have to live again before we get it right, or it may simply concern the humiliation of being confronted in the afterlife with a litany of our sins (possibly presented by our victims). But whatever the scenario is supposed to be, the underlying common theme is that, sooner or later, we'll pay for our wrongdoing, even if we reap some benefits in the short term.

Interestingly, certain forms of modern secular humanism also advocate the theme that you can't fool God, although of course humanists state this theme (and other religious views) without referring to a deity. So instead of saying "you can't fool God," some humanists might argue that people know in their hearts when they are doing wrong, even if they can't articulate exactly what they feel is wrong about their actions. According to these humanists, the price we pay for our wrongdoing is internal. Echoing a viewpoint as old as Plato, they claim that in some sense our minds will be disordered or unsettled, or that we will otherwise be profoundly agitated or unhappy, no matter what sorts of superficial or temporary rewards we enjoy.

A somewhat different humanistic approach would be to say that there are natural laws or regularities governing behavior. These laws are presumably of a statistical rather than universal nature; that is, they have exceptions. But, like statistical generalizations about the dangers of certain foods, we ignore them at our peril. Hence, humanists of this sort might argue that it is generally (even if not universally) true that people eventually pay for their wrongdoings, whether it is in terms of how they make themselves ill, alienate others, or engage in various forms of self-defeating behavior. Of course, some humanists simply reject the notion that there is *any* secular analogue to the claim that you can't fool God. For them, that is simply one of many religious superstitions we should reject.

The evidence from parapsychology adds an interesting wrinkle to this issue. It suggests that physical separateness between people is relatively unimportant and that our psychic interactions link us closely into a kind of global community. The intimidating implication of this is that we seem to have more than the normal ways of gaining information about and affecting—even taking action against—one another. Hence, the data of parapsychology suggest that people might pay for their wrongdoings by means of psychic interventions. But in that case, we can apparently interpret the claim that you can't fool God in a way consistent with both deism and modern humanism (or at least forms of those positions willing to embrace the existence of psychic functioning). And on a related but somewhat less sinister note, the data of parapsychology might also help us understand the apparent (if only sporadic) efficacy of prayer.

What the Evidence Suggests

In his contribution to this volume, Charles Tart surveyed certain kinds of evidence for the existence of ESP and PK. And given the context of his paper, he quite appropriately emphasized the sort of controlled, laboratory, and quantitative data that many scientists (erroneously, in my view) take to be of paramount significance. But some of the most interesting parapsychological evidence comes from venues outside the lab, and I submit that some of this evidence (particularly the best cases of reported large-scale PK) is at least as clean as evidence gathered from traditional and formal controlled experiments. In fact, I believe that non-laboratory evidence promises insights into the nature of psychic functioning far greater than anything we could conceivably learn from laboratory research (see Braude, 1987, 1989, 1997 for an explanation and defense of this general position).

So let us suppose (if only to see where it leads) that I am right, and that non-laboratory evidence for psychic functioning must be taken seriously. And let us consider what that body of evidence suggests about the scope of human intention and the possible purposiveness behind seemingly impersonal events.

To begin with, if we take seriously the non-experimental evidence for PK, then we have reason to believe that humans can intervene in day-to-day occurrences to an extent that most people (in the West, at any rate) would find deeply intimidating. For one thing, once we grant that psi can occur in real-life situations, we must also grant that those occurrences may go undetected. But in that case, there is no reason to think that all instances of observable PK will be as obvious or incongruous as (say) table levitations or other movements of ordinarily stationary objects. Similarly, there is no reason to think that occurrences of everyday PK will be preceded by some sort of overt precursor or warning (a paranormal counterpart to a flourish of trumpets). For all we know, everyday PK might blend smoothly into ordinary surrounding events. Moreover, both laboratory and non-laboratory studies suggest that psi phenomena can have both conscious and unconscious causes. And since human intentions and desires are all too frequently malevolent, it may be that psi effects are not always innocuous or benign. In fact, real-life PK might affect or cause events of a sort that we believe usually occur in the absence of PK (e.g., heart attacks, car crashes, good or bad "luck," ordinary decisions and volitions, healing). The magnitude of PK presumably required for such effects is no greater (or at least not substantially greater) than that for which we already have good non-experimental evidence. And since there seems to be no way to determine conclusively whether psychic intervention played a role in the underlying causal history of an event, it might be impossible in principle to distinguish a psychically caused or influenced event from one that occurred in the absence of psychic influence.

If this view of things is on the right track, then it looks as if we might have to adopt what most Westerners would consider to be a magical world view, one which we associate (usually condescendingly) only with so-called primitive societies. According to this world view, our conscious and unconscious desires can surreptitiously influence a wide range of surrounding events, including those we think we are merely observing rather than helping to cause. Hence for all we know, we might be wholly or partly responsible for a wide variety of occurrences, both local and remote.

Clearly, a similar set of observations can be made about the forms of ESP. Just as occurrences of PK might inconspicuously permeate everyday events such as car crashes and heart attacks (whether or not those events seem to connect with our own interests), our mental lives might conceal a rich vein of telepathic and clairvoyant interactions. Occurrences of ESP, like occurrences of PK, needn't announce their paranormal ancestry beforehand or in some other way display their paranormal nature. For example, although some of our psychic experiences might stand out like a sore thumb, in general there needn't be anything about psychic experiences that—like a marker or label—distinguishes them from ordinary subjective experiences. And it does not matter whether those paranormal mental events are continuous or discontinuous with our ongoing inner episodes. In either case, there may be no way in principle to distinguish ordinary sorts of thoughts and feelings from those that have an underlying paranormal causal history. For example, although a telepathic experience might disrupt our train of thoughts and appear incongruous, that incongruity proves nothing about the nature of the experience. The reason, of course, is simply that not all incongruous thoughts have paranormal causes. Our thoughts might be (or merely seem) disconnected for a variety of mundane reasons.

Furthermore, the non-experimental evidence for ESP—particularly, the evidence from mental mediumship and precognition—suggests that the cognitive forms of psi may be considerably more extensive and refined than we might have thought simply on the basis of laboratory studies. The non-experimental evidence also buttresses laboratory data suggesting that telepathy and clairvoyance are at least two-stage processes. The initial interaction might occur unconsciously, and then later the information received might bubble up to the surface in a form that is both convenient and appropriate (e.g., a feeling, or an image, or an urge or impulse to act). Similarly, telepathic influence needn't manifest immediately. Like post-hypnotic suggestions, the effects of such influence might be delayed until an appropriate time.

Ironically, once we grant the possibility (in fact, the likelihood) that psi occurs outside the lab or seance room and plays a role in everyday life, we must concede that it might also be an unrecognized causal factor in ordinary scientific experiments. And if so, it is easy to see how this would complicate the interpretation of normal and apparently straightforward scientific research. After all, it is absurd to think that PK (for example) occurs only in experimentation conducted by parapsychologists. If PK occurs in laboratory situations and can affect the sensitive and delicate equipment designed to test for it, *and* if it can occasionally occur unconsciously in those situations (as some studies suggest), one would expect this to be possible—if not probable—in ordinary laboratory work. Hence, for all we know, psi influence might have been biasing the results of centuries of scientific experimentation. That possibility might be one reason why many scientists resist taking a serious look at the evidence from parapsychology. It is part of a more general concern that extends well beyond the scientific community. Many people seem to think that by admitting the reality of psychic functioning, especially day-to-day and inconspicuous psi, we are conceding that things could really get out of hand. And it is not simply that scientific experimentation may be deeply unreliable. For all we know, we might be living in a world in which we need to fear the malevolent thoughts of others, and also the responsibility of dealing with the possible psychic efficacy of our own unsavory impulses and desires. The problem of the resistance to psi is extremely complex and fascinating, and some writers have had interesting and provocative observations to make about it (see, e.g., Eisenbud, 1970, 1982, 1983; Tart, 1986; Tart & LaBore, 1986). But for now, we need only note that this resistance exists on a broad scale, and that it may plausibly be attributed to the fears and concerns just mentioned. For present purposes, what matters is how the basis for those concerns also fuels a secular interpretation of the claim that you can't fool God.

Sneaky Psi

So how might an appeal to psychic functioning help flesh out the claim that you can't fool God? One approach would be to view psi as a psychologically safe way of expressing certain feelings (for example, guilt and anger) that have other, and probably more familiar (or at least less threatening) negative consequences.

Consider guilt first. Most of us are probably all too familiar with the ways in which feelings of guilt can prevent us from "getting away with" our reprehensible acts. For example, guilty feelings may prevent us from lying convincingly, or from exhibiting other behaviors appropriate to the innocence we are feigning. Or, we might simply be overcome with remorse and confess our sins. Or, we might unconsciously sabotage some later activity and thereby symbolically atone for our earlier behavior. Or, we might make ourselves sick, by utilizing in a destructive way the dramatic control of our bodies so impressive in the case of placebo effects, hypnosis, and biofeedback.

But what if we manage to surmount or avoid these ordinary sorts of obstacles to successful sinning? Let us assume (perhaps without justification) that placebo effects, hypnotic control of bodily functions, and psychosomatic ailments are not expressions of PK. How (or how else) might we psychically express our guilt?

Perhaps the most obvious tactic would be to subject ourselves to various calamities that appear to originate from external sources. We could have an apparently inexplicable run of "bad luck"; or (if our troubles are not continuous) we might simply find ourselves confronted with a single major annoyance or tragedy (e.g., a serious accident, expensive car repair, lost wallet, etc.). By externalizing psi influence—that is, by obscuring its emotional origins and making our misfortune appear to emanate from outside us, we make it easier to view ourselves as victims of simple impersonal bad luck at best, and cosmic justice at worst. In either case, however, we would be attempting to deflect responsibility, both for our original reprehensible behavior and for our psychic retaliation against ourselves.

If these suggestions are on the right track, they might alter our perspective on a view of humanity captured by the Yiddish distinction between a *shlemiel* and a *shlemazel*. According to one familiar version of that distinction, a shlemiel is someone who spills soup on himself; a shlemazel has it spilt on him. So the shlemazel is a person who seems to be the victim of impersonal forces or the universe at large. Shlemazels are paradigmatic unlucky souls, and they really exist. I actually lived next door to some a number of years ago. I don't know if they were shlemazels before they met (and I wish I could now find that out); but their life as a married couple was a living hell of aggravations and accidents. For example, it seemed that nearly everything they bought was defective. Appliances and other electronic equipment almost invariably failed to operate out of the box; an apparently solid wooden rocking chair fell apart within their first week of ownership (with their infant sitting on it), and their cars were always in the shop (even though they owned brands noted for their reliability).

My favorite incident, however, is when the wife enthusiastically invited me over to see the photo she had just purchased of the Golden Gate Bridge. But when I saw it, I had to tell her, "Donna, that's the Brooklyn Bridge." My neighbor, in other words, had both symbolically and (in a sense) actually purchased the Brooklyn Bridge (which, as many readers will realize, is a classic—although perhaps now somewhat quaint—image of the "sucker" or "loser").

Now it might be that my neighbors, and shlemazels generally, are not merely unlucky. Instead, their misfortune might be a psi-mediated expression of their own self-hatred. Through the use of psi they might be arranging their lives to reinforce their own negative self-image, and they might accomplish this with the same degree of refinement found in more familiar forms of self-destructive behavior. And, like other types of unconsciously-driven self-destructive behaviors (for example, the way in which so many people seem to find themselves repeatedly in the same kinds of unhealthy romantic entanglements), all this would be accomplished in a way that deflects responsibility away from themselves.

In fact, acts of psychic self-aggression might be analogous in certain respects to phenomena elicited in studies of biofeedback control. For example, Basmajian (Basmajian, 1963, 1972) found that subjects could learn to fire a single muscle cell without firing any of the surrounding cells, although of course the subjects had no idea *how* they did this. Analogously, our psychic expressions of guilt or self-hatred might exhibit a similar degree of precision or refinement, and they might be executed with a similar degree of ignorance concerning the processes involved. Moreover, just as conscious willing often interferes with success in biofeedback tasks, it may likewise thwart our attempts at psychic influence. And the spectre of responsibility may, again, be one reason why it is advantageous for us to remain consciously ignorant of our roles in the process.

Having said all this, it is now easy to see how we might psychically (and unconsciously) express our anger toward others. Instead of expressing our hostility overtly, we might help arrange an accident or other nuisance for our victim. In fact, the more obscure the connection to us, the better. If a total stranger hits our victim in a car crash, we can conveniently deny any complicity in the event. After all, we didn't know the offender. Furthermore, if we allow for *symbolic* expressions of hostility, the issue becomes quite complex and even scarier. Probably, many mental health professionals would say that their patients often express hostility toward surrogates, in order to deflect responsibility for what they are really feeling. So suppose that we are very angry (say, at a parent), and suppose that instead of taking out our anger directly at the parent, we express the anger against someone who symbolically stands for the parent—say, another parent, or someone with the same initials. But if we can symbolically express our hostility paranormally, we could do so by causing an accident to a stranger who (at least for the moment) represents the parent. And of course, because we don't know the victim, we can tell ourselves that we had nothing to do with it.

It may be, then, that at least part of the force behind the claim that you can't fool God concerns the way in which psychic influences make it difficult to escape the anger of others or the wrath we feel toward ourselves.

The Efficacy of Prayer

On a slightly more positive note, the possibility of telepathic influence and PK might offer some insight into the apparent (if only occasional) efficacy of prayer. Obviously, psi-sympathetic secular humanists could maintain that it is through these forms of psychic influence that our prayers are sometimes answered. Even deists could hold that, at least on some occasions, prayers that seem to be answered by God are in fact answered through human psychic intervention. But if the efficacy of prayer results from psi rather than divine influence, the underlying causal story would seem to be anything but straightforward, and the prospects may not be quite as cheery as one might have thought.

Most readers, I imagine, would argue that prayers are frequently (and perhaps usually) *not* answered. So if an apparently efficacious prayer is not merely a coincidence, what needs to be explained is not simply why prayer occasionally succeeds, but also why it sometimes fails. And it is at this point that a secular explanation of prayer as psi-mediated might have certain theoretical advantages over conventional deistic interpretations.

The problem is this. For any attempt at psychic influence to succeed (whether or not it's a prayer), it must presumably navigate through an unimaginably complex web of underlying and potentially countervailing psychic interactions and barriers. On the assumption that people do function psychically, it is reasonable to assume, further, that their psychic activities have a natural setting—indeed, a natural *history*. In other words, psychic functioning would not be the sort of thing that we call forth just to meet the demands of parapsychological research, or for other sorts of overt solicitations, such as police investigations, seances, or for the purpose of entertainment. But if psi has a natural history, it's reasonable to suppose that it is typically driven by our deepest genuine or perceived needs and interests. That is why it is implausible to regard psi as the sort of capacity that is likely to be elicited (or elicited in a full-blown form) in response to the contrived and superficial needs created by formal experimentation (Braude, 1997). Moreover, it is reasonable to assume that because people can presumably use their psychic capacities unconsciously, they might be attempting to use them continually. In fact, it is also reasonable to assume that people will (again, possibly unconsciously) erect psychic barriers or defenses against the psychic interventions of others, just as we normally go about our daily affairs with a normal armor of defenses against the more familiar and overt activities of our peers. But in that case, there is no reason to believe that our attempts at psychic influence are likely to succeed. Even if there is no limit in principle to what we can accomplish psychically, those activities may be subject to serious case-by-case practical constraints. (See Braude, 1989, 1997, for a discussion of this point.)

An example should make this clear. Consider, first, what has to happen before we can carry out an ordinary plan of action. Suppose I am a virtuoso assassin (whose high fees reflect the skill and regularity with which I succeed at my job), and suppose I am contracted to carry out a "hit" on a Mr. Jones. No matter how good I am at my profession, there are nevertheless a number of factors that can confound even my best efforts. For one thing, Mr. Jones may anticipate my actions and go into hiding, hire bodyguards, or make some other sort of security arrangements. But even more relevantly, other people will be going about their daily business, and even though these people do not have me or my job on their mind, some of their actions may inadvertently get in my way. My assassination attempt could be thwarted by elevator repairs, traffic jams, pedestrians getting in the line of fire, or even a mugger. And there are innumerable other, and presumably impersonal, sorts of countervailing factors that can likewise interfere with my course of action. I could be stymied by a flat tire, ruptured fuel line, faulty telephone, allergic reaction, ingrown toenail, airport weather delays, or an attack of the flu.

Now if our unconscious psi can be active all the time, imagine how dense the underlying nexus of interactions will be. Our prayers (or any other attempt at psychic influence) would have to penetrate a vast array of psychic activities, any one of which could interfere with or neutralize our own efforts. The obstacles to success might be so numerous and so great that there is no way to predict when any of our psychic efforts might actually succeed. Hence, even if our successes are not entirely fortuitous (because, after all, they would be related to real volitions and efforts, like those of the assassin), they might nevertheless seem quite random. Moreover, the prospect of collective prayer does not seem appreciably better. Both a lone assassin and a team of assassins can be thwarted by an enormous number of countervailing influences.

Furthermore, it is not simply the difficulty in navigating the underlying nexus of psychic interactions and barriers that might frustrate attempts to fulfill our prayers. Our failures might also result in part from the familiar and natural unreliability of our capacities and the inevitable difficulty of summoning our own best efforts. Analogously, athletes and actors cannot always perform as well as they would like (or as well as they usually do), and the best writers sometimes suffer writer's blocks and attacks of ineloquence. Nevertheless, there is no reason to suppose that this formidable array of obstacles is always insurmountable. Our efforts might sometimes succeed, and when they do it may have to do with the resoluteness of our volitions or a fortuitous clearing in the customary array of hindrances. Hence, the secular interpretation of prayer as a kind of ritual for invoking our psi capacities actually makes some sense of its mixed but rather underwhelming record of success. By contrast, if we try to explain the efficacy of prayer in terms of divine intervention, then many might feel that we need to tell a variety of ad hoc, convoluted, and antecedently implausible stories about why a presumably loving God withheld his grace from us at all those times our prayers were not answered.

Of course, these considerations do not clinch the case for psi-enlightened secular humanism. For example, I realize that the so-called problem of evil is quite complex. But I believe they show that this position has more explanatory power and empirical support than some might have thought.

Chapter 7
Intuition: A Link Between Psi and Spirituality

Jeffrey Mishlove

Over the past 110 years, the discipline of psychical research and its offshoots have defined and investigated a variety of mental phenomena with labels ranging from apparitions to xenoglossy and including mediumship, telepathy, precognition, clairvoyance, extrasensory perception, psi, remote viewing, anomalous cognition, out-of-body experience and near-death experience. Some of these terms are derived from popular culture, others from field research and others from laboratory experience. Yet, in every case, it appears as if the effort has been made to describe phenomena which could somehow be understood as distinct from normal experience. Hence, for example, the term "parapsychology"—suggesting the study of experiences that are beyond those of normal psychology.[1]

It has long been recognized that a wide range of extraordinary phenomena occur, and can be studied, in the fabric of daily life. But even then the attempt has generally been focused on rigorous procedures for excluding conventional hypotheses. The procedures for field studies in the area of psychical research are most explicit on this point. A veridical dream of a future event, for example, was considered of little value to the research community if the dream itself had not been well-documented before the predicted event actually occurred.

We already know that anomalous cognitions occur in the laboratory and in certain pronounced types of life experience. The very word *anomalous* implies that the reasonable possibility of conventional explanations has been eliminated. This term is finding increasingly more common usage among psi researchers. Yet, once we acknowledge that anomalous experiences do occur, there is little merit in applying Occam's Razor to such a degree that we accept the existence of anomalous experience only in those rare circumstances in which elimination of other hypotheses is possible.

The emphasis on verification has meant that psi researchers have almost completely ignored a large class of experiences—those in which the validity of extrasensory perceptions are not, in principle, verifiable. This can occur for two primary reasons: (1) Extrasensory perception may be directed toward realities that are not presently testable through empirical methods, or (2) Extrasensory perception may be inextricably intertwined with normal sensory perceptions, or to use the more recent rubric, anomalous cognitions may be inextricably intertwined with normal cognition. One apt term for the types of experiences to which I am referring is *intuition.* It is the premise of this article that we can learn a great deal about psi through the indirect approach of monitoring the use of the term *intuition* in various cultural contexts.

Intuition is a wonderful word because it means so many different things to different people. It has a long tradition of use in philosophy, mathematics, business, psychology, engineering, linguistics, music, literature, religion, and science—particularly with reference to the creative process (Mishlove, 1994). Some of the many definitions and understandings of intuition are mutually inconsistent. Still, the basic definition is simple. According to the *Random House Dictionary of the English Language* (second edition, unabridged), intuition is "direct perception of truth, fact, etc., independent of any reasoning process; immediate apprehension." Another definition from the same dictionary refers to intuition as "a keen and quick insight." Other definitions stress that the intuitive process is itself unconscious. Intuition, then, is "knowing without knowing how you know."

Naturally, attempts have been made to reduce the intuitive process to something less mysterious. Norman Simon, the Nobel laureate economist and cognitive scientist, has suggested that intuition is nothing more than the brain's capacity for subliminal computation (Simon, 1989). Some social scientists view intuition as nothing more than learned habits and social conditioning. This is what they mean when they express delight that their studies have resulted in "counter-intuitive" results. Others believe that intuition is predicated upon biological instinct—for example, the intuition of a salmon in locating its spawning ground. If we eliminate the "nothing more," it is apparent that all of these hypotheses are of some merit. The fabric of intuition may well include these threads, as well as others.

The Meaning of Intuition in Different Walks of Life

While we can learn more about intuition by examining instances of its operation in daily life, we are in the ironic position of being unable to identify times in which intuition is not operating. Philosophers such as Immanuel Kant, for example, maintain that it is through intuition that we construct and maintain the basic elements of our world—our sense of space and time, our sense of identity, our sense of the truth of things, our sense of beauty and goodness. Intuition, derived from the very structure or essence of our minds, is viewed in philosophy as being prior to all perception and all reasoning. In linguistics, intuition is understood as the process by which listeners recognize the meaning of words and sentences, and speakers form words and sentences to create meaning. From these perspectives, our intuitions serve as the Hindu deity Vishnu, the sustainer of reality, providing continuity and meaning in our lives, moment by moment. All of our sensory perceptions and rational cognitions would fall apart like cards in the wind were it not for the glue of intuition holding the house of our lives together.

This fundamental form of intuition which Kant labeled, *a priori*, cannot be reduced to such mechanisms as subliminal computation—since all computations begin with premises and axioms that are, themselves, ultimately beyond computation. Nor can we reduce *a priori* intuitions to the effects of social conditioning. Developmental psychologists have documented the existence of both spatial awareness and "innate grammar" in infants, prior to any possibility of social conditioning (Pinker, 1994). In other contexts, intuition requires, and then adds to, years of experience and training filled with thoughtful reasoning and social conditioning.

Virtually every profession distinguishes between the highly intuitive sense of the virtuoso or genius as opposed to the competent, workmanlike performance of other professionals. In many diverse fields of endeavor—including music, dance, drama, comedy, athletics, gambling, psychotherapy, financial management, and marketing—the factor that seems to distinguish great intuitive genius is that of *timing*. It is as if, at this level, one's whole being is fully engaged in the apprehension of the nuances and rhythms of the relevant activities, both internal and external. Intuition is an exquisite sensitivity, within one's deepest being, to the pulses of life's energies.

Mathematical intuition is an interesting case. The realm of pure numbers and geometrical forms is Platonic in nature—it does not exist in the natural world and cannot be directly observed. Yet one significant aspect of mathematical intuition is the ability to apprehend, and even visualize, this realm. Cases are on record of mathematicians who have developed the capacity to accurately visualize the details of geometrical forms in four dimensions of space (Coxeter, 1972). Interestingly, however, these visualizations are subject to verification—not through empirical methods—but through the logical proofs of mathematics and geometry.

In ancient times, the Pythagoreans, Kabbalists, and Neo-Platonists saw similarities between the intuitions of mathematicians and those of mystics and visionaries. In the nineteenth century, this comparison began to take on momentum as mathematicians began exploring the fourth dimension of space. In 1884, a delightful little book titled *Flatland: A Romance in Many Dimensions*, by schoolmaster and theologian Edwin A. Abbott, (Abbot, 1963) popularized the idea that higher dimensions of space influence our three-dimensional sensory world and may provide a logic basis for accepting the ontological status of our spiritual intuitions.

One contemporary writer intrigued by this idea is Martin Gardner. Although he is generally known as a hardline debunker of matters psychic and mystical, in 1983 Gardner wrote a fascinating essay titled "IMMORTALITY: Why I Do Not Think It Impossible." Here Gardner argues that from the perspective of higher dimensional space, the process that we think of as death may be no more significant than a snake shedding its skin. Perhaps no one has taken intuitions regarding hyperspace and consciousness further than physicist Saul-Paul Sirag (1993).

It is generally believed by physicists working on unified field theory that space-time is hyperdimensional, with all but four of the dimensions being invisible. The reason for this invisibility is a major subject of research. Beside space-time dimensions, there are also other internal (or invisible) dimensions called gauge dimensions. The reality of these gauge dimensions is also a topic of controversy and research. If the extra space-time dimensions or the gauge dimensions are real, this provides scope for considering ordinary reality a substructure within a hyperdimensional reality. This idea has, of course, been suggested before—e.g. it is implicit in the Cave Parable of Plato.

The field of invention is an area in which intuition plays an essential role in searching out undiscovered possibilities. From the perspective of psi research, one might think of inventors as exercising precognition, i.e., looking into the future to a time when they themselves can observe the concrete demonstration of their own ideas. In this sense, the intuitions of inventors are subject to empirical verification. In another sense, inventors are like mathematicians, exploring a world of logical relations.

For some years, the Intuition Network has been receiving support from an inventor, Lynn Charlson, who made his fortune in the field of hydraulics. He cultivated a daily habit of spending thirty minutes every night before going to sleep in visualization and contemplation of specific technical problems. It was this process that led him to develop the first hydraulic power steering unit and other fundamental patents in the area of hydraulic motors.

I think it is of significance that Charlson, in retrospect, has come to view his intuitions as having a connection with higher spiritual sources. This is a viewpoint shared by other inventors, such as Chester Carlson (inventor of the Xerox process) and Arthur M. Young (inventor of the Bell Helicopter)—who have also made significant financial contributions to psi research and related fields. These inventors join the company of Henry Ford and Thomas Alva Edison in having a deep and abiding interest in the subject of reincarnation.

All of this suggests to me a continuum of perceptions. At one end of the spectrum, we have verifiable extrasensory perceptions of two- or three-dimensional, physical targets. Then, we see intuitive apprehensions of engineering and design concepts. These receive their verification at some future point in time through empirical tests of the inventions themselves. Next, there are direct intuitive apprehensions of mathematical realms that can be verified only through logical inferences. There is the intuition that expresses itself in excellent timing, and is generally verified in the context of a strikingly successful professional career. From here, we enter into a realm that, in modern times, has been relegated to metaphysics—beyond all possible verification. This is the realm that positivist philosophy once suggested we should "pass over in silence."

Is there any possibility of rationally investigating spiritual intuitions? Can we begin to reasonably probe the realm of spirits and the mysterious journeying of the human soul? Modern scholarship is divided on this issue. In spite of the diverse perspectives offered through different cultural lenses, the penetrating minds of Aldous Huxley and Huston Smith claim that they can recognize a "perennial philosophy" or a "primordial tradition" that flows through all esoteric thinking. This common ground, they maintain, involves a pattern in which the human soul grows in depth and wisdom as it approaches its ultimate destination of divine union. Other scholars, such as Ninian Smart, in the post-modern deconstructivist tradition, maintain that the experiences of the world's mystics are unique and cannot be compared.

It is not new that scholars disagree. But we can resolve this disagreement if an adequate method can be found. There are hints of possible new methods on the horizon. The concept of "state specific sciences," originally proposed by Charles Tart in 1972, suggests that we view advanced practitioners of various esoteric disciplines as engaging in a type of systematic observation very much akin to science (Tart, 1972). If there are differences in the portrait of reality painted by the various schools of esoteric practice, they may well be the result of cultural projections. However, Tart's model implies that we might also consider these differences to be akin to the differences we might find between the various approaches we know of in psychology, biology, chemistry, and physics. The fact that there are differences between these perspectives offers no grounds for invalidation of any particular perspective. We are still seeking principles of unification of our conventional sciences. Ultimately, I believe, our search will lead to a larger worldview in which we will begin to see the unity between the knowledge brought forth by intuitive disciplines and that produced through mainstream science.

In fact, reported intuitions of spiritual dimensions constitute an enormous area of study. The ancient literature includes *The Egyptian Book of the Dead*, the Old Testament and New Testament, the *Zohar*, the *Talmud*, the *Upanishads*, the *Dammapata*, and *The Tibetan Book of the Dead.* Each of these works has for generations commanded the lifetimes of countless scholars.

Modern religions have also been founded upon such intuitions. The Church of the New Jerusalem is based on the writing of Emanuel Swedenborg, an eighteenth-century scientist whose detailed writings of spiritual worlds fill encyclopedic volumes. Witness the Kardecian *espiritistas* of Brazil, whose teachings result from the systematic effort of a nineteenth-century French pedagogue to correlate accounts of the afterlife provided by different spirit mediums. Kardec's rule was to admit no finding that was not verified by seven different mediums.

These converging insights and methodologies from psi research, the testimony of spiritual experience, and the broad field of intuition suggest to me that we have the potential to use intuitive consensus in a disciplined fashion as a tool for exploring realms of consciousness that have previously been relegated to philosophy, mythology and theology.

Notes:

1. Although I hold a doctoral diploma in "Parapsychology," I used to be very concerned that this was a very poor name that has done more to harm than to help the discipline which I then preferred to think of as "psi research." When one considers the original Greek meaning of the term *psychology* to be "the study of the soul," it struck me as odd that Rhine felt a need to define his area of study as being of another order of experience. Now, having become more acquainted with the Buddhist *prajnaparameta*, I have gained a deeper appreciation for the implications of the root "para."

Chapter 8
Parapsychology and Spirituality: Implications and Intimations

William Braud

There is no need for science to justify spirit. Nor can it do so.

As suggested long ago by Hugh of St. Victor and Bonaventure, and elaborated by Ken Wilber, there are at least three realms of being and three ways of accessing these realms.[1] There is a physical, sensory realm accessed by the *eye of the flesh;* a mental realm of ideas, thoughts, and images perceived by the *eye of the mind;* and a transcendental or spiritual realm known through the *eye of the spirit.* Each *eye* reveals a different aspect of reality, and what is revealed to one eye is not necessarily available to the others. Wilber reminds us that we commit category errors when we unwisely attempt to see everything through one eye only and allow one form of vision to usurp the domains of the other two. To approach a complete picture of reality, we must have, at least, triple-vision.

Psychologist Lawrence LeShan (1974) likewise describes three alternate realities—the *sensory*, *clairvoyant*, and *transpsychic*—within which one encounters different ways of being, different modes and objects of knowing, and different values. Different things are possible and impossible within each reality.

To attempt to justify the spiritual through science (as science is conventionally understood) is to attempt to see the realm of the transcendental through the eye of the flesh or to know clairvoyant or transpsychic realities while remaining firmly within the bounds of the sensory reality. The shoes of the one do not fit the feet of the other. There is, however, *at least some overlap* among the three realities and among what is available to the three eyes. There are regions in which science, psychology, and spirituality intersect. Here, science—in the form of psychical research and parapsychology—can encounter reflections of aspects of reality that are of value to those interested in spirituality. Here, science may have something useful to say.

The Realm of the Sensible and Rational

Charles Tart's "Western Creed" (pages 41-42 of this volume) epitomizes a dominant scientistic worldview. According to this view, we are individual entities, dwelling and moving in our unique, isolated paths through a world of space and time, a world of limits. When we interact with one another or with other parts of nature, we do so by means of language and other physical signals and by means of conventional physical forces and energies. What we know of the world and of each other we have learned though our senses and through the patterns imposed upon earlier sensory information by our faculties of reason and intellect. We live in a world in which causality rules, in which causes always precede effects, and in which time flows inexorably from past, to present, to future. Our thoughts, images, feelings, and wishes are private, sometimes entertaining, often painful, but never able to exert *direct* influences upon others or upon the physical world. Reason and language are valued and require distinctions, limits, and boundaries for their functioning and maintenance. The world is not only a realm of dualities, but also a realm in which contraries duel for supremacy, in which stands are taken for and against, in which the middle is excluded.

In this world, there is a reluctance to examine embarrassing facts that do not accord well with currently accepted theory. There is a tendency to attribute reality only to the physical, to the objectively measurable. There is a privileging of the nomothetic, the general law, the universal pattern, over the idiographic, the unique, the individual instance. There is a mistrust of the subjective, of the personal.

The masculine way of action, power, and doing is elevated above the feminine way of receptivity, relationship, and being. Not only this scientism, but the scientific enterprise itself is often tinged with this masculine flavor in its pursuits of explanation, prediction, and control. Today's scientists often echo the sentiments of Francis Bacon, whose writings contain statements such as "knowledge and human power are synonymous," "nature is only subdued by submission," "nature, like a witness, reveals her secrets when put to torture."[2] Bacon (1561-1626) was one of the earliest and staunchest advocates of the inductive and experimental method.

He also was Attorney-General, and later Lord Chancellor, under King James I, and his close familiarity with the prosecution of witches may have influenced some of his favored metaphors. Huston Smith (1992) reminds us that we can control only what is inferior to us and that any discipline that studies solely what is subject to control and limitation cannot reveal anything transcendent—i.e., superior to us in intelligence, awareness, compassion, or any other criterion of worth (pp. 119, 151, 200).

In common Western science, theory, mechanism, and rational explanation are valued over mere description and appreciation. The usefulness and practical application of knowledge is emphasized. There is consensus that meaningful personal experiences should be excluded from the arena of science and that, indeed, their admission may be grounds for suspicion of scientific objectivity and reliability.

Western science, when not corrupted into a rigid scientism, is a wonderful, self-correcting system for the acquisition of valid knowledge. The praise that it receives for its magnificent triumphs is rightly deserved. Yet, even in its unadulterated form, much is omitted. There is no place for values, purposes, meaning, quality, or spirit. Jacques Monod (1972) wrote: "The cornerstone of scientific method is . . . the systematic denial that 'true' knowledge can be got at by interpreting phenomena in terms of final causes—that is to say, of 'purpose'" (p. 21). Ludwig Wittgenstein (1961) wrote: "We feel that even when all scientific questions have been answered, the problems of life remain completely untouched" (p. 73). Steven Weinberg (1974, p. 42) wrote: ". . . there is an essential element in science that is cold, objective, and nonhuman," and "The more the universe seems comprehensible, the more it also seems pointless" (1977, p. 154).

Another Realm

It was partly to combat pessimistic tendencies similar to those just highlighted, and those made explicit in Charles Tart's "Western Creed," that psychical research arose toward the end of the nineteenth century.[3] Its aim was to replace a philosophical and scientific view of "nothing but" with one of "something more."

Psychic phenomena are like flowers whose distinctiveness, brightness, beauty, and perfume attract attention, inspire awe, and compel approach. The early psychical researchers were fascinated by many of these flowers, and they sought to collect them and explain them using the methods of science. There were near-death experiences, out-of-body experiences, apparitions of the living and of the dead, hauntings, poltergeist disturbances, past-life recall, mental and physical phenomena of mediumship. When part of psychical research transformed itself into experimental parapsychology, the quest continued; but now the methods became more limited, and attention was focused upon certain flowers only. The method of choice became the controlled laboratory experiment, and the studied phenomena were limited almost exclusively to telepathy, clairvoyance, precognition, and psychokinesis. Indeed, often the search was limited to only certain parts, or to certain petals, of particular flowers. Much was ignored and lost. But scientists could now declare, with great confidence, that this and that petal did, indeed, exist.

Part of spirituality may be likened to a garden, which some say exists, and which is said to be filled with certain species of flowers found nowhere else. To the extent that science verifies the existence of some of these flowers, there is growth in evidence that is consistent with the existence of the garden itself and of its other contents. If minor miracles such as telepathy, clairvoyance, precognition, and psychokinesis do indeed occur, then *perhaps* other, grander miracles, healings, and powers (*siddhis*) described in the various mythological, religious, and spiritual traditions can occur as well. At the very least, they become far less outrageous and impossible than before. And, it can be argued, if some of the curious phenomena have a reality, perhaps there also is a reality to the ontologies and epistemologies of our spiritual traditions; perhaps there are levels and ways of being and of becoming, of entities and processes, of knowing (revelation, gnosis) and of doing (creation, emanation), that complement the more mundane forms of life as we know it.

This may be the major implication and promise of parapsychology: If certain exotic flowers exist, might not others? And if such flowers exist and thrive, may there not also be larger and more extensive plant and root systems that support and nourish them, systems of which these flowers are impressive but transient manifestations or emanations?

It is remarkable that science, itself, using its own methods, has validated the reality of the four major psychic phenomena. Instances of telepathy, clairvoyance, precognition, and psychokinesis have been verified repeatedly in thoughtful laboratory research projects.[4] Further, such abilities are not rare, but seem to be widely distributed among the population. The Gnostic and alchemical symbol of Ouroboros—the image of the serpent curled into a circle, tail in mouth—comes to mind. The dragon devouring its own tail, consuming itself, may symbolize how science, in investigating paranormal phenomena, has used its own methods to turn on itself, thereby proving the limitations of those very methods. Using its criteria for studying what is material and physical, using its framework that only what is material and physical exists, science has demonstrated there is something other than the material and physical. This is a wonderful illustration of Heraclitus' law of *enantiodromia* (a running contrariwise) according to which everything tends, sooner or later, but especially when carried to extremes, to become its opposite. The Ouroboros also suggests a coming together, a bridge; and parapsychology is, indeed, a bridge that joins the scientific with the spiritual.

The psychic realm resembles that common ground inhabited by quantum physicists and mystics—a world more like a giant idea than like a giant machine.[5] It is a world in which sensation and reason no longer reign supreme, in which boundaries dissolve, in which limits are replaced by the limitless, in which space and time no longer seem to be critical factors. Here, persons, distantly separated and seemingly without the mediation of conventional informational and energetic exchanges, can share thoughts, feelings, images, movements, and physiological activities. Here, persons can gain access to the future through means other than rational inference, seemingly able to remember the future as well as the past. Here, mental processes of attention and intention can interact directly with and directly influence physical and biological systems. Here occur mutually arising meaningful coincidences or synchronicities, in the absence of conventional causality. Persons evidence direct knowing of remote events. Effects precede causes. Thoughts become things. Like Jung's psychoid level, it is a realm where mind is like matter and matter is like mind.

Beyond Limits and Contraries

The findings of experimental parapsychology suggest that the human mind can do things, can reach through space and time, in ways that human brains and bodies alone, conceived as purely physical organs, cannot do. We are our brains and bodies but are also something more. Under certain conditions, we may transcend limits, including the limits of individuality.

The findings suggest the existence of natural phenomena and processes that cannot be adequately encompassed by our current scientific framework nor fully addressed by current scientific methodologies. Therefore, that framework and those methods need extension and expansion if they are to claim fullness of understanding of our universe. A strange principle may guide us in extending our understanding—the principle of "standing it on its head." For every concept and every law, there may be a contrary concept or law that is equally valid. For example, in modern physics, it is true that light is a particle; but it is also true that it is not a particle. Light is a wave, yet it is not a wave. It is true that matter is material, concretized, localized in time and space; but it is also true that matter is virtually entirely space and energy and is spread out nonlocally throughout time and space (before "observation" or "measurement" occurs). It is true that heavy bodies sink in water and cannot fly; but heavy bodies also can float in water and *can* fly. For any principle within the natural and human sciences, we can probably find an opposite or complementary principle that is equally true and that, under certain conditions, may supersede the first. It has been remarked, "The opposite of a truth is a lie. The opposite of a profound truth is another profound truth."[6] Science may currently be aware of only half of the complementary realities and principles necessary to complete the whole. Whereas it may be true that there are certain limits to processes, it is also true that those limits may be transcended. Events may be determined, and yet there is freedom. Causality is a well-established principle of nature, and yet nature sometimes may operate acausally.

Many psychic phenomena, but especially psychokinesis, indicate the efficacy of intention, volition, and purpose, and suggest that it may profit us to put goal-directed, teleonomic processes and concepts back into our science. And, if intention and purpose are truly present within us, should they not also be present outside of us, in the universe at large? Transtemporal phenomena such as precognition invite us to question the adequacy of our conceptualizations of time and of causality itself. Mutually arising meaningful coincidences or synchronicities suggest an acausal connecting principle in Nature that complements causality.

Interconnectedness

The occurrence of psychic phenomena seems to require a condition of profound and extensive interconnectedness among people and also between people and all of animate and inanimate Nature. Such interconnectedness has important implications for our understanding of who we really are, of our individuality, of our true selves; and from these implications flow other, ethical implications for appropriately interacting with others and with our environment.

Nearly sixty years ago, Henri Bergson (1858-1941) used the image of "our large body"—co-extensive with our consciousness, comprising all we perceive, reaching to the stars—to describe this interconnectedness. Bergson (1935) wrote: "The habit has grown of limiting consciousness to the small body and ignoring the vast one" (pp. 246-247). Could it be that the localized consciousness with which we are intimately familiar and which we know as our "ego"—the convincingness of locality and individuality—is simply a quirk of our ordinarily limited attention? And could a shift in attention reveal the extended range of our true, nonlocal consciousness, allowing direct knowing and direct mental influence of "remote" events? Patanjali favored such a view in the *Yoga Sutras*, and that view is consistent with the findings of contemporary parapsychology.[7]

We could, no doubt, treat one another with kindness, understanding, and compassion even if we were not profoundly and intimately interconnected in nontrivial ways. However, having direct knowledge and direct experience of our interconnections can greatly increase our love for one another and enhance our ethical behaviors toward one other. We can learn from parapsychology the factors and conditions that are more or less likely to lead to such direct experiences and use this knowledge to facilitate their occurrence.

It may be that our deep interconnectedness with each other and with all of Nature is *the* major conclusion that issues forth from the many findings of parapsychology. Perhaps this is what we are really telling ourselves by means of the myriad psychic phenomena that we allow ourselves to experience. All psychic phenomena may be impressive and sometimes elaborate indicators of an already-present connectedness. What better way to dramatize to ourselves that we are truly one than to share—especially at great distances and in defiance of powerful conventional barriers—each other's thoughts, feelings, images, sensations, and reactions? And what better way to demonstrate that we are in intimate contact with all of reality than to touch and move things with our minds? Perhaps the apparent transfer of information and the apparent forces that we seem to see in psychic functioning are not really what they appear to be. Rather, they may be quick yet effective and convincing indicators, that are readily at hand (paths of least resistance, so to speak), when we wish to remind ourselves of our forgotten interconnections.

In general, psi experiences may be self-created metaphors and dramatizations—extremely real and concrete teaching stories that hold important latent meanings, lessons, and reminders that may have little to do with the more obvious literal and "informational" content of the experiences. It could be fruitful to ask ourselves: What is the real message, and what is merely the medium?

Experimental parapsychology reveals interconnectedness only indirectly. Its impact is primarily upon the intellect and is but a shadow of the fuller, more direct impact of oneness felt and known in the mystical experience. One may increase parapsychology's typically dilute yield by venturing into the broader area of psychical research, and it may be increased further still by exploring an even greater range of exceptional human experiences, as advocated by Rhea White (see page 83). Therein, one may learn not only from science, but also from the rich sources of art, poetry, metaphor, mythology, and direct experience. But for the greatest yield, one goes, as well, to the spiritual traditions themselves.

Reflective Patterns

From the laboratory have emerged findings and patterns that reflect observations and patterns of spiritual teachings. At the most obvious level, the finding that persons can exhibit direct knowing of, and direct mental interactions with, other living and nonliving aspects of the world is consistent with the many claims of clairaudience, visions, prophetic dreams, healings, and "miraculous" physical events reported in virtually every spiritual tradition.

From research that has demonstrated that persons are able to influence the bodily systems of other persons, mentally and at a distance, emerge clear implications, and possibly applications, of mental or spiritual healing for purposes of physical wellness and psychological well-being. Studies indicate that attention and intention may be focused upon other persons to either facilitate or impede various biological processes. For example, we have conducted a long and extensive research program in which we found that persons are able to increase and decrease the autonomic nervous system activity of other persons, mentally and at a distance. We monitored electrodermal activity, which reflects the activity of the sympathetic branch of the autonomic nervous system. The monitored person was stationed in one room and the "influencer" was stationed in a separate, distant room. Under the conditions of the experiments, sensory and other conventional forms of communication between the two persons were eliminated. The influencer attempted to influence the distant person's electrodermal activity according to a random schedule unknown to the person being influenced. The experimental procedure was computer-controlled and the electrodermal measurements were scored objectively by computer. We found that, compared to noninfluence, control periods, the distant persons did indeed evidence greater autonomic activity during periods when the influencers were mentally intending for this to happen, and showed lowered autonomic activity when reduced activity was the aim. We also found preliminary indications that persons are able to "block" unwanted influences upon their own physiological systems through their own interfering intentions and imagery. The mental strategies used by the successful influencers included: (a) producing the desired bodily changes in themselves, using self-regulation techniques, while intending for the distant person to change similarly; (b) visualizing or imagining the distant person in situations that would be expected to produce the desired bodily changes if the distant person actually were to find himself or herself in such situations; and (c) intending and wishing for the polygraph indicator (which reflected the electrodermal activity) to behave appropriately (i.e., in line with the influencers' intentions). Using similar designs, we found that persons were able to protect their own and others' red blood cells (i.e., to decrease the rate at which the cells broke down and died under osmotic stress), mentally and at a distance, using strategies of attention, intention, and visualization of the desired outcomes. In these hemolysis studies, the rate of death of the blood cells was monitored in a blind fashion and objectively by means of a spectrophotometer that detected the state of health of the cells. Complete details of hundreds of these biological psychokinesis experiments may be found in three of our summary publications,[8] and similar work by other investigators also has been reviewed (Benor, 1990; Solfvin, 1984).

This work on direct mental interactions involving living systems has two important implications for spirituality. First, the findings are consistent with the reported outcomes, within many spiritual traditions, of mental healing, spiritual healing, and intercessory prayer. Second, the fact that one person's physiological activity can be shown to reflect or mirror that of another person, even when the two people are physically separated by distance and by shields, suggests that at certain levels the two apparently separate and distinct bodies are really one. Certain states of mind and stations of being can facilitate entrance into this realm wherein merging with another is possible.

It seems likely that a much greater range of processes could be similarly influenced. In any dyadic situation (teacher/student, therapist/client, nurse/patient, trainer/trainee), the mental "practice" by the first member of the dyad may directly facilitate what the second member of the dyad is attempting to do or learn. Thus, our states of mind and conditions of being can have important and direct influences upon the thoughts, feelings, images, actions, and being of others.

Some years ago, I was amazed and delighted to find that a large number of factors known to facilitate psychic functioning sorted themselves into three clusters that closely matched the three familiar virtues of faith, hope, and love—virtues emphasized in virtually all spiritual traditions. This analysis was reported in Braud (1990-91) and was mentioned in Braud, Honorton, Schlitz, Stanford, and Targ (1991). *Faith* is related to belief, confidence, and trust, and it is known that these factors tend to enhance psychic functioning, whereas attitudes of disbelief, distrust, doubt, and suspicion are inimical to successful psi performance. There are indications that the more thoroughgoing the belief, the greater are the psi effects. Many parapsychologists hold that feedback (knowledge of successful outcomes) is important to the participant in a psi experiment. Perhaps at least part of the usefulness of feedback may be attributed to the belief-encouraging and confidence-enhancing results of such feedback information. The presence or absence of belief, on the part of investigators themselves, may be, at least in part, responsible for the well-known "experimenter effect" in which certain experimenters consistently tend to obtain positive results in their experiments, whereas other experimenters consistently tend to obtain chance or even negative experimental outcomes.

An attitude of *hope* or confident expectation appears to facilitate psychic functioning. Hope is desire accompanied by expectation of fulfillment. The desire component can provide motivation and incentive, which can drive the psi process. At the same time, the expectation component can focus the process, directing it to one particular goal or outcome, as opposed to another. The role of hope, in its guise of wishing and wanting, is especially evident in psychokinesis, wherein a specific outcome is desired and expected—and comes to pass. Some of the mental strategies employed by successful practitioners of psychokinesis (e.g., imagery or visualization of the desired goal, focusing, concentration, attention-training) may themselves contribute to the expectation process.

The relevance of *charity* or love to successful psi functioning is most evident in cases of psychic healing and in healing analog studies in which the healer's feelings of love for the healee or for the healee surrogate, and strong positive feelings of merging and interconnectedness, may facilitate successful outcomes. In parapsychological experiments generally, positive dispositions toward the experimental situation and toward all persons involved in the study are found to be psi-conducive. The reduction of egocentric motives and methods is believed to be favorable to psi success. It has been suggested that altruistic motives facilitate positive outcomes of applied psi endeavors, whereas egocentric motives interfere with success.

Other sets of laboratory findings, especially those that emphasize the psi-facilitating qualities of spontaneity, absence of striving, and release of effort, are consistent with spiritual teachings of the importance and power of "grace." These findings also are congruent with spiritual beliefs that wonderful and miraculous things can happen when one is "at one with the Tao."[9]

Laboratory research has suggested that various forms of sensory disruption, restriction, or deprivation and the experimental induction of various "altered states of consciousness" may increase one's access to the psychic realm. This is consistent with reports from spiritual traditions that access to spiritual realms may be enhanced by reducing worldly distractions, withdrawing attention from the fleshly, sensory eye, and entering nonordinary consciousness.

"If the doors of perception were cleansed," wrote William Blake, "every thing would appear to man as it is, infinite." Many spiritual disciplines have been developed to help attain such a cleansing, to achieve "lucidity" and an awareness of what is beyond appearances. Many of the components of these practices have been studied by parapsychologists and have been found to facilitate psychic functioning. A common characteristic of these components is that they are accompanied by a freedom from distractions and from internal and external constraints upon the bodymind, and that they result in deep quietude, stillness, and calmness at many levels of the organism. The methods would be quite familiar to followers of Patanjali's Eastern system of purification and control of the mind,[10] as well as to followers of the Western mystical tradition so ably described by Evelyn Underhill (1969). Underhill presented a Western model of spiritual development characterized by stages of awakening, purification, illumination, the dark night of the soul, and unification with the divine. Parapsychologist Charles Honorton (1977) translated the Eastern model of Patanjali's Raja yoga into "a progressive system of psychophysical noise reduction."

The first five stages were designed to systematically reduce the external causes of mental distraction. The first two stages (*Yama* and *Niyama*) involve the reduction of distractions associated with emotion and desire. The second two (*Asana* and *Pranayama*) involve reduction of somatic distractions. The fifth stage (*Pratyahara*) involves detaching attention from the sensory organs in order to isolate consciousness from external perception.

"Freed from external somatosensory noise, the last three stages of Patanjali's system involve the elimination of internal cognitive distractions. This is accomplished by maintaining attention on a single object or image. These three stages designate increasing durations of concentration. The object of concentration serves to focus and limit attention within a narrowly-defined area. Concentration (*Dharana*) is achieved when attention is confined within the boundaries of a single object or image for a specified period of time. In this stage, attention is free to fluctuate within the defined area but may not wander outside of it. Meditation (*Dhyana*) involves the maintenance of concentration for a longer period of time. It is characterized by less movement of attention within the boundaries of the object or image, which is experienced with greater continuity. In the final stage (*Samadhi*), concentration is maintained for a still longer period. This stage is characterized by total continuity of attention on the object or image. Attention is said to be 'absorbed' in the object and there is a dissolution of subject-object differentiation which is associated with an experience of transcending space-time. Collectively, these last three stages constitute a process which Patanjali calls *Samyama.* According to Patanjali, paranormal phenomena may be produced by performing *Samyama*" (Honorton, 1977, p. 438).

Numerous parapsychological studies have been conducted in which the components of Patanjali's model have been simplified, secularized, and tested for possible psi-favorable effects. External sensory "noise" or distractions are minimized by sensory restriction procedures. Typically, this is accomplished through the use of a *Ganzfeld* technique that involves uniform visual and acoustic stimulation and that leads to an experimentally-induced hypnagogic condition. Attention is freed from external stimuli and is directed inwardly toward ordinarily ignored thoughts, feelings, and images. The density, vividness, and reality of imagery is greatly enhanced. Muscular noise/distractions are reduced by means of progressive muscular relaxation and biofeedback procedures. Autonomic and emotional noise/distractions are reduced through autogenic training exercises. Cognitive noise/distractions are reduced through concentration, attention-training, and proto-meditational exercises. All of these techniques, alone or in various combinations, have been associated with good psychic functioning in laboratory tests (see Braud, 1975, 1978; Honorton, 1977).

Spiritual traditions suggest that too much attention to the eye of the mind (rational thought) may limit or even actively interfere with seeing through the eye of the spirit. Laboratory research has demonstrated that too much rational, analytical, interpretative thought can indeed interfere with accurate psychic functioning. Investigators of "remote viewing" (a combination of telepathy and clairvoyance testing involving more natural targets such as geographical sites) have found that logical, interpretative thought ("analytical overlay") can lead one astray, psychically, and they have developed means of identifying and reducing such interferences (see Targ and Puthoff, 1977; Targ and Harary, 1984). Overly structured, linear thinking ("cognitive constraints") has been shown to be psi-antagonistic, whereas a more fluid, spontaneous, creative mode of mental functioning (typically, one that is also rich in imagery) is psi-favorable (Braud, 1982b; Stanford, 1987). As we saw in preceding paragraphs, excessive mental activity of any kind may similarly interfere. Psychic access improves when the drunken monkey of the mind is tranquilized and calmed through meditation and meditation-like techniques familiar to all spiritual seekers.

Glimpses of a Greater Realm

Experimental parapsychology has provided tantalizing intimations of a greater reality; but, to date, nearly all of these findings demonstrate simply that the mundane can be accomplished in extramundane ways. In order to meet the verification criteria of current science, parapsychologists interested in extrasensory perception have focused almost exclusively upon the novel, psychic conveyance of mundane information that can be verified by conventional senses and therefore is redundant with sensory knowledge. We have virtually ignored possible psychic access to aspects of reality that are not readily evident to the senses. Suppose I hide a small object in a box and ask someone to "psychically peer into the box" and describe its contents. Heretofore, we have limited our questions about psychic functioning to ones concerned with accuracy in describing the sensory realm. In the present example, if I am able to accurately describe beforehand what I and others will see when the box is later opened, then I have exhibited psychic functioning. Anything else that I might learn is ignored or discounted. But I already have eyes and ears and other senses to deal with these readily apparent (evident) aspects of the physical realm. Why would Nature have bestowed upon us a "second sight" or "sixth sense" that is so redundant with our regular senses? We could expand our questions about psi to ask: What can psi tell us about the world that is *not* immediately obvious or evident to our conventional senses? Going back to the example, perhaps psi can tell me something about the history of the object, rather than simply about its sensory qualities. Or perhaps I can know something about future events in which the object will participate. Perhaps psi can tell me about relationships, associations, or connections in which the object has previously participated, in which it is presently involved, or in which it will play some role in the future. Perhaps psi can inform me not only about a distant, hidden person's clothing or appearance, but also more interesting things about that person's history, future, relationships, condition of physical and psychological health or illness, emotional condition, state of consciousness, potential, achievements, stage of spiritual development, current goals and challenges, and the best ways to help that person in his life and along her spiritual path. I suspect psi is helping all of us learn such things all the time and that this is part of the "art" of education, medicine, nursing, and therapy. But such questions, curiously, have been ignored by experimental parapsychology. No doubt, one reason for this is that these qualities are not easy to measure, compared to the readily assessed color or shape of an object hidden in a box. Although challenging, we could ask psi to help us perform much more interesting tasks such as discerning hidden meanings, purposes, significances, and relationships. We ask psi to tell us about the physical realm—to duplicate the eye of the flesh. But what can psi help us learn about non-ordinary realms? Can it tell us about qualities of the physical universe at its extremes of largeness, smallness, emptiness, fullness, very high and very low temperatures or energy levels? Can we "remote view" the ultimate constituents of matter and energy?[11] What can psi tell us about the nature of time and of causality? Can psi inform us of the existence and nature of realms other than the physical? Can we discern, psychically, characteristics of persons, objects, or events in "psychic space" that are not immediately obvious to our senses? And can we agree on these? Can we venture, individually or in groups, into nonordinary realities, make "observations" there, remember and bring back what we have learned, compare notes and reach consensus with others who have made similar journeys?[12] What can psi tell us about psi itself? What might we learn, psychically, about our own true natures, our human beinghood? In asking such questions, we would be asking psi to function not as the eye of the flesh, but rather as the eye of the mind and of the heart, and perhaps as even more novel eyes. These new questions are challenging ones, but they are questions of extreme interest and importance. Should it choose to investigate such issues, parapsychology's overlap with spirituality would increase greatly. Further discussions of these issues may be found in Braud (1994a, 1994b).

Researchers who are presently exploring certain forms of psychokinesis are playing a somewhat more exciting game, for we are studying mental ways of doing what cannot be done by ordinary means, such as influencing radioactive decay or rapidly influencing complex biological processes. Still, we can raise our sights to more meaningful goals of even greater spiritual significance. Rather than restrict ourselves to producing physical or physiological changes via our intentions, we might also explore direct mental influences upon psychological, social, cultural, psychic, and spiritual processes in ourselves and in others. We have taken a few feeble steps in this direction in our own research. We have found that persons are able to help other persons improve their mental imagery skills and attention-focusing skills, mentally and at a distance (Braud and Jackson, 1983; Braud, Shafer, McNeill, and Guerra, 1995). It would not be difficult to extend this work to more interesting dyadic interactions, nor is it difficult to see possible useful educational, medical, therapeutic, and social applications of "mentally helping" others with their mental, emotional, imaginative, creative, and spiritual work.

Perhaps most importantly of all, we can begin to explore, deeply and intensively, the *meanings* of psychic and other exceptional human experiences to those who have these experiences. We can study the impacts of such experiences upon the lives of the experiencers. We can interest ourselves not only in the fact that such experiences exist, but also in why they happen to particular persons at particular times and in particular ways. What are their outcomes, their consequences, their fruits? How are they and how are they not assimilated into the experiencer's life, self-concept, growth, being and becoming? Our goal can become, in the words of the epigraph of Carolly Erickson's *The Medieval Vision,* "Not to prove, but to discover" (1976).

Parapsychological findings can be useful to those on spiritual paths as they can provide a certain degree of confidence and trust that at least some of the processes and concepts encountered are "real" in a more traditional sense and are not delusions, projections, or misinterpretations. They also can serve to remind us that we are not alone in having exceptional experiences; such experiences are normal, natural, and remarkably widespread. But these scientific reassurances, though of value, are only partial. A great deal of what is encountered along the spiritual path is quite beyond the reach of current science. Here, one must be armed with trust, faith, hope, love, discernment, and a tolerance for ambiguity and for contraries, rather than with the feelings of safety, certainty, familiarity, and understanding that science can provide.

Spirituality addresses one's highest values and ultimate realities and how one lives one's everyday life in congruence with those values and realities. Spirituality also deals with the Beyond, that which is other and greater than surface appearances, and with how we relate to that Beyond. Thus, spirituality cannot be restricted solely to the sphere of intellect. Spirit permeates the material and impacts upon all facets of our lives, both exceptional and mundane—upon our bodies, our emotions, our relationships, and our expressions of creativity. The findings of parapsychology currently address a small part of this whole. Even the ethical implications of interconnectedness remain merely academic until they are directly and fully experienced and assimilated into our being, our actions, and our personal worldview. Parapsychology may provide confidence that there is, indeed, *something else*. Parapsychology may even provide hints about accessing that *something else;* but these hints are only invitations to enter other realities, to experience them directly, and to bring back what we can to enrich our everyday world.

Notes

1. The Abbey of St. Victor, on the outskirts of Paris, was the cradle of the Scholastic theology of the twelfth century. Hugh of St. Victor and Richard of St. Victor were two of the best-known Victorine mystics. John of Fidenza (better known as Bonaventura or St. Bonaventure) was a thirteenth-century Franciscan. The "three eyes" (and their "three lights") are described in Bonaventura (1953, pp. 7-10, 34-38). The more modern treatment may be found in Wilber (1990, pp. 1-81).
2. The quotations may be found in Bacon (1971, p. 107) and in McKenzie (1960, pp. 82-83). Useful background information may be found in Merchant (1980).
3. Historical accounts of the British Society for Psychical Research may be found in Beloff (1993), Gauld (1968), and Haynes (1982).
4. Excellent discussions of the methods and findings of modern experimental parapsychological research may be found in Edge, et al. (1986), Krippner (1977, 1978, 1982, 1984, 1987, 1990), Kurtz (1985), and Wolman (1977).
5. The original quotation is: "The universe begins to look more like a great thought than like a great machine." It may be found in Jeans (1930, p. 158).
6. The quotation has been attributed to quantum physicist Niels Bohr.
7. Accessible treatments of Patanjali's model may be found in Mishra (1967), Prabhavananda and Isherwood (1953), Taimni (1961), and Vivekananda (1955).
8. Summaries of our work on direct mental interactions with living systems may be found in Braud and Schlitz (1989, 1991) and in Braud (1993, pp. 149-188). Accounts of more recent experiments

in which effects of remote staring were registered autonomically are reported in Braud, Shafer, and Andrews (1993a, 1993b).

9. All references supporting the conclusions of the last four paragraphs regarding faith, hope, love, and grace are given in Braud (1990-91).
10. See note 7.
11. Reports have been published in which it is claimed that gifted psychics are able to clairvoyantly "view" and describe the basic, subatomic constituents of matter. The interested reader may consult Besant and Leadbeater (1951), Phillips (1980), and Smith (1982).
12. These were epistemological and methodological challenges posed in Tart (1972).

Chapter 9

Spirituality in the Natural and Social Worlds

Hoyt L. Edge

In his lead article, Charles Tart describes the conflict between science and religion, arguing that scientific materialism often ends up as scientism, and as such needlessly emphasizes the differences between science and spirituality. Tart's solution is that science and spirituality can mutually benefit each other, parapsychology having shown the inadequacy of materialism.

As Tart suggests, any attempt to further support this thesis requires an understanding of science (and materialism) as well as spirituality, and I will attempt to sketch each in this paper. I will offer first an historical analysis which develops the concepts of science and religion in the modern world with the point of showing that the conflict Tart describes was virtually inevitable. In the second half of the paper, I will offer a few suggestions on the implications of parapsychology for spirituality, although I will not work these out in any detail. In particular, I will argue that parapsychology suggests a more relational world view, denying the interior, privatized view of self and spirituality developed in the modern world; in turn, this approach to self implies a more natural and social spirituality.

My argument in the first part of the paper is presented in two stages: (1) Modern science was intentionally defined as an approach that was the antithesis of religion; this analysis incorporated dualism and atomism. (2) Atomism rejects the possibility of parapsychology; in fact, it attempts to define parapsychology a priori out of existence. In turn, atomism suggests an epistemology which undercuts a major function of spirituality, i.e. the experience of the connectedness of life.

Mind, Matter, and Science

As modern science was developing in the sixteenth and seventeenth centuries, there were specific problems facing Europe. Everyone is aware of the dominating influence of the Catholic Church over science, with the resultant recantation and house arrest of Galileo. Thus, science needed to find a way to free itself from this control, for very practical reasons. In particular, there were growing problems with the expansion of the population and the resultant need to increase the food supply. World trade was increasing with the desire to develop more efficient trading practices; Hadden (1994) has even argued that it was trade practices which gave rise to the mathematical and mechanistic world view. Additionally, there was a growing middle class and a group of wealthy merchants who demanded greater political freedom. The ideas of dualism and atomism were introduced to solve these practical problems.

Let me simply sketch the effect of dualism on science and religion. In arguing for dualism, Descartes declared that both mind and matter were substances, medieval terminology which in essence asserted that they each had opposing characteristics. These can be set up in schematic form:

MIND	**MATTER**
thinking	non-thinking
non-spatial	spatial
purposeful	mechanical
free	determined
private	public
seat of value	avaluable
subjective	objective

This argument effectively solved the practical problem of freeing science from the Church by bifurcating reality into radically different domains. On the one hand, there was the mind, which with its rationality could know moral and religious truths, and which by definition survived bodily death. Obviously, this was the real domain of the Church. On the other hand, there was matter, which was non-thinking and had nothing to do with values (an atom is neither good nor bad). The material world was simply a machine that was determined, and the only stake that the Church should have in it was the assertion that it was the creation of God.

Otherwise, religion, with its interest in the immortal soul, had no concern with the material world. This conclusion was so clever and solved the practical problem of scientists so well that it was not until after Descartes' death that the Church realized the negative implications of this philosophy for religion and put the *Meditations* on its Index of banned books.

Notice, however, another implication of this dualism. We have seen that this approach defined matter as non-thinking, mechanical, determined, etc. What may not be so clear is that this schema also defined the nature of science. Therefore, although I believe science should more correctly be characterized in terms of its careful approach to experimentation, nevertheless, it has been taken implicitly as a discipline that studied spatial, avaluable, unthinking material bits, and necessarily assumed that these bits acted in a determined and mechanistic manner. This view has become, I think, a paradigmatic assumption of science that can be changed only by a major revolution.

One can already see how science could naturally develop into scientism, and how science by its very nature became juxtaposed to the spiritual. It was not by accident or happenstance that science and the spiritual came into conflict; they were each defined as conflicting domains! Such was the price of freeing science from an over-domineering religion. Hence, it follows that our understanding of science and spirituality must change if we are to find them not only compatible but mutually supportive.

I will later explore how our understanding of the spiritual was also affected by this dualism. Now, however, let us take a closer look at how science conceived matter.

Medieval science was a mixture of Aristotelian teleology and alchemy, which stressed sympathetic connections among things, mental and physical. Roman Catholic doctrine had been reinterpreted through Aristotelian philosophy, and in its attempt to separate from the Church, as well as to employ the technological power of the New Science, natural philosophers rejected Aristotle's more organic and teleological view of the world in favor of atomistic mechanism. Atomism, of course, was an ancient doctrine, but it was revived at this time because of its non-teleological approach to nature. However, based on its conceptual power, it was employed in an astounding variety of ways totally unrelated to the material world (Edge, 1994). There were a variety of atomisms, but the English (Newtonian) interpretation eventually won the day, and it consisted of several straightforward components:

(1) Reality ultimately consists of basic units—in the material world these are indivisible material bits; (2) Atoms exist in a void; the purpose of the void is to separate the atoms, which are self-sufficient and inherently not connected to or dependent on other atoms; and (3) Action occurs through contact, one atom bumping against another, and the job of science is to explain how atoms become associated (and thus built into molecules, etc). According to this mechanistic view, there is no teleology, no sympathetic relations, and no action at a distance. Work in nature occurs only through contact.

Notice that this understanding of the world seems to exclude parapsychology *a priori*. Remember that each mind is considered a separate atom, but parapsychology asserts that in telepathy information is transferred from one mind to another without any "bumping" or intermediate processes. Analogously, clairvoyance assumes that information is received from the environment in a nonsensory way. In other words, as opposed to the traditional sensory understanding of light waves traveling between the object and the eye and then being transformed into a mental experience, clairvoyance asserts that no physical intermediary is necessary. One can simply have information from another mind or from a distant part of the world without any "bumping." All parapsychological actions seem to be action at a distance, precisely what was ruled out *a priori* by modern science (see Griffin, 1993).

The basic point here is that the atomistic approach to the world separates and breaks it down into discrete elements. The implication of parapsychology, however, is just the opposite. Connectedness, of person with person and of person with the environment, seems to be the implication of these data. Parapsychology suggests an emphasis on relatedness.

What Is Spirituality?

We have examined the nature of matter and of science; let us now look at spirituality. I find it quite difficult to characterize the nature of spirituality—its manifestations are so diverse—but one common element of the world's great religions is the attempt to engage the human in experiences in which the individual self is connected to a more encompassing reality. What seems to be asserted is the inadequacy of our ordinary individual selves. Connection, therefore, is basic. The Judeo-Christian tradition has tended to personify this force, but many other religious traditions do not. For instance, mystical experiences often do not point to a personified larger force; indeed, nature mysticism seems to imply a more spiritualized (and perhaps even personal) but certainly not personified nature. What I think is important is that humans are put into a larger context in which human nature is congruent with a greater nature. William James (1967), in his "Conclusions to the Varieties of Religious Experience," puts it this way: "He becomes conscious that this higher part [of the person] is conterminous and continuous with a MORE of the same quality, which is operative in the universe outside of him, and which he can keep in working touch with" (p. 774). Spirituality brings us fundamental meaning in life because we find ourselves connected with—related to—a larger context.

Parapsychology and the Spiritual

Having given a characterization of the spiritual, let me now relate it to parapsychology. It strikes me that parapsychology as a scientific enterprise does not derive meaning from its data in any direct way. First, its language is not consistent with this view of spirituality—a chi square will never be part of religious language. But more importantly, the information-gathering aspect of ESP experiences does not suggest ultimate meaning. After all, I can be connected by telephone to all areas of the world; soon we will be connected by an information highway whose memory perhaps will approach the volume of the so-called Akashic Records. Simply having access to information does not provide fundamental meaning. However, parapsychology is importantly related to spirituality for two reasons. The first is less theoretical and more practical. For the general public, I think that paranormal phenomena are symbolic and paradigmatic cases of the mysteriousness of the universe and of its failure to be grasped by contemporary rationality. Scientism excludes transcendence, and paranormal phenomena stand in defiance of such reductionism.

On a more theoretical level, however, parapsychology is importantly related to spirituality, but the connection is indirect. Parapsychological phenomena are no more spiritual than any other phenomena in themselves, but there is an implication of the paranormal that is profound: the data of parapsychology provide evidence for the view that there is a connectedness to all things, and that this relatedness is natural, not a result of human artifact (i.e. the telephone); but as opposed to atomism, parapsychology suggests that the world is relational, and relational in such a way that its nature is conterminous and continuous with mine. Individual bits of ESP bring information, but if psi indirectly suggests that all aspects of the cosmos are intimately interrelated and I am a significant part of this unity, then spiritual meaning can be developed out of this view.

In the Judeo-Christian tradition, we tend to think of meanings being the creation of persons—hence ultimate meaning requires an Ultimate Person. But fundamental meaning does not require this cosmology. My friend, for instance, had a mystical experience in which she "saw" the sweep of history, with its wars, its crises, its progress, its civilizations, and she had the overwhelming feeling that things were as they were supposed to be. As a part of the symphony of life, the melody was played as it should be—with its beauty and its cacophony. All were parts of the symphony of life, including the individual life. The overwhelming feeling was one of meaning based on the connectedness of things.

The same feeling was expressed by a student in one of my early experiments into producing mystical experiences. He said: "I was at the source of awareness, enlightenment, and existence, manifested in a form of energy linking all objects animate and inanimate. . . . I felt morally elevated to a state of pure and simple existence flowing like a continuous current through a waterfall, going deeper and deeper within all existence while feeling more and more at peace and content. . . . I was surrounded by meaning and freed from the despair of meaninglessness, guilt, and time."

Both experiences were spiritual ones in which fundamental meaning was derived from the ultimate connectedness of all things. Engaging in parapsychology does not bring this experience, but its data do suggest that connection is more primary than separation, that we are interrelated with others and the world, that we are "conterminous and continuous with a *more* of the same quality."

In this regard, the teleological nature of parapsychological experience is particularly pertinent since it implies that the world responds on the basis of the same principle that human consciousness employs. The mind and the world are not radically distinct realms, each employing separate principles, but consciousness and the world share the same working principle. The cosmological *more* that parapsychology implies, therefore, is continuous with our own nature. No cosmic consciousness is necessarily implied, nor does one have to postulate a world soul. What is required is that the world is not alien to my nature, but that it is continuous (but not necessarily identical) with my nature.

Juxtapose this view of spirituality with the traditional Western view that has emphasized the difference between mind and body. This distinction did not begin with Descartes, but has at least two other sources in ancient thought. In the *Phaedo,* Plato argued that philosophy was a preparation for death; analogous to the spirit separating from the body (this was not understood in Cartesian terms) at death, so a philosopher was supposed to engage in the process of purifying his spirit. Since it was the appetites and the senses that distracted one from philosophical purity, the philosopher should distance himself or herself from these concerns. Hence, the mental/spiritual world was good, and one should guard against the negative influence of the body.

Likewise, stoicism focused on the distinction between what one had control over and what one did not have control over. In essence, one could control one's internal attitudes toward the world but not control external events in the world. The effect of this stoic distinction produced a further emphasis on the essence of the self being its interiority, and to be happy one ought to make this interior self as cut off from the dominance of the senses and the world as possible. Cartesian duality reified these distinctions into atomistic entities, thus emphasizing the disjunction between mind (the interior), and body/matter (the exterior).

The reason I am emphasizing the separation between mind and body so greatly is that this division has had an interesting effect on our view of spirituality. As the distinction between mind and body has been emphasized, so has the distinction between the spiritual and the nonspiritual. In distinguishing mind from body, spirituality was conceived as the act of attaining greater and greater purity of the spirit, with spirit understood to be interior and nonphysical. To be spiritual meant that one had to inhabit a purely mental, nonphysical, transcendent world. This view resulted in an emphasis on the distinction between the sacred and the profane, between the spiritual and the nonspiritual.

Thus, to become spiritual implied two kinds of separations. On the one hand it meant that one had to separate oneself from the physical world and achieve some sort of spiritual transcendence; thus, disconnection from the world (and our bodies) was emphasized rather than our being continuous with the natural world. On the other hand, it meant separating oneself from the daily affairs of the community. Once spirituality was viewed as the purity of interiority, in order to be spiritual one had to separate oneself from physical and from social. I have already talked about the first point; let me discuss the second point quickly.

If spirit dealt with the purity of the private, interior self, then the public world concomitantly assumed lesser importance. For both theological and practical reasons, this distinction was emphasized more in Protestantism, but the emphasis on the separation of church and state in America exemplifies its cultural importance. The public realm and the private realm are different arenas in this view. This approach is radically different from most other cultures in the world in which the spiritual and the nonspiritual, while maintaining a distinction, are not viewed as disjointed. For instance, Balinese culture is one of the more religious cultures in the world, with its plethora of temples and religious ceremonies. One can hardly go ten or fifteen miles without seeing a religious procession or ceremony; the daily offerings made in one's compound, sometimes as many as 100, testify further to the importance of religion. However, when one questions the Balinese about their religious practices, something odd (from our perspective) is noted.

Temples do not ordinarily house divinities, but for a three-day period every 210 days the gods descend to enjoy a celebration in a particular temple. If asked which divinities are being worshiped in the temple ceremonies, the Balinese are unlikely to be able to respond with any specificity. It is astounding to the Westerner that so much religious ceremony can occur without the participants knowing the particular divine objects of the worship. When this is pointed out to the Balinese and they are asked why, if the divinities seem so unimportant, they continue with their celebrations, their answer is likely to be that it is simply Balinese to engage in the religious ceremonies. Indeed, it is the religious pageantry which defines what it means to be Balinese; the religious and the social are so intertwined that a comfortable distinction cannot be made.

I do not want to deny that there is a difference between the spiritual and the nonspiritual in Balinese culture. The rhythms of Balinese life display a difference; there are times and occasions which are clearly designated as more spiritual than others. The point is, however, that the distinction is not a hard and fast one and that the two, indeed, are intertwined in ways that we find curious in the West. Only when we can emphasize a private, interior self does this distinction between the spiritual and the social assume importance.

The position I am taking has at least one radical implication, and that is that the traditional paradigmatic case of the connection between parapsychology and spirituality—evidence for survival—has little importance. There are four reasons that count against its importance, the first one coming from the data itself, while the remaining three are more implied by my approach to spirituality. I take my first point from C.D. Broad, who described mediumistic communication as being "a blend of twaddle and uplift," a depiction that is both accurate and damning. But the theoretical reasons are more to the point of this paper.

Why has survival been taken to be religiously important? Surely one answer is that it shows that life is eternal. Christianity often has emphasized time to such a degree that life on this earth does not achieve meaning without it being put into a context of an afterlife. This may be one of the reasons why so much emphasis has been put on mediumship, trying to prove survival after biological death. It may have been thought that if one could prove continuing survival, then one's life would automatically achieve meaning. But, in what way does length of life itself bring any meaning? Why would living eternally bring meaning? The Myth of Sisyphus, in which Sisyphus is condemned by the gods to roll a boulder up a mountain, only to see it roll back down as it almost reached the summit, is an adequate illustration of meaninglessness occurring eternally. Far from time bringing meaning, it is precisely the eternal length of time involved which makes the Myth so poignant and displays the absurdity—the ultimate absurdity—of continued life. If one is going to achieve meaning from an afterlife, it must come from a different source than sheer time; indeed, time may be irrelevant.

Further, without atomism, and the concomitant view of the self as an independent, separate entity—without what I have called previously (Edge, 1980) an entity metaphysics—it is not clear that it makes sense to talk about a separately independent surviving spirit. After all, if we cannot be designated as separate entities in this life, why would we want to do so in a view of the afterlife?

Finally, we need to consider carefully the kind of meaning that has been part of the traditional Christian view, of which survival was a part. The idea was that meaning is given to an object—a chair, a pencil, etc.—by the creator of the object, and we simply accept the meaning that is given. When we ask ourselves what is the meaning of life, itself, we looked for the same answer: God created the world and all peoples in it according to a plan, and it is our job to find our individual purpose in it, one that had been designated by God. We find our "calling." However, it is not clear that questions we can ask of individual things in the world can intelligently be asked of the world itself. Because pencils have purpose, or because I act with purpose, does not imply that all of life itself can have a purpose. It makes sense to ask the color of the pencil, but does it make sense to ask the color of the cosmos? I believe it was Bertrand Russell who said that it does not follow from the fact that all of us have mothers that there is a mother of us all. The traditional approach to the meaning of life, the kind given by a Creator, is questionable, but that does not in any way undercut the idea of fundamental meaning—that each of us can make sense of our lives or large portions of it. I have argued elsewhere (Edge, 1980) that we create meaning rather than find it, but the point is that traditional meaning (which gave importance to the survival question) is a questionable idea.

Conclusion

I pointed out earlier that parapsychology in no direct way leads to spirituality, but only indirectly. While maintaining that view, it is also appropriate to point out that with the rejection of dualism, the distinction between the spiritual and nonspiritual (and between the scientific and the spiritual), is blurred. My suggestion is that a more holistic and non-dualistic spirituality is going to be more naturalistic and more civic than we have conceived it in the West. The point of the spiritual is not to separate oneself from the world; it is not to purify an interior element of the person and view the other elements as debasing this purity. Rather, the natural will become sacrilized. The point of spirituality is not to separate oneself from the natural world and from others; rather, it is to make one's own actions in the natural world and one's interactions with others sacred. If a function of religions has been to connect our isolated selves with others and with the rhythms of life more fully, then spirituality must derive from these connections.

Parapsychology gives evidence that supports a more relational and connected view of the world, thus undercutting atomism and dualism. With this accomplished, our understanding of the natural and the spiritual become less disjunctive and more connected. This approach resonates with the grand religious traditions and mystical experiences which emphasize relatedness and connection, and which spiritualize the natural world and our ordinary actions in it.

Chapter 10
Phenomena Suggestive of Life After Death: A Spiritual Existence

Karlis Osis

The neurosciences have lately been admirably successful and useful—except in seeing the limitations of their reach: that part of us which transcends physiological functioning. Nothing stands so clearly in the way of the neurosciences' overclaims than parapsychological findings on phenomena suggestive of life after death. No wonder it releases passionate debates, even by scholars who are otherwise clear and rational!

In this age of science, death is still a mystery left to our ever-changing belief systems. Dante, the towering genius of his time, describes his beliefs in *Convito*: "I say, that of all idiocies, that is most stupid, most vile, and most damnable which holds that after this life there is no other." However, people have also been criticized for holding to a belief in afterlife, especially as this view has come under attack in the modern era. The fact is that a large majority of Americans (73 percent) do affirm such a belief (National Opinion Research Center, 1986).

But the strength of conviction in both camps appears to be weak. When death comes to oneself or one's immediate family, many want to know, rather than depend on belief alone. For these people, empirical information might be of some interest.

How reliable is such information? It has its own limitations, like the frailties in all human sciences that tackle very complex phenomena, such as creativity, mental illnesses, and the depths of human personality itself.

Studies of Apparitions ("Ghosts")

Phenomena suggestive of afterlife have been reported throughout the history of various cultures; for example, Plato, in *The*

Republic, described out-of-body journeys of a soldier, Er, who was thought to have been killed in action. Pliny the Younger described a ghost case in Athens.

Well-organized, systematic studies of apparitions started after the Society for Psychical Research (SPR) was founded in England in 1882. The SPR was soon joined in this quest by the American Society for Psychical Research (ASPR) and by smaller research groups and individual investigators in continental Europe. Scholarly journals were established to publish ongoing research as well as theoretical speculation and fierce debates. The basic idea of these efforts was to apply scientific method to data collection, evaluation, and interpretation of psychic phenomena—an area which nineteenth-century materialistic sciences had ignored up to that time.

Apparition experience was one of the first phenomena studied. In a pioneering survey, 17,000 respondents were contacted. This "census of hallucinations," as it was called, netted many apparition experiences as well as other phenomena that were purely psychological. Reports were analyzed and published in two major works: Gurney et al. (1886) and Myers (1903). Several other collections appeared later, such as those by Bennett (1939), Green & McCreedy (1975), Jacobson (1973), and Jaffe (1979).

An apparition experience is awareness of the presence of a personal being whose physical body is not in the area of the experiencer, provided the experiencer is sane and in a normal waking state of consciousness. In contrast to extrasensory perception (ESP) of a distant event, the apparition is felt to be in the immediate vicinity of the experiencer. Unlike daydreams, apparitions are experienced as part of the immediate real world and cannot be readily created, altered, or terminated at will, except by physical actions such as closing the eyes, running away, or hiding under bedcovers. (For a detailed conceptualization, see Osis, 1986.)

Methods for researching apparition experiences were developed largely by the SPR and have now reached a high level of efficiency. Modern advances in psychology, psychiatry, sociology, and forensic sciences are incorporated, as well as techniques of qualitative and quantitative investigation. Mere hallucinations, hypnagogic and hypnopompic imagery, mistaken identity, illusory reshaping of normal stimuli, deliberate hoaxes, and chance coincidences have had to be identified and sifted off in the process of serious research. Journalistic books usually bypass methodological rigors and can be misleading as to actual observations.

Apparitions are experienced in many ways. "Seeing" is the most frequent sense modality that furnishes this experience. The apparition might look so lifelike that it is mistaken for a flesh-and-bones person—only sudden vanishing gives away its ghostly nature. Sometimes, however, the images represent only parts of the body, or appear as vague and misty outlines. They might portray the dead, the living, or unidentifiable strangers. Sounds, such as steps approaching and doors opening, are often heard. Touch, smell, and temperature sensations may be reported, but sometimes the experience is of a "felt presence" without any specific sensory qualities. Apparitions usually are of short duration, less than a minute. They can be a once-in-a-lifetime experience, or recurrent.

Not all apparitions are of interest for the afterlife issue. Many have been traced to various different roots. Some were thought to be hallucinations whose cognitive content was derived from a telepathic message which is then projected out like a mental slide, retrocognition or sudden glance of events in time long past (e.g., D-Day in Normandy, or a scene from Marie Antoinette's time). If a mother sees her son walking through the kitchen with drenched clothes at the time he was drowned, that experience could hardly be separable from her own ESP projection of her son's image in the kitchen. But if neighbors see him entering the kitchen door at the same time, that would be of interest.

ESP, like our other thoughts and feelings, is a private experience that is directly observable only by the experiencer. Some apparition phenomena, however, have been collectively experienced by several persons. About one-third of those apparition experiences where more than one person was present, awake, and in a position to see, were collective (Hart, 1959). Often, animals also react: dogs growl, cats bristle. In haunted houses, phenomena may be reported as occurring repeatedly over the years to the distress of the family and the surprise of visitors. For example, in a house near Pittsburgh, sixteen witnesses have reported observations of some ghostly phenomena over a period of twenty years. The exact nature of stimuli in collective cases is still unknown, but apparitions that are collectively seen do suggest a disembodied agency. Numerous attempts have been made to explain them, such as by the super ESP hypothesis. However, these explanations have been severely criticized (Gauld, 1982), because ESP of the magnitude and reliability needed to account for the observed phenomena has not been found.

Usually an apparition appears to perform physical actions, such as opening doors, but nothing is later found to have been moved. The noises of opening and closing doors turn out to be an imitation of the sounds of real events. On rare occasions, however, physical objects are affected: lights or gadgets are switched on or off, locked doors are reported opening, and so on. L.E. Rhine (1957) advances an explanation that does not presume a discarnate agency. She claims that psychic forces (psychokinesis, PK) of the observer could do the same as the ostensible ghost. The formidable burden of this hypothesis is to explain why such a mighty psychokinetic effect occurs at the moment of an apparition experience to people who have never exerted such an effect before or after in their lives.

In two-thirds of poltergeist (literally, "noisy ghost") cases, a living agent has been identified. However, such cases are very rare in comparison with the frequency of reported hauntings, and the patterns of both phenomena differ markedly. Poltergeist phenomena are linked to persons who must be present for the effects to occur. Furthermore, the time sequences and movements of objects seem to be different (and much more destructive). Apparition cases that involve physical action are very unnerving to the experiencers because they cannot be readily explained away as hallucinations and, instead, forcefully suggest an external agency. It would be a strange hallucination, indeed, that could open windows, say, in a mental hospital.

Out-of-Body Experiences

The out-of-body experience (OBE) is another phenomena which, in its best examples, seems to suggest something akin to short-term disembodied existence. The main characteristic of OBE is the experiencer's feeling that his or her other viewpoint and center of perception are located somewhere outside the body, at the ceiling, for instance. Some researchers also include a state of intense attention deployment, such as the feeling of being right on the stage when one is absorbed in watching a play. C.T. Tart (1977) has attempted to sharpen the criteria delineating "discrete OBE states." The literature on OBE is less extensive than on apparition experiences. As with apparition experiences, only some types of OBE could be considered suggestive for disembodied existence, namely those in which the experience is not completely private, but accessible also to observers and registering instruments.

There are cases on record where one or two external observers "see" the person experiencing an OBE as an apparition at the same time as the person experiences himself as visiting the observers. It is more impressive if the "visit" is not announced beforehand but comes as a surprise.

In very rare cases, animals also have been reported to react to the OBE apparition. Only experiments with gifted subjects have been suggestive. In one experiment, a kitten in the laboratory was measurably quieter at randomly selected intervals when its master made OBE "visits." In another experiment, strain gauge measures in the projection area gave some indications of OBE presence. Experiments with unselected subjects usually give no indications suggesting that anything "goes out" during OBE.

Parapsychological phenomena have also been reported to occur in states near death. These may have indirect bearing on the survival hypothesis because they shed some light on spontaneous OBEs. One cross-cultural study was designed to contrast the phenomena according to a model of postmortem survival versus a model of death as extinction (Osis & Haraldsson, 1977, 1986). The experiences of not only revived patients but also those who actually were dying were sampled in the United States and in northern India. The reported data fit the survival model much more consistently than they do the extinction counterpart.

Messages Ostensibly from the Dead

Messages interpreted as coming from the dead are reported in many cultures. They captured the interest of Western intellectuals in the heyday of spiritualism from the middle of the nineteenth century to the first decade of the twentieth century. Scholars struggled to develop methods for separating the ostensibly real from chance coincidences, believers' excessive claims, and the often fraudulent practices of mediums. William James, the great thinker in American psychology at the time, discovered a psychic genius, Eleanor Piper, who was extensively studied by scholars in the United States and England. The literature is too voluminous and complex to be abstracted here (e.g., Myers, 1903; Hart, 1959; Gauld, 1982). Many luminaries have been impressed by the emerging evidence for the survival hypothesis. For example, a past president of the American Psychological Association, Gardner Murphy, wrote (1961, p. 273), "Where, then, do I stand? To this the reply is: what happens when an irresistible force strikes an immovable object?" As a psychologist of his day he could not accommodate the pressure of evidence and remained "unmovable" until his death—so far as I know. His *Challenge of Psychical Research* (1961) provides an excellent description of that "irresistible force."

Messages coming in dreams are sometimes suggestive. For example, J.L. Chaffin (Anon, 1927) appeared to his disinherited son, giving clues for finding a second will. Following the dream message, the will was found and recognized by the court, restoring the inheritance to the dreamer. Most clearly identifiable messages come from specially gifted psychics such as Eleanor Piper, G.O. Leonard, and E.J. Garrett. While some psychics have claimed to identify the sources of their information as coming from spirits of the deceased, it soon becomes clear that they may give the wrong address. Without being aware of it, psychics incorporate in their messages bits of information that have come from their living informants, the persons seeking to communicate with beloved dead. It has been argued that if messages from the dead are to be verifiable, they have to be checked either with a living person, records, or objects. Psychics can also access these "living" sources by their ESP—without requiring any information obtained from the dead. This, roughly, is the super ESP hypothesis. The best mediumistic data are hardly interpretable in this way. ESP from this-world sources was indeed available but it had to be pieced together from various obscure documents found in different places. Gauld's *Mediumship and Survival* (1982) provides the best contemporary overview.

Reincarnation Memories

Reincarnation is a long-standing belief held mostly by people in India and Buddhist countries. Scientific studies of the phenomena pointing to reincarnation have been conducted in recent years by Ian Stevenson, a well-known psychiatrist at the University of Virginia, and his collaborators. Stevenson took a hard look at the claims of hypnotic age regression to previous lives and found nearly all of them unimpressive. But he was intrigued by cases in which preschool children seem to remember having been somebody else from a distant location and family. He developed a network of informants in India, Burma, Sri Lanka, Lebanon, Turkey, and among the Alaskan Indians, to lead him to cases he could investigate. Stevenson has developed efficient methods for interviewing the child, his or her family, and other witnesses, as well as for locating and interviewing the alleged family of the previous incarnation. Normal sources of ostensible past life memories are considered and possible selfish motives weighed. Sometimes Stevenson has been able to take the child to the family of previous life to see if he or she would identify persons, places, and possessions. Stevenson carefully evaluates his data and presents alternative explanations. Most impressive are the very detailed descriptions and analyses of forty individual cases published in four volumes with a total of 1,439 pages: *Cases of the Reincarnation Type, 1975-1983.* Stevenson also presents various quantitative analyses of more than 1,000 cases in his files. Stevenson's overview (1987) gives enough information for most readers.

His findings indicate that a large sample of children did give verifiable information about their ostensible previous lives: names of family members, locations, descriptions of houses, objects, and cause of death. Errors also abound. Some children exhibit behavior consistent with previous family and alien to present family, such as an Indian child preferring the food of a different caste. Phobias and preferences for clothing also seem to come from remembered past lives. Previous lives ending in violent death seem to be more frequently remembered than others.

Stevenson also found birthmarks in some cases that coincided with the location and shape of fatal wounds in a previous life. Birthmarks were photographed and, whenever possible, checked against autopsy reports and other medical records. In his cautious style, Stevenson (1987, p. 260) concludes: "Although the study of children who claim to remember previous lives has convinced me that some of them may indeed have been reincarnated, it has also made me certain that we know almost nothing about reincarnation."

Conclusions

Evidence for possible survival of bodily death comes mainly from research on the following phenomena: apparition experiences collectively perceived, some types of out-of-body experiences, certain aspects of near-death experiences, selected communication ostensibly coming from the dead, and reincarnation memories. Assessments of the evidence vary greatly among researchers, ranging from those who find no acceptable evidence for survival (Siegel, 1980) to those who find certainty (Hart, 1959). The researcher's own philosophical outlook seems to have a strong influence on the conclusions that are reached, as is evident in studies of spiritual exercises, practices, and beliefs. Most researchers take a position somewhere in the middle, and various theories of survival are presented by Thouless (1984). Apparently, the evidence is not yet strong enough to sway scholars whose philosophy has no place for disembodied existence. It is my experience, however, over long years of interactions with people, that evidence here offered does bolster spiritual convictions of many, regardless of their religious background. It was most apparent in people who came to me in severe crises of their lives, where beautiful spiritual writings alone did not help.

Most Americans, regardless of their age or level of education, say they believe in life after death. When death approaches us or our dear ones, the research findings mentioned above might be useful to these believers and possibly to some others, especially if they themselves have experienced phenomena suggestive of afterlife. Of course, when counseling, one's own opinions and beliefs should be given less emphasis than the background, ideas, and feelings of the client.

The spiritual and the psychic have often been pictured as enemies. The animosity between them stems from aberrations in both fields and from not knowing much of each other. At the heart of the matter, they are neighbors and friends, able to help each other.

Chapter 11
Who or What Might Survive Death?

Charles T. Tart

[This chapter is based on an invited address entitled "Who Might Survive The Death Of The Body? You? Who Are You?" at a 1994 Chicago conference, The Sacred Source: Life, Death, and the Survival of Consciousness, sponsored by the Institute of Noetic Sciences.]

Discussing who or what might survive death is difficult to do adequately. It is hard because there are so many important things I would like to cover, but in this chapter there simply isn't enough space to do it fully. More importantly, it is hard because I do not really know the answers in any final way. I am not blessed to be one of these people who have had such profound personal experiences that there is no question of doubt of any sort, the kind of person who, as a result of some altered-state experience such as a near-death experience (NDE), *knows* at an extremely deep level what the meaning of life is about. I have had some little hints here and there, but I do not write from that space of doubt-free knowing, although I respect and try to learn from such people. At times I wish I did *know*, at other times I am glad that I have to live my life without the possible fetters of apparent certainty. I suspect that those who completely know do not bother to come to the kinds of conferences at which I speak or read the kind of books I write, though; so, in not knowing, we, dear reader, have a bond in common, and we can share something about our doubts as well as what we think we know.

It is also difficult to discuss who or what might survive death because I would also like to be able to write about it from my heart, not just from my head. I am a scientist, but that is only a part of being human. To illustrate: While I was finalizing my notes on survival just a few days before the Institute of Noetic

Sciences' (IONS) conference talk on which this chapter is based, I was forcibly reminded of how little I really know about the topic of death, and how important it is. My daughter Cindy was spending the day taking care of a friend's baby, a cute little nine-month-old girl I'll call Ruby. Ruby's mother was in the hospital, quite ill: she is HIV-positive,[1] and Ruby is also HIV-positive. I was acutely aware of this tremendous contrast: I was supposed to get up and say some comforting and also objective, scientific words about death, and here is this sweet, nine-month-old who is not going to have a very long life.

Death really reminds us how little we know, and yet how important it is to try to understand. So I can't give you any ultimate answers in this chapter, but I hope I can reduce some of our automatic preconceptions about death and possible survival and get us thinking constructively about it on the basis of *data*, both psychological and parapsychological, data with which we are usually not familiar, but which are important in thinking about death.

IONS sponsored an earlier conference on survival and death in 1985 in Washington, DC. In my talk attempting to summarize the evidence for survival then, I said that what I had come to conclude after thirty years of studying it could be summed up in two sentences. (1) After a period of confusion, fear, and unconsciousness that I will probably experience in the process of dying, I won't really be too surprised if I regain consciousness in a *post mortem* state. (2) On the other hand, I will be very surprised if *I* regain consciousness. I say this because so much of what my ordinary self consists of is dependent on having a familiar physical body and constantly getting sensory and informational input from a familiar physical environment. Without that sort of a "mold" to shape the particulars of my consciousness, I suspect things are going to become very different—and very interesting. That is a very quick summary on my understanding of more than a hundred years of research on the possible survival of death.

As I said, I am trying to be objective and scientific about it. On the other hand, I am an ordinary human being, and I have my biases. For one thing, I am afraid of death—at least sometimes. Socially it is not considered a very polite or impressive thing to admit to being afraid of something, yet when we do not admit to our fears, they control us all the more. When we do not admit to and understand our desires and fears, even to ourselves, they become implicit, unconscious kinds of prejudices, pre-judgments that distort the way we think, perceive and feel, the way we live our life, and probably distort the way we live our death. So I want to be honest with you, that I may not be able to write in a completely objective way about death, as much as I try, because there are times when I am afraid of it.

Now I also know I am not alone. When I admitted this fear in my IONS talk and asked how many other people of the 2,000 in the audience would raise their hand to publicly admit their fear of death, just about every hand went up. I can entertain the idea that there are people who really have never had any fear of death, but I suspect they are very rare.

I also have to qualify that while I can say I am afraid of death, I am speaking about my ordinary conscious self. There is a part of me that is looking forward to death and thinks it is going to be a great adventure! My ordinary self is quite ambivalent about that part; it says, "Whoa, what kind of freaky psychodynamics are operating in there?" But, at some deeper level, I am not at all afraid. That lack of fear in some other part of me is *data*. I can't explain it well, but that is data, and data, fact, is more important than theories and beliefs when you practice science—or exercise common sense.

So, I am going to try to be objective about death and survival, but I want to encourage us to recognize that fear we have of it, not just now while reading, but throughout life. Also recognize that it is all right to be afraid of death; it is not strange or shameful.

To preview my argument a little more, I think that there is a *something else* that "incarnates" in a body. When you get a body it is like getting a personal computer, a personal computer that comes with some programs already installed in it; they are already on the hard disk or in, as it were, ROM, permanent read-only memory. One of those brain/computer programs is fear of death and fear of pain in the physical body. When threatening and stressful circumstances happen in life, this program is activated and we are afraid of death and suffering. That is just the way the brain is programmed. Ordinarily we are very identified with that physical body—it is *me*—so it is perfectly normal and natural to be afraid sometimes. But be careful about taking it as some ultimate truth, even though it is a useful program that can really get our attention!

Scientific Evidence for Survival

I want to first give a brief summary of what I think is the main scientific evidence about survival—Karlis Osis gives this in more detail in Chapter 10—then put that in the special context of this chapter, the question of "Who" might survive death.

The easiest position on survival to cover, one that is supposed to be a scientific position, is the materialist position. Life equals biology, mind equals biology, your thoughts, your feelings, your hopes, your fears, they are all nothing but electro-chemical reactions in the mind, in the brain. The brain obviously disintegrates into mush after you die, so no more thoughts, no more feelings. So why worry about survival? From that position, people who come to conferences such as the IONS survival conference or read books such as this are unrealistic people, people who are afraid of death and can't face the facts that we just have to tough it out and know we are going to die and that is the end, period.

Materialism is a very dominant position in today's world and, because we are Westerners, to some extent we believe it strongly, whether we know it or not. That position is drummed into us all the time, as if it were scientific *fact.* It is not actually scientific fact; it is a hypothesis with some evidence for it, but hardly an overwhelming amount of evidence.

Why is this materialistic position so predominant? For one thing, it is associated with science, and science has been remarkably successful. Also we should recognize a certain psychological factor. The background of many of our beliefs about survival, especially what we were taught in childhood, was that yes, there was survival, post mortem survival *in which you were judged and you had an excellent chance of going to Hell because you weren't good enough!* The materialist position is thus psychologically appealing because it leads to thoughts like, "Oh, I am *not* going to go to Hell, there is nothing that survives to be judged, at last that fear is gone!" I do not think we recognize that psychological dynamic often enough and calculate how much it affects the way we think about things, i.e., we have very strong personal biases that can incline us toward materialism: it is not just a matter of rational thought.

Now the main thing I, speaking as a scientist, want to say about the materialist position is that it is not good science. The first rule of science is that you have to account for *all* the data, all the experience, all the information, all the facts you can gather about something. If your theory cannot account for all the facts, it is not very good: it is a limited, even if useful, way of thinking about things, but not the final truth. The materialist equation of mind with *nothing but* the brain simply doesn't take into account all the facts, including some quite important facts that I am going to go over, so, as a scientific theory, it is clearly inadequate. Yes, the brain, the material stuff, has a lot to do with the mind as we ordinarily experience it, no doubt about it. We are working this bio-computer, and it has its inherent style it adds to consciousness. But that is not all there is to mind, and it's important for us to know that. It is poor science to simply accept materialism without having looked at all the evidence.

The area of science that specifically looks at the things that do not fit materialism is parapsychology. In a parapsychology experiment, basically you take all you know about the material world, the dominant materialistic understanding, and you set up a situation that is "impossible," where nothing can happen. If something happens, there is something wrong with the apparent or claimed completeness of your materialistic theories. So parapsychology has, for example, set up telepathy experiments. Two people are put in different rooms or different buildings, sometimes thousands of miles apart from each other. Given all we know about the physical world, and the fact that these people do not have telephones or radios, there is no way they can communicate with one another. Yet you can do very careful, precisely controlled experiments to show that sometimes a receiving person picks up something that somebody else is trying to send. It almost never works 100 percent of the time; the results are often at a low level, but they are greater than chance expectation too often for it to be coincidence.

People can pick up information from another living person's mind, and there are hundreds of really well-controlled experiments demonstrating this. In fact, I would say that experiments in parapsychology are generally far better controlled experiments than in ordinary branches of science. The criticism has been so intense over the last century that the methodology has gotten extremely good.

The Big Four of Psi Phenomena

Telepathy is one of what I call the Big Four—four psychic kinds of effects, *psi* phenomena, that we can't have any reasonable doubts about if we really look at the evidence. It leads me to conclude that mind is something more than brain, because while "mental radio" is a comforting analogy, telepathy is not some kind of mental radio. It does not follow the kind of laws that would happen if telepathy were based on some kind of electromagnetic radiation such as radio waves.

A second major psi phenomenon is *clairvoyance*—the direct perception of the physical world. In the old, classical clairvoyance experiments, an experimenter would thoroughly shuffle a deck of cards dozens of times *without looking at it*, put it in a box, and lock the box in a drawer. Nobody in the world, no mind, knows what the order of that deck of cards is. A person then comes into the laboratory and is asked to "guess" what the order of the deck of cards is. This procedure works well enough above chance to know that sometimes the human mind can directly "reach out," directly know the state of physical matter without any of the physical senses involved. Now already we can start to ask the question, "Who am I?" Who am I if I have the potential to at least occasionally reach out into another mind, in spite of barriers of space? Or reach directly into the material world, and know what the state of affairs is?

Precognition is the third of these major four psi phenomena, where you ask someone to predict the future when that future event is controlled by inherently random, inherently unpredictable processes. An experimental subject is told something like, "Two hours from now, after you leave, I am going to very thoroughly shuffle this deck of cards without looking at the card faces as I shuffle. Would you write down *now* what the final order of the cards will be?" When subjects score significantly above chance, that is precognition. That means that our ordinary ideas about time are very useful for all sorts of ordinary things, but they are not ultimate. There is something the human mind can do that puts it outside of ordinary time in some sense.

Finally, the fourth of the big four is *psychokinesis* (PK)—the direct ability of the mind to affect matter. In the old days, they had people try to mentally make dice fall in a certain way when a randomizing machine was throwing dice. Now it is all done with electronic devices and computers. As the *agent* in a PK experiment, you see a little black box with solid state circuits in it—a total mystery to everyone who is not an electrical engineer—and it is making a red light and a green light blink at random. You are told something like, "Make the green light blink more than the red light for the next minute." In spite of the impossibility of this from a materialistic view of the world, it works a good deal of the time. It is a small shift: instead of the chance expected success rate of 50 percent, agents shift the rate up to 51 percent or 52 percent, but it is significantly elevated. What I find most interesting psychologically is that none of the agents know what they are doing. Which chip do you mentally "push" on, which electron do you try to slow down or divert in the crystal structure of the chip? It is incomprehensible. And yet sometimes simple desiring has a direct effect on the physical world.

Again, what kind of creatures are we? Who am I if my mind can transcend time? If at times my mind can have a direct effect on the physical world? It doesn't happen that often—which is probably fortunate, as people sometimes get frightened when psychic abilities work too well, a topic there is no space to go into here (but see Tart & LaBore, 1986; Tart, 1982; 1984; 1986)—but it happens often enough that I have no scientific doubts about its reality.

Psi happens enough that we can't ignore it. As people who have been taught to respect science, we have to know that we have very sound scientific data, well over 1,300 experiments, that show that *the human mind can do things that a human brain can't conceivably do.*

Out-of-the-Body Experiences

There are other phenomena that may be kinds of psi, even though they haven't been investigated nearly as well as the basic four psi phenomena, and some of these bear more directly on the survival question. For example, consider out-of-the-body experiences (OBEs). I am not talking about near-death experiences (NDEs) now, where the experiencer gets into an altered state of consciousness as well as feeling out of their physical body, but what we might call old-fashioned, garden-variety OBEs, experiences where you find yourself out of your body, but your state of consciousness is pretty much as it is now. You are still you, thinking and feeling in your usual sorts of ways; you just happen to be up near the ceiling, looking down at your body lying in bed—and probably having a rational argument with yourself about how this can't possibly be happening! People who haven't had an OBE, if they've even heard of them, tend to dismiss them as some funny kind of dream. People who have experienced an OBE, though, often say something like, "I no longer *believe* that I am going to survive death, *I know I am going to survive death.* It is not a belief, I have had a direct experience of functioning without my physical body." For these lucky people, as well as the NDErs, the debate about survival seems rather academic; they *know*.

I want to describe an experiment I was able to do years ago. I was very fortunate in meeting a young woman who, ever since she was a child, had experienced OBEs routinely many nights of the week. In fact, as a child, Miss Z, as I have called her (Tart, 1986), thought what was "normal" was that you go to bed, you fall asleep, you have a dream, you float up near the ceiling for a few seconds, you have another dream, and you wake up and go to school.

Miss Z's OBEs were still happening occasionally, and although she was moving from the area soon I was able to have her spend four nights in my sleep research laboratory. I was very curious about what happened psychophysiologically as well as parapsychologically in OBEs. I knew about NDEs. This was before NDEs had "come out of the closet" for our culture, but I had been reading a lot of unusual literature, so I wondered, is she getting near death during her OBEs, or what?

For several nights Miss Z would sleep in my laboratory through the night. She would have electrodes attached to her head to measure her brain waves. She couldn't get up without pulling off these electrodes, which would create a huge, artifactual signal on the brain wave (EEG, electroencephalogram) machine. But there was enough slack in the wires so she could turn over normally, so she was comfortable. When she was ready to go to sleep, I would go off to another room and open a book of random numbers, randomly select a five-digit sequence, write it on a piece of paper, slip it in a folder, and then put it up on a shelf near the ceiling of Miss Z's room, a high enough shelf so that even a person walking around in the room couldn't see what was lying flat on it. I would pull the folder off, remind her that there was a number exposed to the ceiling up there and that she should read and memorize the number if her OBEs took her in that vicinity. I also reminded her to look at the clock near the number and memorize the time while she was out.

Miss Z had several OBEs over the few nights I was able to experiment with her, and she was a pleasure to work with. Occasionally she would wake up and report things on the order of, "It took me about two to three minutes to wake up, and the floating experience lasted about thirty seconds," so I would know where to look on the record.

The first thing that became clear was that she was not near death. No physician looking at her brain waves or heart rate recordings would get excited. The second thing that was interesting was that she was in a brain-wave state that I had never seen before. I had studied a lot of records of people sleeping and dreaming, and this was like, but not the same as, the normal dreaming state, which is termed stage 1 EEG with rapid eye movements (REMs). Miss Z's OBE state was like a stage 1 EEG state in many ways (primarily a predominance of irregular, low voltage theta waves), except there was a lot of slowed down alpha rhythm mixed in. I showed the EEG records to one of the world's foremost EEG experts on sleep, and he had 100 percent agreement: he said, "Looks weird to me too." I wish we had actually known what this pattern meant, but she certainly wasn't near death.

On all nights but one, though, she reported that while she had floated out of her body, she was not at the right position in the room, near the ceiling, to look at the target number, so she had no idea what it was. On the one occasion when she said she saw the number, she correctly reported that it was 25132. Now that is odds of 100,000 to 1 to guess correctly like that, by chance alone, on a single try. So Miss Z not only *experienced* herself as out of her body, floating near the ceiling, but she also gave a very impressive demonstration of seeming to perceive the physical room correctly from such a location. A single experiment doesn't prove anything in any final sense, but this does make the question of whether an OBE can sometimes indeed be what it seems to be, the mind being really located in space elsewhere than the body, a most interesting question!

I should note that I often get a funny reaction to reporting these results with Miss Z when I lecture, a reaction which shows the level of sophistication nowadays. Someone is liable to ask, "Did you know the number?" and when I admit to it, they say, "Oh, it was just telepathy." It is true, at this beginning stage of experimentation, we can't control for *mere* telepathy yet!

Miss Z was a very rare person who could have full-scale OBEs like this almost at will and I have never been able to study anyone else who could do it quite so well as that. I would have thought that, in a rational world, investigators all over the world would want to find the people that can have OBEs voluntarily and study them extensively, but not much happened, a good reminder that biases and emotions play a strong part in our approach (or lack of approach) to death. At any rate, judging from this study, a few others that have been done (for some interesting selections in this literature, see Gabbard & Twemlo, 1984; Harary & Weintraub,

1989; Irwin, 1985; McMoneagle, 1993; Monroe, 1971; Monroe, 1985; Monroe, 1994; Osis & McCormick, 1980; Tart, 1967), and reports of people's spontaneous OBEs, people can sometimes have the experience of being out of the body, with their minds still functioning in a pretty ordinary way, and, sometimes, come up with clear perceptions about the state of the physical world that make you think that perhaps in some real sense the mind actually can get "out."

Mediumship

The most direct parapsychological research on survival are studies of mediumship, most done in the nineteenth and the early part of this century. Millions of people believe that special people, mediums, can go into some kind of altered state where the spirits of the deceased can communicate through them. There was a fair amount of investigative work done in the past, but the subject is almost entirely dead as a research area today.

One of the first findings was that most ostensible[2] spirits of the deceased are long-winded and terribly general in what they say, so their communications are not particularly evidential. In a wry sense this is consistent with survival, because if you listen to most people's conversations they are often long-winded and do not have anything terribly profound to say. But some spirits, when asked to give information to prove they are who they claim to be, have done very well. I will give you an example of the kind of mediumistic communication that is high quality.

> After the war I went to a Scottish medium to see if she could pick up something about a friend, a German diplomat whom I feared had been killed either by the Nazis or the Russians. I simply didn't know what had happened to him. The medium very soon got onto him. She gave his Christian name, talked about things we had done together in Washington, and described correctly my opinion of his character. She said he was dead and that his death was so tragic he didn't want to talk about it. She gave a number of striking details about him and the evidence of personality was very strong . . . (Heywood, in Roll, 1985, pp. 178-179).

There are many cases with detailed, correct communications like this, besides all the long-winded kinds of things. They make extremely impressive reading. They are consonant with a basic claim that spiritualism made, which was that basically it was a scientific approach to the question of survival. Many mediums said, in effect: "You shouldn't *believe* or not *believe* in life after death; you should *test* it. We can put you in touch with spirits; you check them out. See if they are who they claim to be."

I said most of this research was done in the last century and the early part of this century, and that practically none is done anymore. Why? Let me read you the rest of this particular case, which had a very unusual outcome.

> If I had never heard any more, I would have thought it very impressive.
>
> But after the sitting, I set about trying to find out something about him. Finally the Swiss foreign office found him for me. He was not dead. He had escaped from Germany and had married an English girl. He wrote to me that he had never been so happy in his life. So there I think the medium was [psychically] reading my expectations. She was quite wrong about the actual facts, but quite right according to what I had expected (Heywood, in Roll, 1985, pp. 178-179).

This and other kinds of complexity led the few people researching survival to see an alternative explanation for the good-quality mediumistic evidence. First, living human beings can use psi, especially ESP. Furthermore, we have not found any kind of clear *limits* to ESP; that is, we can't say that ESP can pick up this kind of information but *not* that kind, so potentially any deceased person's personal history is accessible to ESP. We also know from laboratory studies that *you can use ESP without consciously knowing you are using ESP*. We further know from psychology that human beings have an unconscious mind, and that the unconscious can create an impersonation of another personality. If you add these possibilities together you produce what is called the *super psi* hypothesis, the super ESP hypothesis. Perhaps no one's mind or personality survives death; perhaps the apparently evidential cases occur "merely" because the mediums' unconscious minds use ESP to produce very good imitations in order to make us, the living, feel better about our mortality, as well as supporting the mediums' own belief systems.

It was so unclear how to prove that the super ESP alternative was *not* true, that most of the few researchers there were got discouraged, and survival research basically ground to a halt. Very few investigators devote any attention to survival today[3]—a very strange situation, given the importance of the question and our fear of death!

Personally, I am not too worried about the super-ESP alternative to survival. Go back to our question of "Who am I?" If I am someone who potentially has psychic access to all the information in the universe, what makes me want to completely identify with the narrow version of myself that says I am nothing but my physical brain to begin with? I actually find the super-psi hypothesis gives excellent *a priori* grounds for expecting some sort of survival.

Reincarnation Research

While I have noted that the classical mediumistic research has largely died off, there has been one major new development in the last twenty to thirty years, which adds a new light on the picture, namely research on reincarnation. I speak primarily here of the excellent and careful work of Professor Ian Stevenson and his colleagues at the University of Virginia in Charlottesville, where they have now collected well over a thousand cases of children who spontaneously remember past lives. In many of these cases, the memories can be fitted to someone who has recently died and who the child claims to be the reincarnation of. Here is a fairly typical example of one of Stevenson's cases:

The Case of Thusitha Silva:

Thusitha Silva was born near Payagala, Sri Lanka, on July 29, 1981. Her parents were Gunadasa Silva and his wife Gunaseeli. Gunadasa Silva was a tailor. Thusitha was the sixth of the family's seven children.

When Thusitha was about three years old she heard someone mention Kataragama, and she began to say that she was from there. She said that she lived near the river there and that a dumb boy had pushed her into the river. She implied, without clearly stating, that she had then drowned. (Thusitha had a marked phobia of water.) She said her father was a farmer and also had a boutique for selling flowers which was near the Kiri Vehera (Buddhist stupa). She said that her house was near the main Hindu Temple (Devale) at Kataragama. She gave her father's name as Rathu

Herath and said that he was bald and wore a sarong. (Thusitha's father wore trousers.) Thusitha did not give a name for herself in the previous life and indeed gave no proper names apart from "Kataragama" and "Rathu Herath." She never explicitly said that she had been a girl in the previous life, but she mentioned frocks and also objected to having her hair cut; so her parents inferred that she was talking about the life of a girl.

Tissa Jayawardane learned of this case in the autumn of 1985 and visited Thusitha and her family for the first time on November 15, 1985. Having recorded the above statements and some others he went to Kataragama. Here we should explain that Payagala is a small town (population in 1981: 6,000) on the western coast of Sri Lanka south of Colombo, and Kataragama, a well-known place of pilgrimage, is in the southeastern area of the island, in the interior (Obeyesekere, 1981; Wirz, 1966). Kataragama is approximately 220 km by road from Payagala. It is also a small town (population in 1987: approximately 17,500) and consists almost entirely of temples and supporting buildings together with residences for the persons who maintain the temples and supply the needs of the pilgrims. A moderately large river, the Manik Ganga, runs through the town.

T.J. went first to the police station in Kataragama, where he inquired for a family having a son who was dumb. He was directed to a double row of flower stalls along the pavement of the main road to the Buddhist stupa, known as the Kiri Vehera. (The vendors at these stalls sell flowers to pilgrims for their use in worship.) Upon inquiring again among the flower vendors he was told to go to a particular flower stall, and at that one he asked whether a young girl of the family had drowned. He was told that a young daughter of the family had drowned in the river some years earlier, and one of her brothers was dumb. According to T.J.'s notes, Thusitha had made 13 verifiable statements and all but three of these were correct for the family with the dumb child who had lost a girl from drowning.

In the second phase of the investigation (in December 1985), G.S. learned about 17 additional statements that Thusitha had made, and he recorded these. The two families still had not met (and, so far as we know, this is still true), so that, as mentioned earlier, we consider our record of these statements uncontaminated by any contact between the two families. Two of these 17 additional statements were unverifiable, but the other 15 were correct for the family of the drowned girl. A few of these statements, such as that one of the houses where the family had lived had had a thatched roof, were of wide applicability. A few others, such as that there were crocodiles in the river, could be regarded as part of information generally known about Kataragama. However, several of the additional statements that G.S. recorded were about unusual or specific details, and we will mention these. Thusitha said that her father, in addition to being a farmer and selling flowers, was also a priest at the temple. She mentioned that the family had had two homes and that one of them had glass in the roof. She referred to the water in the river being low. She spoke of dogs that were tied up and fed meat. She said her previous family had a utensil for sifting rice that was better than the one her family had. She described, with imitative actions, how the pilgrims smash coconuts on the ground at the temple in Kataragama.

Western readers unfamiliar with Sri Lanka may not immediately appreciate the unusualness of the details in several of these statements. For example, there are plenty of dogs in Sri Lanka, but most of them are stray mongrels who live as scavengers; few are kept as pets. Also, most Sinhalese who are Buddhists would abhor hunting, although Christian Sinhalese might not. It happened that the family of the drowned girl had neighbors who hunted, and they fed meat from the animals they killed to a dog chained in their compound. This would be an unusual situation in Sri Lanka. Another unusual detail was that of a glass (skylight) in the roof of the house. Devotees at Hindu temples other than the one at Kataragama may smash coconuts as part of their worship; however, Thusitha had never had occasion to see this ritual.

In the third phase of the investigation, I.S. (accompanied by G.S. and T.J.) went to Thusitha's family and then to Kataragama. Each family was visited twice in this phase, once in November 1986 and again in October 1987. We learned that the girl who had drowned, who was called Nimalkanthi, had been not quite two years old when she died, in about June 1974. Nimalkanthi had gone to the river with her mother, who was washing clothes there. She was playing near her mother with two of her brothers, one of whom was the dumb one. Her mother apparently became absorbed in her washing, and then suddenly noticed that Nimalkanthi was missing. The brother who could speak could not say where she had gone. Nimalkanthi's mother raised an alarm, a search was made, and Nimalkanthi's dead body was recovered from the river. It is unlikely that the dumb brother had pushed

Nimalkanthi into the water, but all three children had been playing around just before she disappeared. It seems probable that she lost her footing and slid or fell into the water; she could not swim. Thusitha's statement that the dumb brother had pushed her into the river thus remains unverified, and it is probably incorrect. However, the brother may have pushed her playfully just before she drowned accidentally.

Two of Thusitha's verifiable statements were definitely incorrect. She said that her father of the previous life was bald, but Nimalkanthi's father (whom we interviewed) had a good head of hair. She said his name was Rathu Herath, but it was Dharmadasa. There were, however, two bald men in the family—Nimalkanthi's maternal grandfather and a maternal uncle—and Nimalkanthi would have seen them often. And a cousin by marriage, whom Nimalkanthi saw from time to time, was called Herath (not Rathu Herath). Thus one could argue that Thusitha's memories included some confusions of the adult men in her family, but we do not wish to emphasize this explanation.

Another of Thusitha's statements was incorrect for Nimalkanthi's lifetime, but not for the period after her death. She said that she had sisters (but did not say how many). Nimalkanthi had one sister, and about 18 months after her death, her mother gave birth to another daughter.

Concerning the possibilities for previous acquaintance between the families concerned, we are confident that they had none. Nimalkanthi's family had never even heard of Thusitha when we first met them. Nimalkanthi's father had never been to Payagala; he had passed through it only on his way to a larger town called Kalutara, also on the west coast of Sri Lanka. Thusitha's family had never gone to Kataragama in an effort to verify her statements. Gunadasa Silva said he had hoped to do this, but for various reasons-largely the needs of his tailoring business—he had never got around to this.

In the years 1980-81 Gunadasa Silva had gone "very often" to Kataragama. On one visit only, when she was two months pregnant with Thusitha, his wife, Gunaseeli, had gone with him. Gunadasa had bathed in the river in the usual way of pilgrims and had purchased flowers from the flower stalls near the Kiri Vehera. He could not remember the name—if he ever knew it—of the flower vendor from whom he purchased most of the flowers he bought. Thus he had gone to Kataragama after Nimalkanthi's death, but had stopped going there before Thusitha's birth. Thusitha, incidentally, said that she had seen her father at Kataragama, a reference on her part to a presumed discarnate existence between the death of Nimalkanthi and her own birth.[4]

We made inquiries in Kataragama about the frequency of drownings in the river. The police station had records available only for the three years of 1985-87. There had been one drowning in 1985, none in 1986, and one (up to October) in 1987. The coroner of Kataragama had died in 1986 and his records were not available. The coroner of the neighboring town of Tissamaharama, who had been acting coroner at Kataragama for almost a year (since the death of its regular coroner), had no detailed figures of drownings in the river at Kataragama; however, he estimated that one occurred about every two years, mostly among pilgrims. The registrar of births and deaths at Kataragama did not keep records beyond each year, at the end of which the records were sent to the government office (kachcheri) of the next largest administrative area. The records were not classified according to causes of death. The registrar said that there had been no drownings so far in 1987 (contrary to the police records). She estimated that two children drowned in the river each year, a much higher estimate than other sources suggested.

There were 20 stalls of flower vendors on either side of the broad avenue that leads to the Buddhist stupa (Kiri Vehera) in Kataragama. On the day of our inquiries one stall was unattended, but we asked the vendors at all the others whether any member of their family was dumb and whether any member had drowned. One vendor's family had a cousin who was dumb; no other family (apart from Nimalkanthi's) had any dumb member. No family except Nimalkanthi's had lost a member through drowning.

Comment. Despite Thusitha's failure to state correctly any proper names other than that of Kataragama, we have no doubt that we have identified the only family to which her statements could refer. The single detail that her (previous) father had a flower stall near the Kiri Vehera in Kataragama immediately restricted the possibilities to about 20 families. Of these, only one had both a son who was dumb and a daughter who drowned in the river. The various other details Thusitha mentioned are hardly necessary for increasing the correctness of the identification of the family to which Thusitha's statements correspond, although they do provide additional confirmation (Stevenson & Samararatne, 1988, pp. 221-225).

Stevenson is cautious and conservative about drawing conclusions from his research, but cases like this certainly make the possibility of reincarnation a fair probability, even if not proven yet.

There are some fascinating patterns that come out of Stevenson's reincarnation research. For example, it is generally preschool children that make these claims, and once they start school they talk less and less about it and may finally forget these memories. That makes sense, because school is not simply an education, but also an indoctrination into the belief systems and limitations of their particular culture (Tart, 1986b; 1994).

Most of these cases happen in cultures that are supportive of reincarnation, such as Hindu India, some Muslim cultures, and some Eskimo cultures. Is this some sort of cultural artifact, kids making up stories to support the beliefs of the culture? There is little support for this idea, however, as generally the parents are highly upset and embarrassed when their child starts spontaneously talking about a past-life memory. Psychologically, parents might see it as meaning their child doesn't really love them when they ask to be taken to live with their *real* family! In India there is the additional embarrassment that the child might remember a life as a lower caste person than her present family! Parents frequently try to get the child to forget and stop talking about these memories.

Parents usually put off any attempt to check the veridicality of their child's memories. But when they do, they often find that many details about a past family are true. Sometimes the meetings with relatives from a past life are heart-wrenching kinds of things, meetings between loved ones who thought they were forever lost to one another.

A particularly interesting pattern that emerges from these cases is that somewhere between a quarter and a third of these children who spontaneously remember a past incarnation have very peculiar kinds of birthmarks, and these birthmarks seem to correspond with wounds on the deceased persons they claim to be. Someone was shot to death, for example, and there is on the child who remembers this person's life a birthmark that is round on the front of his chest, like a bullet entry wound, and a much more ragged birthmark on his back, like the kind of scar a bullet exit wound makes. In fact, I have heard Stevenson joke that if you want to remember this incarnation the next time around, given what we know now, the best thing to do is have an especially violent and horrible death, which will probably fix it in your mind more firmly! You do not have to follow that advice, but for those who are really curious and want to set up your research project next time around . . .

Who Am I? The Ordinary Experience Perspective

Now I want to focus in on the big question of "Who am I?" We have already been talking about that when I summarized some parapsychological material. At least part of who I am has to do with psi abilities to sometimes get information that seems to transcend the ordinary barriers of space and time, ESP, and to affect things at a distance, PK.

Let's look at another perspective on "Who am I?"—what we might call the ordinary experience level. "Who am I?" Well, I am a man, I am a father, I am a scientist, I am a writer, I am an amateur carpenter, etc. I have these identities, we all have many identities. We might call them *personas*, to use Jung's psychological term: they are appearances we manifest, except they usually go deeper than just appearances; we become identified with these roles. These personas, these roles, have plenty of reality; they usually control most of our lives. Each can occupy center stage and totally control who we are for anywhere from a few moments to a lifetime, so we mustn't underestimate their power. Even though I have spent many years working with various psychological growth processes, for example, and have learned enough about *dis*identification that sometimes I can get behind them, most of the time *I* do not use my personas, my personas use *me*; they pop up automatically.

Many of our personas, if not all of them, are very much based in the body. Being a "man" or a "woman," for instance, is based on certain kinds of bodily structures. Being an "athlete" is based on certain kinds of bodily structures, as is being "beautiful" or "ugly." Furthermore, these bodily structures do not exist in isolation; they are used within environmental and social contexts that reinforce certain aspects of them and inhibit others. We know, unconsciously as well as consciously, a great deal about the physical and social worlds, how they work, what to expect as a result of our actions. These bodily and social familiarities and expectations support our identities as the skeleton supports the body.

If you think about this from a survival point of view, it is probably going to be pretty difficult for any of these personas to survive. You are not going to have a body to constantly make your internal sensations have a certain familiar kind of pattern and flavor. You are not going to have your usual friends and acquaintances around to call you by the same name, who give you familiar responses to familiar actions. Habits *per se* may last for a while after death, but the molds, the bodily, physical world and social world constancies that created those habits and reinforce them, will be gone. Without reinforcements for these familiarities, these habits, there is a good chance that they won't last very long.

Who Am I? The Materialist Perspective

The materialist position we have already talked about, that your personas, your identities, are nothing but what is generated by your brain and your body, is clear on this: there is no survival. Remove the skeleton and the body cannot live, much less maintain its familiar stance. Interestingly, some mediums in the last century, dealing with materialists who had died, reported that it was interesting when somebody asked them to get in contact with such people. They said it was hard to find these people and when they did find them, they had sort of made themselves a little "black hole" in after-death space, where they remained in a state of minimal consciousness, because they were convinced they couldn't survive death, so nothing was happening for them. I do not know how true that is, but it is an interesting idea. Sadly, some people do something like that in life. They create artificially bounded psychological spaces to live in where they try to allow nothing to happen that doesn't fit within their preconceptions and beliefs. My *Waking Up* and *Living the Mindful Life* books deal with that (Tart, 1986b; 1994).

Who Am I? The Cultivated Experience Perspective

Now, let's take another perspective, instead of the kind of ordinary experience of "Who am I?" We'll take the perspective of what we might call *cultivated experience*, or *disciplined experience*, the kind of perspective resulting when people systematically practice a meditative discipline designed to get deeper insights into themselves. I do not mean merely thinking about yourself, one of the too common, but highly inaccurate, ways people can use the word *meditation*. I mean the kind of meditative discipline where you learn to still the agitation in your ordinary mind and more directly perceive the state of internal and external reality, for example, or the Gurdjieffian self-remembering, skills that have interested me for many years.

If you ask people who practice these kinds of disciplines "Who am I?" they get "behind" their ordinary identities of father, mother, citizen, etc., and come to realize their more fundamental identity is something like *a capacity to experience* rather than any particular manifestation of that capacity. You might say, in a sense, that I am nothing, no*thing*, that I am not frozen into any one, concretized pattern, but that there is fluidity underneath these patterns, there is spaciousness there. There is a capacity to experience particulars, to experience change, to flow with change, although the ordinary identities are still there, and there is a little more choice about "putting on" personas or identities, *deliberately* using them consciously, and taking them off when they are not appropriate. It is like having a variety of uniforms or name tags, recognizing they are just uniforms and name tags, not really you, and putting them on and taking them off when they are appropriate.

Another way of talking about this cultivated perspective is as a quality of mind that can be developed, a quality that we can call *spaciousness.* Some people call it "detachment," but I do not like that word because of associations with a pathological form of detachment that I am not talking about here. The pathological form is "I do not care about anything and so nothing can hurt me." There is a kind of healthy spaciousness that comes from teaching yourself to be more objectively aware, to not be as caught in your experience, to pay clearer attention to all events, that makes life more vivid, more clear. Thus you can have a clearer understanding of the particulars of the moment, and there is this spaciousness, there is this basic capacity to experience, which is a more fundamental identity. Note that I use words clumsily here, as this "spaciousness" is something beyond strict verbal definition, even though it can be experientially, observationally clear.

I think this kind of answer to the question of "Who am I?" from the cultivated experience perspective is much more about the kind of "something" which has the capacity to survive death. It is not as dependent on bodily, social, and environmental conditions as ordinary aspects of personality, where "Things must be exactly like so-and-so or I am going to be upset!" It is also a kind of mental position that accepts change as natural.

This cultivated experience position is not an easy position to get to for most of us, unfortunately; you have to work to develop it.

Who Am I? The Beliefs Perspective

Another perspective on the question of "Who am I?" involves our many theories about who we are, our belief systems. These theories might be, to illustrate, "I am a sinner" or "I am a child of God" or "I am a Christian" or "I am a Buddhist," etc. If we have these theories purely as *theories*—if we say, "I have a certain set of beliefs, and I do not know if they're really true, but I act on them sometimes"—life wouldn't be so bad. But the problem is these theories become thoroughly conditioned in us as children. The process of being enculturated is not only passing on the knowledge of the culture, but also passing on the restrictions and literally training and automatizing the way you think, the way you have emotional feelings, the way you perceive the world and yourself.

I do not think our theories of who we are will survive death very well. But, more importantly, our theories do become automatic belief systems and they control how we live, they suck up our energy, they suck up our vitality. So, to jump ahead to the question of what do we do in life to live a better life and prepare better for death, one thing is that we had better find out what those theories are that have been conditioned into us, and we had better learn to be able to take some perspective on them and make some adult decisions about whether to continue to automatically believe them. "Do I want to believe that *that* is what I am?" Because these theories do *work* in a psychological way while we are alive. Do not confuse the theories you have about yourself, even though they may run a lot of your life, with who you actually are and what you can find out by direct observation. As I said above, from the survival perspective, from the mode of cultivated experience, from self observation, from meditation, I am no*thing*; I am not a thing. I am a process, and it is open to change.

Who Am I? The Altered States Perspective

Now let's switch to another perspective that is very important in considering who or what might survive death, the perspective on "Who am I?" from altered states of consciousness (ASCs). Most of what I have said so far makes good sense in our ordinary state of consciousness and is based on that kind of "rational" thinking. And yet, as William James put it,

> Our normal waking consciousness . . . is but one special type of consciousness, whilst all about it, parted from it by the filmiest of screens, there lie potential forms of consciousness entirely different. We may go through life without suspecting their existence, but apply the requisite stimulus, and at a touch they are all there in all their completeness, definite types of mentality which probably somewhere have their field of application and adaptation. No account of the universe in its totality can be final which leaves these other forms of consciousness quite disregarded. How to regard them is the question—for they are so discontinuous with ordinary consciousness. Yet they may determine attitude though they cannot furnish formulas, and open a region though they fail to give a map. At any rate, they forbid a premature closing of our accounts with reality (James, 1929, p. 378-379).

We all know this to some extent from a very common altered state of experience, dreaming. We spend about 20 percent of our sleep time dreaming, in which we are generally not quite the same person we are now. Frequently we think differently, we act differently, we are afraid of different things and attracted to different things, and so forth. Unfortunately, our culture has brainwashed most of us into thinking dreams are not important. Get up and get out to work and increase the gross national product; do not be a dreamer! So we throw away a part of our mental life which is interesting in and of itself and which is interesting in the terms of the possibility of survival.

In the dream you are much less psychologically connected to your body than you are in your waking state, so you have a partial preview of a state of consciousness that is less "embodied" in a very important kind of sense. It behooves us to study our dream lives, not just to interpret dreams, but to take dreaming as a kind of life—then what does it mean?

Dreams could be called a rather "ordinary" altered state of consciousness, experienced to various degrees by most people. Then there are the extraordinary ASCs, induced sometimes by meditation, sometimes by psychedelic agents, sometimes by extreme stress, etc., altered states which are much more difficult to talk about; words really begin to fail us there. But in terms of the question of "Who am I?" the spectrum of altered states is a dramatic reminder that we may be much more, much different than just our ordinary state, our ordinary self.

Near-Death Experiences

Let's look at near-death experiences, NDEs, for a moment as one of the more unusual ASCs. The NDE may start with a "straightforward" out-of-the-body experience. But generally, it changes into a profound altered state of consciousness, not just ordinary consciousness where you happen to be up near the ceiling of the room. People think differently, experience emotions differently, know differently, and so forth in the typical NDE.

Let me read you the beginnings of a very interesting OBE case of a woman named Vicki. She had this OBE when she was thirteen.

> In that near-death experience, I would describe it as going through a pipe or a tube type of feeling, and I was shocked, I was just totally in awe, I mean I can't even describe it, because I thought "So that is what it is like," and I saw my body, just before I got sucked into the tube, I was up on the ceiling and I saw my body being prepared for surgery and I knew that it was me.

This is a fairly typical start for NDEs for many cases, and Vicki went on to have many of the other elements of the classical NDE. She met other beings, she met a deity-like being, she knew things she didn't ordinarily know, and so forth, before coming back to her body.

When people have NDEs it generally changes their life extraordinarily. It is funny—my training as a psychologist says the field of psychology tries to understand what human life is about, particularly behavior, and that would mean, obviously, that you'd want to study the important behavior-changing experiences first, and look on the tiny, minor ones later on. So since an NDE that takes five minutes can produce more change in your life than everything else put together, obviously psychology studies such experiences very intensively? No, no, it is a very funny profession I am in. And, incidentally, if you are into changing your life, while the NDE is generally the most intense and effective way, I do not recommend it. The *near* part is tricky: most people who come that near to death do not give us interesting reports; they get buried.

But now let me return to Vicki's NDE, this tremendous change experience. Vicki continues,

> I was born premature and went down to one pound 14 ounces. They had this new airlock incubator to save babies such as myself, and they didn't realize that they were giving us too much oxygen. . . . There were approximately 50,000 babies in this country who were blinded that way from 1947 through about 1952. My optic nerve was destroyed. . . . I can't see anything. No light, no shadows, no nothing, ever. And so I have never been able to understand even the concept of light . . . (*Vital Signs*, Spring 1994).

Vicki had an NDE, and was overwhelmed because she *saw.* And that is what a lot of what her statements about being so amazed were about. She was amazed at the near-death quality of it, yes, but also because *she saw!* Our skeptical minds might think that perhaps Vicki was imagining this, but I am not inclined to dismiss honest testimony about experience just because it doesn't agree with my preconceptions.

This kind of NDE, as well as many other altered state experiences, reminds us that there are frontiers of the human mind that we can't begin to grasp in our ordinary state of consciousness—but such "impossible" and paradoxical experiences sometimes seem to make perfect sense in some altered states. So when we think about our theme "Who am I?"—who might survive—we have to take into account that while we do almost all our living in a "one-note" style, in this ordinary state of consciousness, there are extraordinary experiences that human beings can have. Unless we really understand the full spectrum of these, we will not fully understand what might survive.

Some altered states involve various degrees of loss of contact with our real physical body. With NDEs and ordinary dreaming, it's an almost total loss of contact. I mentioned earlier that the constant, familiar kind of input from our body is one of the main things that stabilizes our ordinary state of consciousness. If you take that stabilization away by losing your physical body in dying, whatever consciousness is left is probably going to change in some quite profound and interesting ways. Some people may find that thought terrifying, but it need not be. We'll consider this later.

Who Am I? How Should I Live?

To bring our exploration to an end, I want to try to condense more than thirty years of looking at survival, altered states, parapsychology, personal and spiritual growth, etc. from the perspective of a human being as well as a scientist, and draw from it a few suggestions as to who we are and how, given that knowledge, we might want to live. These are suggestions to make you think, not the final word! As I said at the beginning of this chapter, I do not have the blessing of *certain* knowledge on this kind of thing as some people feel they do, but I have what I believe are some good ideas.

In terms of an overview, it is clear to me that whatever that *something else* is that I mentioned at the beginning of this chapter—call it "mind," "soul," "essence," whatever—it is not totally equivalent to the brain or the body. That does *not* mean to neglect the body! One of the great and all-too-common distortions of the spiritual life is to neglect or mistreat the body because of a yearning to develop the soul. Treat your body with great respect; it is the temple of your soul. But do not assume that whatever consciousness after death is, it is just like being in a body, just like now.

I also think we are here, living this embodied life, for a purpose, a purpose that has something to do with learning. Learning knowledge and, more importantly, learning how to love. Sometimes in my more optimistic moments, when I am trying to reconcile some of the horrors that occur on this planet with a spiritual perspective, I hope that we are, in a sense, enrolled in what my friend Robert Monroe, who had many OBEs (Monroe, 1971; 1985; 1994), called an "accelerated learning school." It is a tough school, but if you can graduate from this Earth school, you've got it together!

Altered states such as NDEs and dreams give us some feeling for what consciousness that is less embodied is like. But there is something about states of consciousness where you are very detached from your body that are wonderful in some ways and awfully vague in other kinds of ways, a vagueness and detachment that make it hard to learn things. A physical body gives *focus*, gives you a stable platform from which to get things together, experiment, try some new things. That is my guess as to why we are here, why this embodied existence is an *accelerated* learning school. So the mind, the essence, the soul—

whatever you want to call it—is modified by the learning and growth in this body.

Psi phenomena, the psychic manifestations we see now, such as telepathy, clairvoyance, etc., are probably the basic modes of communication and living in any life after death. In a way it is an unusual and odd circumstance that when we are living here in the body we sometimes see psi phenomena. Interesting as they are, psychic effects are generally unnecessary. For the vast majority of the time in this life, what is important to you is what is in your immediate physical vicinity and we already have a set of physical senses which are amazingly good at keeping you in touch with what's in your immediate vicinity, senses which bring in much more detailed and accurate data than we generally see in psi functioning. I have developed this idea more fully elsewhere (Tart, 1979). Psi is more interesting for its implications than its applications.

To summarize, I have talked about different perspectives on the vital question of "Who am I?" and one especially important aspect of the answer is that I am a psychic being who at times is not limited by the ordinary barriers of time and space. I have talked about a quality to being which is accessible to all of us with a little training and sometimes just spontaneously as a gift, a quality where we become a *process* of experience, open to change, rather than our ordinary little me, tightly holding on to who I believe I am. I have mentioned the altered states kind of me, where, though it is difficult to talk about, extraordinary changes in perception, feeling, embodiment and identity can take place. With these kinds of experiences you can deeply *know* that there is love, there is unity, there is sense and perfection in the universe. You may try to talk yourself out of it afterwards, for the habits of ordinary consciousness, supported by our hopes and fears, are *very* strong. But this kind of knowledge is accessible.

Those who have been personally closest to death and returned, those blessed with NDEs, frequently mention why they came back instead of going on into the bliss they were experiencing. While there are some particularly personal reasons, the most frequent reason given is that they hadn't learned how to love yet, and learning how to love is the most important lesson we are here to learn. The second most important reason was to make a contribution to expanding human knowledge. But there is one reason for returning from death that has never, to my knowledge, been reported. No one has ever come back concluding, "I really should spend more time at the office."

Notes:

1. Ruby's mother has since died as the AIDS became active. We don't know how long Ruby will live, but she's already having problems.
2. I use the qualifier "ostensible" here with spirits, as I am not convinced these apparent spirits of the deceased are exactly what they purport to be, but I will not keep using it explicitly in order to avoid awkward wording.
3. The picture isn't completely sterile. Just before the IONS conference at which the paper this chapter is based on was scheduled, the Fetzer Foundation, IONS, and the Life Bridge Foundation sponsored a small conference of people who are interested in doing research in the question of life after death. I was very impressed with the sophistication brought to it. There is no money to do any survival research yet, and there aren't people working on it to speak of, but there is a new sophistication in how to go about asking the questions. This creates the possibility of a fresh and valuable new approach to this question. Not that it is the *most* important thing in the world to know whether we survive death or not—I would say something like learning how to love and be wise is more important—but, on the other hand, survival research is certainly more important than curing the common cold, and we spend a lot of money on trying to cure the common cold.
4. Most children who claim to remember previous lives say nothing about events after death in the previous life and before their birth. Memories of a discarnate existence are particularly rare in Sri Lanka cases. The case of Disna Samarasinghe (Stevenson, 1977) is exceptional. When the children do make comments about such "intermediate" experiences, they frequently include the child's explanation of how it came to be in its family, instead of in some other family.

Chapter 12

Channeling and Spiritual Teachings

Arthur C. Hastings

In contemporary Western culture, the term *channeling* refers to the ability of persons who claim to speak or write messages coming from personalities other than their own. With the mind or body in a light trance the person appears to be taken over by another personality, who communicates through the individual, often with messages of spiritual or psychological import. The idea is that the person is a "channel" for some other, higher source that communicates through him or her. This source may be understood as having higher spiritual advancement, psychic skills, or special knowledge. It may identify itself as a teacher, spiritual guide, or even a deity, as well as a spirit of someone who has died.

The channeled entity often speaks as a spiritual and psychological guide, giving advice, teachings, information, and ideas to the channel personally or more publicly to others. Besides being spoken aloud, the messages may come mentally, or through automatic writing. Books have been published of these communications, some selling hundreds of thousands of copies; channels speak to large gatherings of interested followers, and people peruse the teachings individually and in study groups. For many individuals seeking spiritual growth in their lives, channeling is providing a source of understanding and guidance. However, channeled messages go beyond this to speak to social and global issues. What can we make of these messages? Are they spiritual truths coming from transcendent beings?

This phenomenon is not a new one. It is known from ancient religions, when the individuals who spoke in trances and ecstasy were considered prophets or oracles for the gods. Even now, in various mainstream and minority religions, within many cultures, possession by the holy spirit, speaking in ecstasy, or possession by spirits is considered a sign of spiritual development, and is often encouraged and facilitated by ceremony and ritual. Channeling may be the current equivalent of ancient prophecy, bringing spiritual guidance and teachings for this time.

Revealed Religions

In the early religions, including the most ancient, the Goddess tradition, the channeling process was used to learn the will of the gods and for divination and healing. This was usually through oracles, which were sacred sites where a deity communicated through a priestess, who was probably in a trance state. The earliest oracle to which I have found reference was a Babylonian oracle of the goddess Astarte in the eleventh century BCE. In Greece, there was an early shrine to Gaia, the Greek earth goddess, at Delphi, and this was likely an oracle with a priestess channeling the words of the goddess. Later, according to myth, the god Apollo came to the shrine and made it his by killing a python there (the python was the animal sacred to Gaia), and it became the oracle of Apollo at Delphi. Apollo spoke though a priestess and gave advice to the ancient Mediterranean world on religious, personal, and political questions. Prophecy does not mean just predicting the future, as is the common impression, but rather speaking under the inspiration of the god or interpreting the will of god. Still, many of the accounts of the oracles of the ancient gods and goddesses report apparent parapsychological messages—a secret revealed, an event predicted, a far off event described.

In the traditions of the three Near-Eastern revealed religions, Judaism, Christianity, and Islam, in which the deity is masculine, prophecy was accepted as inspiration from God. Revelations became the basis of the religion, providing commandments, rules, and transmitting the will of God to the people. The prophet spoke the words of God; either the words were revealed to the prophet in a vision or dreams, or the spirit possessed the prophet and spoke through his or her voice. This is evident in the words of the Biblical prophets, who say "These are the words of God" or "It is I, Yahweh, who speaks." This is meant literally, just as someone on the telephone announces himself by name.

In the prophetic days of Judaism, there were schools for prophecy. Large cities had brotherhoods of prophets who gathered around a leader or major prophet to learn how to go into prophetic states of ecstasy. These were often induced through dancing, chanting, prayer, and music. When a well-known major prophet would visit, the brotherhood would come to meet him dancing and singing and welcome him to the town.

The prophet in those times did not always have an easy task. Some prophets spoke words that the king or the people did not appreciate and were imprisoned or killed because of their message. Others did not wish to be chosen as prophets and protested; they did not embrace prophecy with open arms, but reluctantly or doubtfully.

Jesus was considered a prophet by many of his Jewish followers. However, the Christian scriptures we have do not explicitly describe him in the prophetic mode, but rather as a preacher and teacher. In the early Christian era, the tradition of prophecy continued. In worship services and in preaching, the inspiration of the holy spirit provided the words. Paul wrote in a letter to the church at Corinth that of all the gifts of the spirit, prophecy was the most persuasive because listeners knew their hearts had been seen. Prophecy was a regular part of the Christian services in the early meetings of the churches until a formal liturgy developed.

The third major Near-East religion, Islam, is based on Muhammad's prophetic revelations, which came in ecstatic states and were collected as scripture in the Koran. Islam recognizes Moses and Jesus as earlier prophets and Muhammad as the last of the prophets. All three of these religions are based on revelations from God. In one sense they are revealed teachings not to be questioned, but in actual practice, there may be social and religious negotiation as to which prophets and which messages are the valid ones. If we may judge from current experience, prophetic claims may be ignored or discounted. A claim to speak with the words of God does not necessarily command belief.

As each of the three religions became more solidified, the role of prophecy disappeared. Doctrine and tradition, including prophetic teachings, became settled, and new teachings were not welcome. In Judaism prophecy ceased with the final revision of the scriptures around 600 BCE. As the Christian churches became organized as an institution, the liturgy became set and prophecy, speaking in tongues, and other gifts of the spirit were not emphasized. Now, only in a few churches are the gifts of the holy spirit sought in preaching and witnessing, and they are often considered unsophisticated by more orthodox churches.

Thus in terms of spiritual realities, at the beginning prophecy played a role of communicating the will of the goddesses and the gods, the commandments and expectations, the requirements of faith, justice, righteousness, and worship, and the promises of reward or punishment. These were spoken by the prophets, and accepted as revelation of spiritual truths. Often it would seem that the revelations would include psychic elements in which the prophet would see the future or provide answers and decisions.

True Prophets

The beliefs of those times were that prophets spoke with the voice of God. Therefore, if a prophet was accepted as a true prophet, his messages were given due weight. Once Muhammad was acknowledged as a prophet by his followers, his revelations were written down or memorized. His followers developed criteria for identifying his prophetic trances so they would know when his words were revelation (one sign was sweating, another was when he reported hearing bells). In the Christian churches, the spirits speaking through Christians were to be tested by asking if they came in the name of Jesus. Once the authenticity was established, the words were accepted. The people of the time had little doubt that God could speak through these men and women. Our times are more diverse in beliefs, knowledge, and needs. There are more sources of information as a basis for decisions in everyday matters. Science, psychology, and reason have taken the place of religion for many people. The human unconscious has been postulated as a source of non-conscious impulses, including voices and visions. Particularly since the times of Newton, Darwin, and the scientific revolution, religion has lost its dominant hold on the Western belief system, and so it does not provide a context for channeled inspiration and revelation. God does not have the same immediacy. It is unlikely that God speaking through a channel would be given the acceptance that was true of the ancient prophets. However, at least some members of society are willing to believe that angels, discarnate teachers, spirits, humans in the bardo, and UFO occupants exist and speak through channels. For such people, true prophets can still exist.

Contemporary Channeling

With this background, we can pose the question: are we experiencing a resurgence of prophecy in our time which presents spiritual teachings for the turn of the second millennium? Is the channeling a form of spiritual teaching to revitalize and inspire the religious energy of the era?

The last quarter of the twentieth century produced an increased incidence of channeling, particularly in the United States, and apparently as a part of the general spiritual awakening that began in the 1960s. The teachings of Seth, a personality channeled by Jane Roberts, were published by a major house and became best-selling books. Popular interest led to individuals and groups that studied the messages and conferences were held for followers. *A Course in Miracles*, dictated mentally to Helen Schucman, comprised a 1500-page manuscript of integrated psycho-spiritual teachings and exercises, and resulted in study groups, magazines, and classes. Many other channels and channeled teachings emerged during this period and earlier channelings also became more widely known. Channeled literature, teachings, and inspiration became popular among seekers of personal and spiritual growth. A majority of these followers appeared to accept that the channelers were contacting spirits or outside beings who were speaking through them. There were perhaps thousands of channels and channeled entities at the peak of the interest in the 1980s, but the number dropped in the 1990s.

This is a popular movement, a lay movement. The mainstream religions have not encouraged persons to channel nor do they give their official stamp of approval to channeled messages (though some individual churches had study groups for *A Course in Miracles*). One might not expect churches to approve lay individuals transmitting messages from the angels, Jesus, or God. Channeling is essentially outside the orthodox organizations, a spontaneous spiritual movement. However, it is not all religious in its content. As in the early days of prophecy, the messages ranged through advice on decisions, inspiration, spiritual guidance, generic metaphysics, personality readings, social comment, and warnings, as well as religious matters. Some of the channelers are surrounded by groups of followers, and their fame extends via books, workshops, video and audio tapes, computer communication, and other media not available to the earlier prophets.

Individuals study the messages and use them as guides for their personal searches for inner meaning, psychological insight, and spiritual growth. Many find stimulating ideas, mind-opening beliefs, self-help, and inspiration in the words from channels. Some of the messages show some evidence of ESP, that is, information that seems to come from non-sensory modes. Channeled messages sometimes appear to tune in to the thoughts and feelings of an audience or an individual. Sometimes accurate prophecies are made through channeling, but little research has been done to confirm psychic ability in channeling. There is rarely any attempt to prove the reality of the channeled being, or to prove that a spirit is really that of a deceased human.

Too often channelers and their followers are uncritically accepting of the messages. As in the ancient times, many people unquestionably accept the validity of the process and believe the claims of the channeled personality as to its identity, level of intelligence, spiritual knowledge, and authority. A more discerning attitude is one of testing the messages on the basis of intrinsic value, and the channeled personality on the basis of signs of integrity, psychological health, and track record—in short, applying criteria that might be applied to an embodied teacher. If this is done, much channeled material withers away, leaving no trace. It is repetitious, unsophisticated, wish-fulfilling, perhaps inspirational to some, but with little weight. William James, the great American psychologist at the beginning of the twentieth century, said that 50 percent of the channeled spirit teachings seemed to be written by the same person. This percentage holds true in our time also.

Spiritual Teachings in Channeling

I am not contending that the messages are from God, ascended masters, or enlightened beings from beyond; that is a further question to explore. I am suggesting that the channeling process and the teachings may be contributing to the current spiritual awakening. Here are some of the qualities and implications of channeling that may be of value.

1. Spiritual and inspirational teachings can come directly. With the decline of the prophets, Western religions have taught that the teachings are to be found in written scriptures and church tradition. Only in a few cases (e.g. Latter Day Saints, Society of Friends) are revelations acknowledged. The channeled messages seem to offer direct communication with a realm of inspiration and teaching, implying that spiritual teachings can come directly, even now, from a transcendent realm. This has been missing in orthodox religions.

Many channeled messages say that anyone can become a channel; I doubt this as a realistic fact, but it does suggest that each individual can draw on a source from within. The mystical or spiritual path in general is one that prepares the individual to transform himself or herself to experience the spiritual level personally. People on a spiritual path sometimes report a period in which there are inner voices or communication with a spiritual source, whether this evolves into channeling or not. The entities being channeled do not appear to be enlightened, saintly, or one with God. Rather, they are like human personalities, with particular traits, and presumably come from a more advanced level of knowledge, wisdom, compassion, or clarity. But then, saints and enlightened beings might very well be human also.

2. Channeled messages can speak directly to the individual situations and needs. Scriptures and traditions of necessity present general (and often rigid) values and doctrines, which have to be adapted to particular cases, sometimes in convoluted ways. Some channeled messages are more specific, answering questions from individuals about life issues, problems, personal and career situations. Thus, there is a kind of advising role that might be filled by a therapist, counselor, or minister, but with the claim that the guidance is coming from a source presumably more authoritative and wise than a human being. So far as I know, there are no objective evaluations on the quality of this advice, or comparisons with that of professional therapists, financial advisors, or pastoral counselors. In my research it appears that most of the questions asked are on personal problems and everyday concerns, and perhaps this is the level of most channeled beings. There are few people who ask "how can I live a good life?" or "what is my spiritual challenge?" Still there are some who use channeled teaching to guide their inner work and spiritual search.

3. Channeled teachings incorporate contemporary psychological understanding. Religions claim to embody eternal truths, but the truths that are revealed are based on the images and understanding of human beings at that time and for that locale. Channeled teachings emerging in the twentieth century began to reflect new understandings in psychology, philosophy, language, and physics that are available to individuals and the culture, that were in the collective unconscious pool of knowledge. The teachings are drawing on the increased scientific and psychological knowledge that is part of the culture.

Some examples are these. The writings dictated by Seth through

Jane Roberts include a theory of personality in which individuals are understood as aspects or sub-personalities of a larger self. Seth also proposes a model of the ultimate nature of matter that has similarities to quantum physics. He emphasizes the limiting nature of assumptions and their role in affecting life experiences. There is the potential for changing experience, by changing limiting beliefs and assumptions, a process common to several psychotherapy systems. The Seth teachings state that we can determine our own personal reality—our self-concept, emotions, perceptions, and experience.

A Course in Miracles uses a psychological treatment of attention, belief, assumptions, will, and emotions to change a person's state from fear to love, which it says is the ultimate spiritual condition and goal. The process is not done by faith, prayer, and will power, but through well-described and sophisticated psychological exercises.

Earlier in the twentieth century, the transmitted teachings of Djwhal Khul through Alice A. Bailey gave a definition of seven spiritual essences, called the seven rays, with psychological implications for understanding the personality, and for the divine essences that make it up. Students worked with the model to align their personal qualities with the essences. The Bailey teachings emphasize service for others and humanity as a part of spiritual development. A similar concept emerged later as a part of the enneagram personality system, also claimed to have come through inner revelation, with the idea of a basic essence that is expressed or distorted through the personality. Students of the system took the initial ideas and developed it for general application in psychology, therapy, business, and human relationships.

In the earlier prophetic traditions, people were enjoined to be good, to follow the divine commands, to love one another, and so forth. However, the methods given appear to be prayer, worship, devotion, grace of god, belief, will power, promise of heaven, and threat of punishment. It seems to me that these contemporary channeled teachings are presenting insightful and sound psychological tools for personal change toward higher mental and spiritual levels; from what we know of psychological tools of change, these are more effective than injunctions and admonitions.

4. Channeled messages provide social commentary. The social admonitions from contemporary channeling have been uniform admonitions to change our ways. Whether the source of the message

is said to come from angels, discarnate teachers, or UFO occupants, there are strong warnings that we are heading toward disaster. There are ecological and global concerns and calls for a transformation in consciousness. Perhaps these warnings are similar to those of ancient Hebrew prophets who spoke of the need for righteousness and faithfulness. The channeled beings comment that humans have brought this danger about by their own thoughts, actions, and desires. There is a New Age utopianism in many of these messages.

5. Channeled teachings are part of religious revitalization and inspiration for our contemporary time and culture. At times of crisis or religious inadequacy, religious revitalization movements often occur, giving rise to a new spiritual teaching or inspiration. If a movement speaks to the needs of the time, it may coalesce as a new religion, or it may simply influence the ongoing development of the existing faith. In any event, new inspiration and fresh perspectives of spiritual truths, social reality, and personal status emerge from these movements. In Christian history, the Protestant movement begun by Martin Luther could be an example. In Native American tradition, the Ghost Dance religion in the late 1800s was a revitalization movement. The creation of the Nation of Islam by Malcolm X may also be considered such a revitalization. Channeled messages seem to be presenting new teachings for this Western culture and time, such as the concept of each individual having a spiritual essence, the reality of reincarnation, incarnation as learning, the personal construction of reality, the need for social cooperation, the importance of love, and the necessity of transformation, personal and global. In one sense these are familiar themes, but in channeling they often take on stronger force because they presume to come from beyond the ordinary human realm. Channeling has not emphasized formal worship, obedience to God, and following religious rules, but rather values and qualities to be cultivated by the self and society.

The channeled teachings are not from any single individual or source, nor is there one prophet or spokesperson to represent them. It does not appear that they are leading to a new religion, but rather creating a body of beliefs that may have influence on the common belief system and perhaps thereby on new religions that develop in our time. It seems likely to me that the spiritual awakening movements beginning in the 1960s were the advance waves of spiritual energy around the event of the second millennium, as well as a response to the many crises of the times. Religious energy, e.g. cults, sects, revivals, fanaticism, new movements, are expected to increase before and after the year 2000; the increase in channeling has reflected that energy.

Is Present Religion Inadequate?

I think of religion as an organized response to the manifestation of spiritual energy in a particular time and place. (I also consider religion to have two dimensions: one is authentic spiritual contact, and the second is social facilitation, whether or not it is genuinely spiritual.) Our major traditions were founded in cultures and civilizations much different from the present Western world. Religion crystallizes the spiritual energy in relation to the particular time, with its culture, knowledge and activities. The revelations may not be the same ideas and forms that the spiritual energy would reveal in a different time and place. Thus it is not surprising that there are needs now that traditional religions do not address or do so inadequately. Here is a list of some that come to mind.

1. The world is becoming a global society. Most religions have come from a tribal viewpoint and speak with that perspective and do not address global implications.

2. Gender equality is emerging. Most traditional religious organizations have not accepted this equality fully or willingly.

3. Advances in medicine and health raise issues about prolongation of life, euthanasia, abortion, health, self-responsibility, sexuality, birth control, etc. that were not issues in earlier millennia, where life and death were much simpler.

4. Contemporary psychology offers psychological insights and therapeutic techniques that can change personality, emotions, ideas, and behavior. These affect understanding of spiritual growth, sin, relationships, virtues and vices, action, and responsibility. They also provide tools for pursuing transformative spiritual work.

5. Science provides greater knowledge of natural forces, weather, health, the astronomical universe, biology, evolution, etc., that are not reflected in religious cosmology.

6. Direct experience of the divine is valued. The reality of personal transcendent experience is becoming evident from research on peak and mystical experiences, near-death experiences, and meditation. Despite their belief systems, most religions do little to encourage such experiences that go beyond the conventional ego.

7. For many individuals in the West at least, religion has lost its power to evoke the divine, with its healthy and healing consequences for life, love, and meaning. The ceremonies and myths do not have the power they once had. The social dimension remains important for many but the spiritual level is not experienced.

Some religious organizations and individual congregations have attempted to address these issues, and others have become more traditional and fundamental. In either event, if one takes seriously the above concerns (and many more can be listed) then the doctrines and dogmas created centuries and millennia ago are often of limited guidance. While channeled messages do not present themselves as new religions, they do acknowledge and address some of these concerns. They speak of the need for global community, they are accepting of scientific knowledge, there is a distinct shift from patriarchal values, they offer practical transformative growth, and they often express their messages in words that are genuinely inspiring, that speak in images for this time.

To qualify these statements, it must be stated that much of the channeled teachings is at an emotional level, with no more spiritual content than can be found in television evangelists, though perhaps the values are more compassionate, the tone is less strident, and the money less an issue. Many of the channels communicate a pleasing and acceptable gospel of generic metaphysics, acceptance of self and others, peace, love, and self-development, combined with personal psychic readings of varying quality. Even so, persons have told me that such a channel opened their minds. Still, there are deeper teachings, which lead to more demanding paths, and these are also coming from some channels.

It should be said also that words for the spiritual in our time are coming not only from channels, but also from spiritual teachers, mystics, religious leaders (even politicians), and many individuals who are finding direct experience with spiritual levels through meditation, service, religion, ritual, community, transcendent experiences, and other paths. In the past—even five decades ago—religious experiences were judged eccentric or pathological by much of "science," as though religion were simply a false belief system, and if people had any experiences they must be abnormal. Now transpersonal psychology and other fields of study are recognizing the healthy and developmental values of these experiences and pursuits, and public attitudes are changing to be more accepting.

But Do the Gods Exist and Do Men and Women Channel Them?

In ancient times, the general beliefs were that the gods and goddesses were real and existed, and the prophets could speak with their inspiration. In some contemporary religions—Umbanda and Candomblé in Brazil, Voodoun in Haiti, and the Hindu trance dance ceremonies in Bali—such beliefs still prevail. In our Western culture with diverse points of view, some scientists, psychologists, rationalists, and humanists characterize these religious beliefs as fantasy, wish-fulfillment, opiates, pathology, and projections. These explanations have merit, of course, because belief systems have many origins. These origins can include fantasy as well as reality, and vice versa.

In the case of channeling, some people accept without question the validity of the channeled beings, be they Christ or a discarnate teacher. Others, more critical or "rational," consider them to be personalities created by the subconscious mind of the channel, acting out the fantasies and fulfilling neurotic needs of the channel. Other suggestions include extensions of a greater self of which the channel is also a part, or personifications of the higher self. As it turns out, there seem to be no ways of proving any conclusive answer to this question. There may be deities or teachers or spirits who can contact or be contacted for communication, or the messages may come from more human regions of the unconscious, or the wider collective unconscious. My guess is that most parapsychologists and psychologists believe the messages are from some part of the channel's unconscious, and even respected channels have said that a high proportion of channeled communication probably comes from the mind of the channel, rather than outside entities. The question itself presents complex problems in defining the self, conscious and unconscious mentation, the existence of other realities, and physical vs. mental dualities. These are issues that are not resolved in philosophy itself, and they permeate the questions about channeling. We can explore several possible alternative explanations, but we have no good way to decide among them. There is little doubt in my mind that most channeled communication draws on the mind of the channel for information, vocabulary, and often even the material itself, but there are also messages that seem inspired and informed beyond the individual personality of the channeler. The implications of any explanation are often overlooked; for example, if the material does come from the unconscious of the individual, then we still have to explore how the unconscious can create the more sophisticated and exceptional channeled material.

Whatever the underlying source, the channeled material is coming from outside the conscious ego of the channel. There may be some frauds who pretend to go into trance and spout wisdom, or individuals who free associate and credit it to channeling, but almost all the practicing channels that I have studied appear to be honest and experience the material as coming to them spontaneously in their minds, or as taking over their bodies, often with the stamp of another distinct personality, but not from their own thoughts.

During the late 1800s and the first half of the twentieth century, there were many studies of mediumship and attempts to establish proof of survival of death, which is similar to attempting proof of the discarnate existence of the channeled entities. The evidence for survival from mediumship is stronger than channeling evidence, but certainly not conclusive, in that the argument is intrinsically inferential, and direct proof is not possible. The chapters in this book by Karlis Osis and others and an overview by Gauld (1977) discuss the results of this research.

There have been a few research-oriented studies of channeling. One study using brain wave measures found that the channels showed a particular brain wave pattern when channeling (Hughes, 1990), similar to results from brain wave studies of spirit mediums and psychics. A comparison of ten channels and persons with multiple personality syndromes showed a few overlaps, but generally different patterns of personality and behavior, with channels on the healthy end (though the channels in each of these studies were chosen rather than representative) (Hughes, 1992). An earlier study of mediums (Assailly, 1963) and a more recent one of channels (reported in Hastings, 1991) showed that a high proportion had experienced abuse or traumatic childhoods, but again these were subjects of convenience rather than representative samples; it is difficult to draw any conclusions about causes here.

My own book, *With the Tongues of Men and Angels: A Study of Channeling* (Hastings, 1991), and Jon Klimo's *Channeling: Investigations on Receiving Information from Paranormal Sources* (Klimo, 1987) are studies of channeling that show the spiritual dimension, varieties of channeling, psychological aspects, themes, and other facets of the phenomena.

Conclusion

What we call channeling today draws on an age-old process to communicate messages that come from beyond the individual ego. In ancient times it seems that these were taken as words of the gods. These were eras in which there was little medical, scientific, or psychological knowledge, hence fewer guidelines for decisions, and in which values and spiritual perspectives were still being established for the peoples. The revelations came authoritatively from a source beyond worldly matters and were accepted for practical guidance and spiritual direction. Religious institutions developed from these channeled beginnings into mainstream world religions, and we might postulate that in these teachings are found higher levels of guidance than was possible at an individual ego or societal level. It may be that the prophetic process was tapping a transpersonal reality. However, even in these traditions are revealed teachings that are outdated, trivial (at least to modern eyes), or apparently pernicious. The contributions of channeling to these mainstream religions is thus mixed, from a transpersonal perspective.

The same mixture is true of contemporary channeled messages. In these messages can be found teachings and inspiration that speak to the spiritual needs of our time and its challenges. In the best of the messages there is an intelligence and perspective that can contribute to social values and personal guidance. But channeling also can express the trivial, fallacious, and pretentious and be given credence that diverts attention from authentic transpersonal communication. As with many other sources of spiritual teaching, there is a place here for discernment along with open-minded consideration.

A Channeling Sampler

For the person interested in exploring channeled writing and speaking, here are some places to start.

1. Self-awareness, consciousness, human potentials. The books dictated by Seth through Jane Roberts emphasize that the self goes beyond the ego, with its assumptions and limitations, into alternative states of consciousness, different realities, other identities, and potential transcendence. Seth dictated *The Nature of Personal Reality* (Roberts, 1975) as the basic handbook for this, with concepts and exercises. There are two dozen other Seth books on the self, the soul, past lives and reincarnation, God (All That Is), physics, and our social system of reality. Norman Friedman (1994) compares Seth's concepts of physics with current thinking in that field.

2. A metaphysical, spiritual psychotherapy. *A Course in Miracles* (1985) presents an intensive spiritual training program, intended to change the person's mind by removing obstacles to love and perception of the presence of the divine. The ideas are challenging and the exercises are sophisticated. The course has sold over a million copies of the three-volume set, with no sales campaign. It has developed both serious followers and fanatics; study groups are found in many cities. The language is dense, but carefully constructed. For a person interested in spiritual growth, the course offers a thoughtful and focused path. It seems to me among the most spiritually sophisticated material channeled in our time.

3. Traditional prophecy. The early books of the Bible and the prophets reveal the Jewish revelations, e.g. Exodus, Isaiah. Christian prophetic preaching is recorded in Acts of the Apostles. The verses of the Koran record the revelations of Muhammad.

4. Poetry and Literature. English poet William Blake wrote that much of his poetry was dictated to him from beings outside of time, particularly his long poem *Jerusalem*. Contemporary German poet Rainer Maria Rilke's *Duino Elegies* and *Sonnets to Orpheus* have transpersonal themes and are considered to have come to him from outside inspiration. James Merrill, U.S. poet, received Pulitzer Prizes for his *Divine Comedies* and *The Changing Light at Sandover*, both based on personally channeled material, in this case via a Ouija Board, and containing metaphysical themes. Merrill's work was also the recipient of a National Book Award. Less well-known are the novels and poetry of Pearl Curran, channeling a presumed spirit named Patience Worth. Patience

Worth's best poetry was ranked with that of Amy Lowell and Edgar Lee Masters in the early decades of the twentieth century, and her novels were well reviewed.

5. Research and Theory. My book, *With the Tongues of Men and Angels* (Hastings, 1991), reviews the psychology of channeling including ESP, counseling, ancient oracles, social impact, theories, and transpersonal implications. Jon Klimo's *Channeling* (Klimo, 1987) presents who channels are, their messages, the theories, and reports from interviews with channels and researchers.

Chapter 13
On the Scientific Study of Nonphysical Worlds

Charles T. Tart

This final chapter is intended to be provocative, suggesting that a relatively objective scientific inquiry is possible in areas normally reserved for speculative thought and theology. The suggestions here may still be premature for our current stage of development; when I presented some of these ideas at the Parapsychological Association meeting in 1986 (Tart, 1987), there was very little discussion of them then or subsequently. But they are important for the future study of parapsychology and the spiritual.

A major instigating force behind the nineteenth century's psychical research movement was the desire to test the essential claims of religion. Contemporary parapsychology has almost totally abandoned such an aim in its quest for technical precision and scientific respectability. Technical excellence is fine, but we must not lose sight of what is humanly important about our research endeavor. One aspect of that is to investigate as objectively as possible the reality (or lack thereof) of ostensibly independently existing "nonphysical" worlds (NPWs). The concept of personal survival of bodily death assumes the reality of at least one NPW, for example, at least insofar as we must assume that surviving spirits exist "somewhere." NPWs are not a fashionable concept in orthodox science, to put it mildly, but if they have any reality at all, they are enormously important for understanding our nature and the nature of the world.

The most common contact with ostensible NPWs is during out-of-the-body experiences (OBEs). The OBEr finds him- or herself in an experiential world which is "sensorily" or perceptibly real, vivid, and usually stable, yet is clearly not our earthly physical world. The more lucid quality of OBE consciousness, its immediate clarity (compared to dream consciousness), which is typical of the OBE, inclines the OBEr to take the perceived NPW reality as existing independently of his personal experience of it, in the same way we believe the physical world exists independently of our experience of it; in other words, to answer a classical question, a tree falling in the woods makes a sound whether there is anyone there to hear it or not. Considering such an NPW independently real is especially likely if: (1) it is stable and not changed by arbitrary acts of will on the OBEr's part, as can happen in lucid dreams; and (2) repeated OBE visits to the NPW show it to have consistent, lawful properties.

To illustrate this concept, consider the following descriptions from the OBEs of Robert Monroe, an American businessman who had repeated, usually voluntary, OBEs over many years. Monroe's experiences are described in his three books (Monroe, 1971; 1985; 1994), in my one experimental study with him (Tart, 1967), and in a biography (Stockton, 1989).

> 11/5/58 Afternoon. The vibrations came quickly and easily . . . I tried to lift out of the physical with no result. Whatever thought or combination I tried, I remained confined right where I was. I then remembered the rotating trick, which operates just as if you are turning over in bed. I started to turn, and recognized that my physical was not "turning" with me. I moved slowly; after a moment I was "face down," or in direct opposition to the placement of my physical body. The moment I reached this 180º position . . . there was a hole. That's the only way to describe it. To my senses, it seemed to be a hole in a wall which was about two feet thick and stretched endlessly in all directions . . . The periphery of the hole was just precisely the shape of my physical body. . . . I moved cautiously through the hole, holding on to its side . . ." (Monroe, 1971, pp. 86-87)

During the next couple of years, over a dozen times, Monroe went through that hole. To him it was a repeatable experiment. He waited for the vibrations and did the action that created the feeling of rotating 180 degrees, a hole would appear, and he would go through it. The place he went to had recognizably similar and stable characteristics each time. He called it "Locale III." He could wander around there, invisible to the inhabitants of that apparently real world. To Monroe, the reality of Locale III would be like what any of us could experience by stepping out of our house for a few minutes, wandering around, looking at some things, and coming back. If we went out again, and looked at the same area, it would be pretty much the same place. That's what it was like for Monroe.

He reported that Locale III had a number of stable characteristics that were similar to those of our own, ordinary world. It was a physical-matter world. There were trees, houses, people, artifacts, all the appurtenances of a reasonably civilized society. There were homes, families, businesses; people worked for a living; there were roads, vehicles traveled on the roads, and so forth. And yet it also had quite stable characteristics which were not similar to our world. For instance, he saw nothing that would suggest any kind of electrical devices. No telephones, no electric lights, no TV. He saw no internal combustion devices, nothing that looked as if it ran on gasoline or oil or anything like that. But there was mechanical power in use. For example, he reported:

> . . . Careful examination of one of the locomotives that pulled a string of old-fashioned looking passenger cars showed it to be driven by a steam engine. The cars appeared to be made of wood, the locomotive of metal, but of a different shape than our now obsolete types. The track gauge was much smaller than our standard track spacing, smaller than our narrow-gauge mountain railways.
>
> I observed the servicing of one of the locomotives in detail. Neither wood nor coal was used as a thermal source to produce steam. Instead, large, vatlike containers were carefully slid from under the boiler, detached, and rolled by small cart into a building with massive thick walls. The containers had pipelike protuberances extending from the top. Men, working behind shields, performed the removal, casually cautious, and did not relax their automatic vigilance until the containers were safely in the building and the door closed. The containers were "hot," either through heat or radiation. The actions of the technicians all seemed to indicate the latter.
>
> The streets and roads are different, again principally in size. The "lane" on which vehicles travel is nearly twice as wide as ours. Their version of our automobile is much larger. Even the smallest has a single bench seat that will hold five or six people abreast. . . . Wheels are used, but

without inflated tires. . . . Motive power is contained somewhere in the rear. Their movement is not very fast, at something like 15 to 20 miles per hour. Traffic is not heavy . . ." (Monroe, 1971, 94-95)

NPWs versus Lucid Dreams

The contrast with lucid dream worlds is particularly important here. When an ordinary dream becomes lucid, the state of the dreamer's consciousness changes such that she knows she is dreaming *while* she is dreaming; she has relatively full access to her waking-state memories and knowledge; and she can plan actions and carry them out in a far more active way than in ordinary dreaming. The "sensorily" experienced dream world nevertheless remains real and vivid. The lucid dream world has a major difference from ordinary reality, however, in that "paranormal" (by physical world standards) events become common. Willing an object in the lucid dream world to disappear, for example, will likely cause it to vanish into thin air.

NPWs, compared to lucid-dream worlds, are reported to have a solidity, stability, and lawfulness that resists the OBEr's mental desires. If you want an object to disappear from the NPW scene, wishing is not enough; you will have to pick it up and carry it away, or otherwise follow the laws that appear to apply in the NPW. The possession of lawful properties in a way apparently independent of the experiencer's wishes leads to the ascription of independent reality to the world in both ordinary waking life experiences and NPW experiences.

Such experienced phenomenal independence and lawfulness of NPWs could be accounted for by retaining the hypothesis that the NPWs are still subjective creations and that there are simply more rigid psychological processes (automated habits) underlying their apparent consistency and independence. Some NPWs are probably adequately accounted for by such a hypothesis. But suppose some NPWs really are independently existing realities, not subjective creations of the experiencers' minds. How would we discriminate such NPWs from purely subjective ones?

Are Some NPWs Real?

Let's assume we develop a technology for producing consistent OBE excursions to NPWs, or have consistent meditative techniques producing similar experiences, or can locate people capable of doing so through their own natural talents. Then we may look for *consistency* of descriptions from *independent* observers as a test of particular NPWs' reality. If their descriptions of a particular NPW—NPW-A, for example—were coherent and consistent in major details and not significantly contradictory on important details, we could provisionally grant at least partial independent reality status to NPW-A.

By analogy, I have never been to "Munich," and probably never will go there. I have met a number of people who claim to have traveled to "Munich," and their descriptions of what "Munich" looks like have been, in the main, consistent. Therefore I will accept the idea that "Munich" has an independent existence. I don't know if "Munich" really exists in any absolute sense, but the proof of its existence is good enough for many practical and personal purposes, such as mail ordering something from a company that is purportedly located there, for example. Similarly, if several people claim to have repeatedly visited NPW-A during OBEs, and give consistent descriptions of what it is like, I am inclined to provisionally grant at least some likelihood of independent existence of NPW-A.

Weighing the Evidence for an NPW

Several factors will influence how much likelihood we will grant to NPW-A's independent existence. First, we know that interior experiences can often be strongly shaped by belief and suggestion, so we must ask: Is the reported nature of NPW-A significantly different from what would be expected, given overt cultural beliefs held by our OBErs about such ostensible worlds? Second, we must consider the influence of implicit, covert cultural beliefs. If we have a control group of people from the same culture *fantasize* about having an OBE and visiting NPW-A (with minimal directions for getting there), how different are their fantasy productions from the reports given by the OBErs who claim to have actually been there? It's important to check that the people in the control group do not actually have an OBE as a result of the questioning procedure also, as some naturally talented people might have. Research in hypnosis, for example, was confused for many years because some of the people in the "control" (no formal hypnotic induction procedure) group were highly hypnotizable people who went into hypnosis as a result of the testing procedures, yet were erroneously classified as "unhypnotized."

Third, people influence each other, so we would want to establish strongly that our several OBE explorers have not been influencing each other during normal, physical-world contact. Ideally, they should not know each other's identities and never have any communications with each other. If normal contact is effectively ruled out, the more difficult problem of ruling out psychic influences on each other, influences which might lead to consistent subjective constructions, arises. This is analogous to the problem of the super-ESP hypothesis for explaining survival data discussed in earlier chapters. We cannot rule such possible telepathic "contamination" out at this stage of our knowledge, but such a counterhypothesis itself lends some support to the idea of the reality of NPWs, in the same way that the super-ESP hypothesis lends general support to the possibility of survival of death.

Our analogy between reports of "Munich" and of NPW-A is limited, because we have two distinct advantages in establishing the independent reality of "Munich." First, our travelers can bring back physical evidence such as photographs. Second, we can potentially travel there ourselves. At present we do not have anything analogous to photographs for NPW-A, but if particular NPWs do have an independent existence, perhaps something analogous might develop. Furthermore, as we develop our sciences of altered states of consciousness and parapsychology, we may develop training methods that are reliable and successful enough that we may indeed be able to travel to NPW-A ourselves. This latter potential development does not completely solve the problem of objectively real independent existence, but it certainly raises the stakes in the game!

The proposed lines of research into the existence of NPWs will not be easy ones, running against current scientific prejudice as they do, but it might produce data highly germane to questions about the nature of humanity, our place in the universe, and the possibility of some kind of survival of death.

Glossary

As there are a fair number of special usage terms in parapsychology, the following glossary, reproduced by permission of the *Journal of Parapsychology*, may be helpful. The definitions of most of the following terms have been borrowed or adapted from *A Glossary of Terms Used in Parapsychology* by Michael A. Thalbourne (1982). We highly recommend this book to those who seek a more complete glossary of parapsychological terms.

AGENT: In a test of GESP, the individual who looks at the information constituting the target and who is said to "send" or "transmit" that information to a percipient; in a test of telepathy and in cases of spontaneous ESP, the individual about whose mental states information is acquired by a percipient. The term is sometimes used to refer to the subject in a test of PK.

ANOMALOUS COGNITION (AC): A form of information transfer in which all known sensory stimuli are absent; that is, some individuals are able to gain access to information by an as yet unknown process; also known as *remote viewing (RV)* and *clairvoyance.*

ANOMALOUS PERTURBATION (AP): A form of interaction with matter in which all known physical mechanisms are absent; that is, some individuals are able to influence matter by an as yet unknown process; also known as *psychokinesis (PK).*

CALL: (As noun), the overt response made by the percipient in guessing the target in a test of ESP; (as verb), to make a response.

CLAIRVOYANCE: Paranormal acquisition of information about an object or contemporary physical event; in contrast to telepathy, the information is assumed to derive directly from an external physical source and not from the mind of another person.

CLOSED DECK: A procedure for generating the target order for each run, not by independent random selection of successive targets, but by randomization of a fixed set of targets (e.g., a deck of 25 ESP cards containing exactly five of each of the standard symbols).

CONFIDENCE CALL: A response the subject feels relatively certain is correct and indicates so before it is compared with its target.

CRITICAL RATIO (CR): A mathematical quantity used to decide whether the size of the observed deviation from chance in a psi test is significantly greater than the expected degree of random fluctuation about the average; it is obtained by dividing the observed deviation by the standard deviation; also called the *z statistic*.

Critical Ratio of Difference (CR_d): A critical ratio used to decide whether the numbers of hits obtained under two conditions (or by two groups of subjects) differ significantly from each other; it is obtained by dividing the difference between the two total-hits scores by the standard deviation of the difference.

DECLINE EFFECT: The tendency for high scores in a test of psi to decrease, either within a run, within a session, or over a longer period of time; may also be used in reference to the waning and disappearance of psi talent.

DIFFERENTIAL EFFECT: In an experiment where the subjects are tested under two different procedural conditions: (I) the tendency of subjects who score above chance in one condition to score below chance in the other; and vice versa; (II) the tendency of one condition to elicit psi-hitting from the group of subjects as a whole and the other condition to elicit psi-missing.

DISPLACEMENT: A form of ESP shown by a percipient who consistently obtains information about a target that is one or more removed, spatially or temporally, from the actual target designated for that trial.

Backward Displacement: Displacement in which the target extrasensorially cognized precedes the intended target by one, two, or more steps (designated as -1, -2, etc.).

Forward Displacement: Displacement in which the target actually responded to occurs later than the intended target by one, two, or more steps (designated as +1, +2, etc.).

ESP CARDS: Special cards, introduced by. J.B. Rhine, for use in tests of ESP; a standard pack contains 25 cards, each portraying one of five symbols, viz., circle, cross, square, star, and waves.

EXPERIMENTER EFFECT: An experimental outcome that results, not from manipulation of the variable of interest itself, but from some aspect of the experimenter's behavior; such as unconscious communication to the subjects, or possibly even a psi-mediated effect working in accord with the experimenter's desire or motivation.

EXTRASENSORY PERCEPTION (ESP): Paranormal cognition; the acquisition of information about an external event, object, or influence (mental or physical; past, present, or future) in some way other than through any of the known sensory channels.

FORCED-CHOICE TEST: Any test of ESP in which the percipient is required to make a response that is limited to a range of possibilities known in advance.

FREE-RESPONSE TEST: Any test of ESP in which the range of possible targets is relatively unlimited and is unknown to the percipient, thus permitting a free response to whatever impressions come to mind.

GANZFELD: Term for a special type of environment (or the technique for producing it) consisting of homogeneous, unpatterned sensory stimulation; an audiovisual ganzfeld may be accomplished by placing halved ping-pong balls over each eye of the subject, with diffused light (frequently red in hue) projected onto them from an external source, together with the playing of unstructured sounds (such as "pink noise") into the ears.

GENERAL EXTRASENSORY PERCEPTION (GESP): A noncommittal technical term used to refer to instances of ESP in which the information paranormally acquired may have derived either from another person's mind (i.e., as telepathy), or from a physical event or state of affairs (i.e., as clairvoyance), or even from both sources.

GOAL-ORIENTED: Term for the hypothesis that psi accomplishes a subject's or experimenter's objective as economically as possible, irrespective of the complexity of the physical system involved.

MACRO-PK: Any psychokinetic effect that does not require statistical analysis for its demonstration; sometimes used to refer to PK that has as its target a system larger than quantum mechanical processes, including microorganisms, dice, as well as larger objects.

MAJORITY VOTE TECHNIQUE (MV): The so-called repeated or multiple-guessing technique of testing for ESP. The symbol most frequently called by a subject (or a group of subjects) for a given target is used as the "majority-vote" response to that target on the theory that such a response is more likely to be correct than one obtained from a single call.

MEAN CHANCE EXPECTATION (MCE): The average (or "mean") number of hits, or the most likely score to be expected in a test of psi on the null hypothesis that nothing apart from chance is involved in the production of the score.

MICRO-PK: Any psychokinetic effect that requires statistical analysis for its demonstration. Sometimes used to refer to PK that has as its target a quantum mechanical system.

OPEN DECK: A procedure for generating a target order in which each successive target is chosen at random independently of all the others; thus, for example, in the case of a standard deck of ESP cards whose target order is "open deck," each type of symbol is not necessarily represented an equal number of times.

OUT-OF-THE-BODY EXPERIENCE (OBE): An experience, either spontaneous or induced, in which one's center of consciousness seems to be in a spatial location outside of one's physical body.

PARANORMAL: Term for any phenomenon that in one or more respects exceeds the limits of what is deemed physically possible according to current scientific assumptions.

PARAPSYCHOLOGY: The scientific study of certain paranormal or ostensibly paranormal phenomena, in particular, ESP and PK.

PERCIPIENT: The individual who experiences or "receives" an extrasensory influence or impression; also, one who is tested for ESP ability.

POLTERGEIST: A disturbance characterized by physical effects of ostensibly paranormal origin, suggesting mischievous or destructive intent. These phenomena include such events as the unexplained movement or breakage of objects, loud raps, electrical disturbances, and the lighting of fires.

POSITION EFFECT (PE): The tendency of scores in a test of psi to vary systematically according to the location of the trial on the record sheet.

PRECOGNITION: A form of ESP involving awareness of some future event that cannot be deduced from normally known data in the present.

PROCESS-ORIENTED: Term for research whose main objective is to determine how the occurrence of psi is related to other factors and variables.

PROOF-ORIENTED: Term for research whose main objective is to gain evidence for the existence of psi.

PSI: A general term used either as a noun or adjective to identify ESP or PK.

PSI-HITTING: The use of psi in such a way that the target at which the subject is aiming is "hit" (correctly responded to in a test of ESP, or influenced in a test of PK) more frequently than would be expected if only chance were operating.

PSI-MISSING: The use of psi in such a way that the target at which the subject is aiming is "missed" (responded to incorrectly in a test of ESP, or influenced in a direction contrary to aim in a test of PK) more frequently than would be expected if only chance were operating.

PSYCHOKINESIS (PK): Paranormal action; the influence of mind on a physical system that cannot be entirely accounted for by the mediation of any known physical energy.

RANDOM EVENT GENERATOR (REG): An apparatus (typically electronic) incorporating an element capable of generating a random sequence of outputs; used in automated tests of psi for generating target sequences; in tests of PK, it may itself be the target system that the subject is required to influence; also called a *random number* generator (RNG).

RECURRENT SPONTANEOUS PSYCHOKINESIS (RSPK): Expression for paranormal physical effects that occur repeatedly over a period of time; used especially as a technical term for poltergeist disturbances.

REMOTE VIEWING: A term for ESP used especially in the context of an experimental design wherein a percipient attempts to describe the surroundings of a geographically distant agent.

RESPONSE BIAS: The tendency to respond or behave in predictable, nonrandom ways.

RETROACTIVE PK: PK producing an effect backward in time; to say that event A was caused by retroactive PK is to say that A would not have happened in the way that it did had it not been for a later PK effort exerted so as to influence it; sometimes abbreviated as *retro-PK;* also referred to as *backward PK* or *time displaced PK.*

RUN: A fixed group of successive trials in a test of psi.

SHEEP-GOAT EFFECT (SGE): The relationship between one's acceptance of the possibility of ESP's occurrence under the given experimental conditions and the level of scoring actually achieved on that ESP test; specifically, the tendency for those who do not reject this possibility ("sheep") to score above chance and those who do reject it ("goats") to score below chance.

SPONTANEOUS CASE: Any psychic occurrence that takes place naturally, and is often unanticipated, in a real life situation, as opposed to the experimentally elicited psi phenomena of the laboratory.

STACKING EFFECT: A spuriously high (or low) score in a test of ESP when two or more percipients make guesses in relation to the same sequence of targets; it is due to a fortuitous relationship occurring between the guessing biases of the percipients and the peculiarities of the target sequence.

TARGET: In a test of ESP the object or event that the percipient attempts to identify through information paranormally acquired; in a test of PK, the physical system, or a prescribed outcome thereof, that the subject attempts to influence or bring about.

TELEPATHY: The paranormal acquisition of information about the thoughts, feelings, or activity of another conscious being.

TRIAL: An experimentally defined smallest unit of measurement in a test of psi: in a test of ESP it is usually associated with the attempt to gain information paranormally about a single target; in a test of PK, it is usually defined in terms of the single events to be influenced.

VARIANCE: A statistic for the degree to which a group of scores are scattered or dispersed around their average; formally, it is the average of the squared deviations from the mean; in parapsychology, the term is often used somewhat idiosyncratically to refer to the variance around the theoretical mean of a group of scores (e.g., MCE) rather than around the actual, obtained mean.

Run-Score Variance: The variance around the mean of the scores obtained on individual runs.

Subject-Variance: The variance around the mean of a subject's total score.

References

Aanstoos, C.M. (1986). Psi and the phenomenology of the long body. *Theta, 13-14*, 49-51.

Abbott, E.A. (1963). *Flatland: A Romance in Many Dimensions.* New York: Barnes and Noble.

Allen, G.W. (1967). *William James*. New York: Viking.

Anonymous (1927). Case of the will of Mr. James L. Chaffin. *Proceedings of the Society for Psychical Research, 36*, 517-24.

Anonymous (1985). *A Course in Miracles*. Tiburon, CA: Foundation for Inner Peace.

Assaily, A. (1963). Psychophysiological correlates of mediumship faculties. *International J. of Parapsychology, 5*, 357-574.

Atkins, P. (1992), Will science ever fail? *New Scientist, 8*(1833), 32-35.

Bacon, F. (1971). *Novum Organum*. Chicago: Encyclopaedia Britannica, Inc. (Original work published 1620.)

Balfour, G.W. (1935). A study of the psychological aspects of Mrs. Willett's mediumship, and the statements of the communicators concerning process. *Proceedings of the Society for Psychical Research, 43*, 41-318.

Basmajian, J. (1963). Control and training of individual motor units. *Science, 141*, 440-441.

Basmajian, J. (1972). Electromyography comes of age. *Science, 176*, 603-609.

Batcheldor, K. (1984). Contributions to the theory of PK induction from sitter-group work. *Journal of the Society for Psychical Research, 78*, 105-122.

Beloff, J. (1993). *Parapsychology: A Concise History*. London: Athlete.

Bem, D. & Honorton, C. (1994). Does psi exist? Replicable evidence for an anomalous process of information transfer. *Psychological Bulletin, 115*, 4-24.

Bennett, E. (1939). *Apparitions and Haunted Houses: A Survey of Evidence*. London: Faber & Faber.

Benor, D.J. (1990). Survey of spiritual healing research. *Complementary Medical Research, 4*, 9-32.

Berger, A. (1987). Three unrecognized problems in survival research. In *The Parapsychological Association 30th Annual Convention, Proceedings of Presented Papers*, Edinburgh University, 76-86.

Berger, A.S., Berger, J., Kalin-Deriso, V., & Roll, W.G., (1981). A majority vote test to open the Pratt lock. In W.G. Roll & J. Beloff (Eds.), *Research in Parapsychology 1980*. Metuchen, NJ: Scarecrow Press.

Bergson, H. (1935). *The Two Sources of Morality and Religion*. New York: Henry Holt and Company.

Berry, T. (1988). *The Dream of the Earth*. San Francisco, CA: Sierra Club Books.

Besant, A., & Leadbeater, C.W. (1951). *Occult Chemistry, 3rd edition*. Wheaton, IL: Theosophical Publishing House.

Bogart, G.C. (1992). Separating from a spiritual teacher. *Journal of Transpersonal Psychology, 24*, 1-21.

Bonaventura. (1953). *The Mind's Road to God*. Translated by George Boas. New York: The Liberal Arts Press. (Original work written 1259.)

Braud, W., Shafer, D., & Andrews, S. (1993a). Further studies of autonomic detection of remote staring: Replication, new control procedures, and personality correlates. *Journal of Parapsychology, 57*, 391-409.

Braud, W., Shafer, D., & Andrews, S. (1993b). Reactions to an unseen gaze (remote attention): A review, with new data on autonomic staring detection. *Journal of Parapsychology, 57*, 373-390.

Braud, W.G. (1975). Psi conducive states. *Journal of Communication, 25*, 142-152.

Braud, W.G. (1978). Psi conducive conditions: Explorations and interpretations. In B. Shapin and L. Coly (Eds.), *Psi and States of Awareness*. New York: Parapsychology Foundation, 1-41.

Braud, W.G. (1982a). Lability and inertia in psychic functioning. In B. Shapin & L. Coly (Eds.), *Concepts and Theories of Parapsychology*. New York: Parapsychology Foundation, 1-36.

Braud, W.G. (1982b). Nonevident psi. *Parapsychology Review, 13*(6), 16-18.

Braud, W.G. (1990-91). Implications and applications of laboratory psi findings. *European Journal of Parapsychology, 8*, 57-65.

Braud, W.G. (1993). On the use of living target systems in distant mental influence research. In B. Shapin & L. Coly (Eds.), *Psi Research Methodology: A Re-examination*. New York: Parapsychology Foundation, 149-188.

Braud, W.G. (1994a). Honoring our natural experiences. *Journal of the American Society for Psychical Research, 88*, 293-308.

Braud, W.G. (1994b). Reaching for consciousness: Expansions and complements. *Journal of the American Society for Psychical Research, 88*, 185-206.

Braud, W.G., & Jackson, J. (1983). Psi influence upon mental imagery. *Parapsychology Review, 14*, 13-15.

Braud, W.G., & Schlitz, M.J. (1989). A methodology for the objective study of transpersonal imagery. *Journal of Scientific Exploration, 3*, 43-63.

Braud, W.G., & Schlitz, M.J. (1991). Consciousness interactions with remote biological systems: Anomalous intentionality effects. *Subtle Energies, 2,* 1-46.

Braud, W.G., Honorton, C., Schlitz, M., Stanford, R., & Targ, R. (1991). Increasing psychic reliability. *Journal of Parapsychology, 55*, 59-83.

Braud, W.G., Shafer, D., McNeill, K., & Guerra, V. (1995). Attention focusing facilitated through remote mental interaction. *Journal of the American Society for Psychical Research*, *89,* 103-115.

Braude, S.E. (1979). *Esp And Psychokinesis: A Philosophical Examination.* Temple University Press.

Braude, S.E. (1987). Psi and our picture of the world. *Inquiry, 30*, 277-294.

Braude, S.E. (1989). Evaluating the super-psi hypothesis. In G.K. Zollschan, J.F. Schumaker, & G.F. Walsh (Eds), *Exploring the Paranormal: Perspectives On Belief and Experience.* Dorset: Prism, 25-38.

Braude, S.E. (1991). *First Person Plural: Multiple Personality and the Philosophy of Mind.* Routledge, 1991; revised edition, Rowman & Littlefield, 1995.

Braude, S.E. (1997). *The Limits of Influence: Psychokinesis and the Philosophy of Science*. Lanham, MD: University Press of America.

Brinkley, D., with Perry, P. (1994). *Saved by the Light*. New York: Villard.

Broad, C.D. (1953). *Religion, Philosophy and Psychical Research*. New York: Harcourt, Brace & Co.

Bruner, J. (1990). *Acts of Meaning*. Cambridge, MA: Cambridge University Press.

Buddhaghosa. (1923) *Visuddhimagga [The Path of Purity]*, 3 vols. Translated by M. Tim. London: Oxford University Press.

Carington, W. (1944). Experiments on the paranormal cognition of drawings, IV. *Proceedings for the Society for Psychical Research*, 47, 155-228.

Carington, W. (1945). *Thought Transference*. London: Methuen.

Cassirer, M. (1988). *Parapsychology and the UFO*. London: Author.

Clark, W.H. (1977). Parapsychology and religion. In B.B. Wolman et al. (Eds.), *Handbook of Parapsychology.* New York: Van Nostrand Reinhold, 769-780.

Cohen, J.M., & Phipps, J.F. (1992). *The Common Experience: Signposts on the Path to Enlightenment.* Wheaton, IL: Quest Books.

Coxeter, H.S.M. (1972). Cases of hyperdimensional awareness. In C. Muses & A.M. Young (Eds.), *Consciousness and Reality*. New York: Outerbridge & Lazard, 95-101.

Crookall, R. (1961a). *The Study and Practice of Astral Projection*. London: Aquarian Press.

Crookall, R. (1961b). *The Supreme Adventure*. London: James Clarke.

Crookall, R. (1964a). *More Astral Projections: Analyses of Case Histories*. London: Aquarian Press.

Crookall, R. (1964b). *The Techniques of Astral Projection*. London: Aquarian Press.

Crookall, R. (1972). *Case-book of Astral Projection*. Secaucus, NJ: University Books.

Csikszentmihalyi, M. (1993). *The Evolving Self: A Psychology For the Third Millennium*. New York: Harper-Collins.

de Vesme, Caesar (1931). *A History of Experimental Spiritualism, Vol. 1: Primitive Man*. London: Rider.

Dodds, E.R. (1980). *The Greeks and the Irrational*. Magnolia, MA: Peter Smith.

Dossey, L. (1993). *Healing Words: The Power of Prayer and the Practice of Medicine*. New York: Harper San Francisco.

Drewes, A.A., & Drucker, S.A. (1991). *Parapsychological Research with Children: An Annotated Bibliography*. Metuchen, NJ: Scarecrow Press.

Edge, H.L. (1980). Activity metaphysics and the survival problem. *Theta 8(3)*, 5-8.

Edge, H.L. (1994). *A Constructive Postmodern Perspective on Self and Community: From Atomism to Holism*. Lewiston, NY: The Edwin Mellen Press.

Edge, H., Morris, R., Palmer, J., & Rush, J. (1986). *Foundations of Parapsychology: Exploring the Boundaries of Human Capability*. Boston: Routledge & Kegan Paul.

Ehrenwald, J. (1974). Out-of-the-body experience and the denial of death. *Journal of Nervous and Mental Diseases*, 159, 227-233.

Eisenbud, J. (1970). *Psi and Psychoanalysis*. New York: Grune & Stratton.

Eisenbud, J. (1982). *Paranormal Foreknowledge: Problems and Perplexities*. New York: Human Sciences Press.

Eisenbud, J. (1983). *Parapsychology and the Unconscious*. Berkeley, CA: North Atlantic Books.

Erickson, C. (1976). *The Medieval Vision*. New York: Oxford University Press.

Evans, H. (1984). *Visions * Apparitions * Alien Visitors: A Cooperative Study of the Entity Enigma*. Wellingborough, Northamptonshire, England: Aquarian Press.

Evans, H. (1987). *Gods * Spirits * Cosmic Guardians: A Comparative Study of the Encounter Experience.* Wellingborough, Northamptonshire, England: Aquarian Press.

Fox, O. (1962). *Astral Projection: A Record of Out-of-the-Body Experiences.* New Hyde Park, NY: University Books.

Friedman, N. (1994). *Bridging Science and Spirit: Common Elements in David Bohm's Physics, the Perennial Philosophy, and Seth.* St. Louis: Living Lake Books.

Gabbard, G.O., & Twemlow, S.W. (1984). *With the Eyes of the Mind: an Empirical Analysis of Out-of-Body States.* New York: Praeger.

Gardner, M. (1983). *The Whys of a Philosophical Scrivener.* New York: William Morrow.

Gauld, A. (1968). Discarnate survival. In B. Wolman et al. (Eds.), *Handbook of Parapsychology.* New York: Van Nostrand Reinhold, 577-630.

Gauld, A. (1968). *The Founders of Psychical Research.* New York: Schocken.

Gauld, A. (1977). Discarnate survival. In B. Wolman et al. (Eds.) *Handbook of Parapsychology.* New York: Van Nostrand, Reinhold, 577-630.

Gauld, A. (1982). *Mediumship and Survival: A Century of Investigation.* London: Heinemann.

Gay, K., Salter, W.H., Thouless, R.H., Firebrace, R.H., Phillimore, M., & Sitwell, C. (1955). Report on the Oliver Lodge posthumous test. *Journal of the Society for Psychical Research, 38,* 121-134.

Grad, B. (1965). Some biological effects of laying-on of hands: A review of experiments with animals and plants. *Journal of American Society for Psychical Research, 59,* 95-127.

Green, C. & McCreery, C. (1975). *Apparitions.* London: Hamish Hamilton.

Green, C.E. (1968). *Out-of-the-Body Experiences.* Oxford: Institute of Psychophysical Research.

Griffin, D.R. (1993). Parapsychology and philosophy: A Whiteheadian postmodern perspective. *Journal of the American Society for Psychical Research, 87,* 217-288.

Grosso, M. (1985). *The Final Choice: Playing the Survival Game.* Walpole, NH: Stillpoint.

Grosso, M. (1992). *Frontiers of the Soul.* Wheaton: Quest Books.

Grosso, M. (1994). *The Millennium Myth.* Wheaton: Quest Books.

Gurney, E., & Myers, F.W.H. (1888-89). On apparitions occurring soon after death. *Proceedings of the Society for Psychical Research, 5,* 403-485.

Gurney, E., Myers, F.W.H., & Podmore, F. (1886). *Phantasms of the Living,* 2 vols. London: Trubner.

Hadden, R.W. (1994). *On the Shoulders of Merchants.* Albany, NY: SUNY Press.

Harary, K., & Solfvin, G. (1977). A study of out-of-body experiences using auditory targets. In J.D. Morris, W.G. Roll, & R.L. Morris (Eds.), *Research in Parapsychology 1976.* Metuchen, NJ: Scarecrow Press.

Harary, K. & Weintraub, P. (1989). *Have an Out-of-Body Experience in 30 Days: The Free Flight Program.* New York: St. Martin's Press.

Hardy, A. (1979). *The Spiritual Nature of Man.* Oxford, England: Clarendon Press.

Hart, H. (1959). *The Enigma of Survival.* Springfield, IL: Charles C. Thomas.

Hastings, A. (1991). *With the Tongues of Men and Angels: A Study of Channeling.* Fort Worth, TX: Holt, Rinehart and Winston.

Haynes, R. (1982). *The Society for Psychical Research, 1882-1982.* London: Macdonald.

Heywood, R. (1976). Illusion or what? *Theta, 4,* 5-10.

Hodgson, R. (1892). A record of observations of certain phenomena of trance. *Proceedings of the Society for Psychical Research, 8,* 1-167.

Hodgson, R. (1898). A further record of observations of certain phenomena of trance. *Proceedings of the Society for Psychical Research, 13,* 284-582.

Hoffman, E. (1992). *Visions of Innocence: Spiritual and Inspirational Experiences of Childhood.* Boston: Shambhala.

Honorton, C. (1977). Psi and internal attention states. In B. Wolman et al. (Eds.), *Handbook of Parapsychology.* New York: Van Nostrand Reinhold, 435-472.

Hughes, D. (1990). Change in brainwave activity during trance channeling: A pilot study. *Journal of Transpersonal Psychology, 22*(2), 175-189.

Hughes, D. (1992). Differences between trance channeling and multiple personality disorder on structured interview. *Journal of Transpersonal Psychology, 24*(2), 181-192.

Hyslop, J.H. (1905). The mental state of the dead. *The World Today,* Jan., 1-5.

Hyslop, J.H. (1908). *Psychical Research and the Resurrection.* Boston: Small, Maynard.

Inglis, B. (1977). *Natural and Supernatural.* London: Hodder and Stoughton.

Inglis, B., with West, R. (1989). *The Unknown Guest.* London: Coronet. (Original work published 1987.)

Irwin, H. (1985). *Flight of Mind: A Psychological Study of the Out-of-Body Experience.* Metuchen, NJ: Scarecrow Press.

Jacobson, N.O. (1973). *Life without Death?* New York: Dell.

Jaffe, A. (1979). *Apparitions: An Archetypal Approach to Death, Dreams, and Ghosts.* Irving, TX: Spring.

James, W. (1909). Report on Mrs. Piper's Hodgson-control. *Proceedings of the Society for Psychical Research*, *23*, 2-121.

James, W. (1914). *The Varieties of Religious Experience: A Study in Human Nature.* New York: Longmans, Green & Co.

James, W. (1929). *The Varieties of Religious Experience.* New York: Modern Library.

James, W. (1967). Conclusions [to The varieties of religious experience]. In J.J. McDermott, *The Writings of William James.* New York: The Modern Library, 758-782.

Jeans, J. (1930). *The Mysterious Universe.* New York: Macmillan.

Jung, C.G., & Pauli, W. (1955). *The Interpretation of Nature and the Psyche: Synchronicity and the Influence of Archetypal Ideas on the Scientific Theories of Kepler.* New York: Pantheon Books.

Kastenbaum, R. (1979). Death through the retroscopic lens. In R. Kastenbaum (Ed.), *Between Life and Death.* New York: Springer, 156-84.

Kastenbaum, R. (1984). *Is There Life after Death?* New York: Prentice-Hall.

Keller, E.F. (1983). *A Feeling for the Organism: The Life and Work of Barbara McClintock.* New York: W.H. Freeman.

Kennedy, J.E., Kanthamani, H., & Palmer, J. (1994). Health, well-being, meaning in life, absorption, temporal lobe systems, and psychic and spiritual experiences. *Proceedings of Presented Papers: The 37th Annual Convention of the Parapsychological Association*, 190-203.

Kimbrell, A. (1993). *The Human Body Shop: The Engineering and Marketing of Life.* San Francisco: Harper San Francisco.

Klimo, J. (1987). *Channeling: Investigations on Receiving Information from Paranormal Sources.* Los Angeles: J.T. Tarcher.

Krippner, S. (1977, 1978, 1982). *Advances in Parapsychological Research,* Vols. 1, 2, 3. New York: Plenum.

Krippner, S. (1984, 1987, 1990). *Advances in Parapsychological Research*, Vols. 4, 5, 6. Jefferson, NC: McFarland.

Kurtz, P. (1985). *A Skeptic's Handbook of Parapsychology.* Buffalo, NY: Prometheus.

Landau, L. (1963). An unusual out-of-body experience. *Journal of Society for Psychical Research, 42*, 126-28.

LeShan, L. (1974). *The Medium, the Mystic, and the Physicist: Toward a General Theory of the Paranormal.* New York: Viking.

Lipsyte, R. (1975). *Sportsworld.* New York: Quadrangle/New York Times.

Lodge, Oliver (1909). *Man and the Universe.* London, Methuen.

Lukoff, D. , Turner, R. & Lu, F. (1993). Transpersonal psychology research review: Psychospiritual dimensions of healing. *Journal of Transpersonal Psychology, 25*, 11-28.

Mack, J.E. (1994). *Abduction: Human Encounters with Aliens*. New York: Scribner's.

MacKenzie, B. & MacKenzie, S.L. (1980). Whence the enchanted boundary? Sources and significance of the parapsychological tradition. *Journal of Parapsychology, 44*, 125-166.

Mansfield, V. (1991). Looking into mind: An undergraduate course. *Journal of Transpersonal Psychology, 23*, 53-64.

Maslow, A.H. (1968). *Toward a Psychology of Being*. New York: Van Nostrand.

Matthews, W.B. (n.d.). *The Churches and Psychical Research*.

McKenzie, A.E.E. (1960). *The Major Achievements of Science*. Cambridge: Cambridge University Press.

McMoneagle, J. (1993). *Mind Trek: Exploring Consciousness, Time, and Space Through Remote Viewing*. Norfolk, VA: Hampton Roads.

Merchant, C. (1980). *The Death of Nature: Women, Ecology, and the Scientific Revolution.* New York: Harper & Row.

Midgley, M. (1992). Can science save its soul? *New Scientist, 1*(1832), 24-27.

Mishlove, J. (1994). Intuition: The source of true knowing. *Noetic Sciences Review,* Spring, 31-36.

Mishra, R. (1967). *The Textbook of Yoga Psychology.* New York: Julian Press.

Mitchell, E.D. (1974). Introduction. In E.D. Mitchell & J. White, (Eds.), *Psychic Exploration: A Challenge to Science.* New York: Putnam.

Mitchell, J. (1978). Out-of-the-body vision. In D.S. Rogo (Ed.), *Mind Beyond the Body: The Mystery of ESP Projection.* Middlesex, England: Penguin Books.

Monod, J. (1972). *Chance and Necessity: An Essay on the Natural Philosophy of Modern Biology.* New York: Vintage Books.

Monroe, R.A. (1971). *Journeys Out of the Body.* Garden City: Anchor Books.

Monroe, R.A. (1985). *Far Journeys.* New York: Doubleday.

Monroe, R.A. (1994). *Ultimate Journey.* New York: Doubleday.

Moody, R. (1976). *Life After Life.* Harrisburg, PA: Stackpole.

Moody, R., with Perry, P. (1993). *Reunions.* New York: Villard.

Moody, R., with Perry, P. (1993). *Visionary Encounters with Departed Loved Ones.* New York: Villard.

Morris, R.L., Harary, K., Janis, J., Hartwell, J., & Roll, R.W. (1978). Studies in communication during out-of-body experiences. *Journal of American Society of Psychical Research, 72*, 1-22.

Muldoon, S., & Carrington, H. (1951). *The Phenomena of Astral Projection*. London: Rider.

Muldoon, S., & Carrington, H. (1956). *The Projection of the Astral Body*. London: Rider.

Murphy, G. (1961). *Challenge of Psychical Research*. New York: Harper & Row.

Murphy, M. (1992). *The Future of the Body: Explorations into the Further Evolution of Human Nature*. Los Angeles: Tarcher.

Murphy, M. & White, R. (1995). *In the Zone: Transcendent Experience in Sports*. New York: Penguin/Arkana.

Myers. F.W.H. (1903/Reprint 1954). *Human Personality and its Survival of Bodily Death,* 2 vols. London: Longman, Green.

Nash, C.B. (1958). Correlation between ESP and religious value. *Journal of Parapsychology, 22,* 204-209.

Neher, A. (1980). *The Psychology of Transcendence*. Englewood Cliffs, NJ: Prentice-Hall.

Nelson, P.L. (1990). The technology of the praeternatural: An empirically based model of transpersonal experiences. *Journal of Transpersonal Psychology, 22*, 35-50.

Noyes, R., Jr. (1972). The experience of dying. *Psychiatry*, 35, 174-184.

Obeyesekere, G. (1981). *Medusa's Hair*. Chicago: University of Chicago Press.

Osis, K. (1978). Out-of-body research at the American Society for Psychical Research. In D.S. Rogo (Ed.), *Mind Beyond the Body: The Mystery of ESP Projection*. Middlesex, England: Penguin Books.

Osis, K. (1986). Apparitions old and new. In K.R. Rao (Ed.), *Case Studies in Parapsychology: Papers Presented in Honor of Dr. Louisa E. Rhine*. Jefferson, NC: McFarland, 74-86.

Osis, K. & Haraldsson, E. (1986). *At the Hour of Death*. Rev. ed. New York: Hastings House.

Osis, K. & McCormick, D. (1980). Kinetic effects at the ostensible location of an OB projection during perceptual testing. *Research in Parapsychology 1979*. Metuchen, NJ: Scarecrow Press, 142-145.

Owen, I. & Sparrow, M. (1977). *Conjuring Up Philip*. New York: Pocket Books.

Palmer, J., & Lieberman, R. (1975). The influence of psychological set on ESP and out-of-body experiences. *Journal of the American Society for Psychical Research*, *69*, 193-213.

Persinger, M.A. (1993). Geophysical variables and behavior: LXXI. Differential contribution of geomagnetic activity to paranormal experiences concerning death and crisis: An alternative to the ESP hypothesis. *Perceptual and Motor Skills*, 76, 555-562.

Phillips, S.M. (1980). *Extrasensory Perception of Quarks*. Wheaton, IL: Theosophical Publishing House.

Piddington, J.G. (1908). A series of concordant automatisms. *Proceedings of the Society for Psychical Research*, *22*, 19-416.

Piddington, J.G. (1918). Fresh light on the "one-horse dawn" experiment. *Proceedings of the Society for Psychical Research, 30*, 175-229.

Pinker, S. (1994). *The Language Instinct.* New York: William Morrow and Company.

Prabhavananda, S., & Isherwood, C. (1953). *How to Know God: The Yoga Aphorisms of Patanjali.* New York: New American Library.

Price, H.H. (1939). Some philosophical questions about telepathy and clairvoyance. *Philosophy*, *15*, 363-374.

Price, H.H. (1940). Haunting and the "psychic ether" hypothesis: With some preliminary reflections on the present condition and possible future of psychical research. *Proceedings of the Society for Psychical Research*, *45*, 307-343.

Radhakrishnan, S. (1992). *Indian Philosophy*, 2 vols. (centenary edition). Delhi: Oxford University Press. (Original work published 1923.)

Rao, K.R. (1977). On the nature of psi. *Journal of Parapsychology, 41*, 294-351.

Rao, K.R. (1988). Psychology of transcendence. In A.C. Paranjpe, D.Y.F. Ho & R.W. Rieber (Eds.), *Asian Contributions to Psychology.* New York: Praeger, 123-148.

Rao, K.R. & Palmer, J. (1987). The anomaly called psi: Recent research and criticism. *Behavioral and Brain Sciences, 10*, 539-555.

Raudive, K. (1971). *Breakthrough.* New York: Taplinger.

Reed, G. (1988), *The Psychology of Anomalous Experiences: A Cognitive Approach* (rev. ed.). Buffalo, NY: Prometheus Books.

Rhine, J.B. (1934). *Extra-sensory Perception.* Boston: Boston Society for Psychic Research.

Rhine, J.B. (1945). Parapsychology and religion. *Journal of Parapsychology, 9,* 1-4.

Rhine, J.B. (1947). *The Reach of the Mind.* New York: William Sloane Associates.

Rhine, J.B. (1951). From miracle to experiment. In A.J. Smith, *Religion and the New Psychology.* New York: Doubleday, 13-22.

Rhine, J.B. (1953). *New World of the Mind.* New York: William Sloane Associates.

Rhine, J.B. (1973). Can Parapsychology Help Religion? Paper presented at the Spiritual Frontiers Fellowship Convention, Chicago, 1973.

Rhine, J.B. (1975). The parapsychology of religion: A new branch of inquiry. In *The Centrality of Science and Absolute Values: Proceedings of the Fourth International Conference of the Unity of Science.* New York: The International Cultural Foundation, Inc., 585-596.

Rhine, J.B. & Rhine, L.E. (1978). A search for the nature of the mind. In T.S. Krawiec (Ed.), *The Psychologists*, Vol. 3. Brandon, VT: Clinical Psychology Publishing Company, 181-206.

Rhine, L.E. (1957a). Hallucinatory psi experiences: II. The initiative of the percipient in hallucinations of the living, the dying, and the dead. *Journal of Parapsychology, 21*, 13-46.

Rhine, L.E. (1957b). Hallucinatory psi experiences: III. The intention of the agent and the dramatizing tendency of the percipient. *Journal of Parapsychology, 21*, 186-226.

Rhine, L.E. (1961). *Hidden Channels of the Mind.* New York: William Morrow.

Rhine, L.E. (1977). Research methods with spontaneous cases. In B. Wolman et al. (Eds.), *Handbook of Parapsychology*. New York: Van Nostrand, Reinhold, 59-80.

Ring, K. (1984). *Heading Toward Omega: In Search of the Meaning of the Near-death Experience*. New York: William Morrow.

Ring, K. (1989a). Near-death and UFO encounters as shamanic initiations: Some conceptual and evolutionary implications. *ReVision, 11*(3), 14-22.

Ring, K. (1989b). Toward an imaginal interpretation of "UFO abductions." *ReVision, 11*(4), 17-24.

Ring, K. (1992). *The Omega Project: Near-death Experience, UFO Encounters, and Mind at Large*. New York: William Morris.

Roberts, J. (1975). *The Nature of Personal Reality*. Englewood Cliffs, NJ: Prentice-Hall.

Rogo, D.S., & Bayless, R. (1979). *Phone Calls from the Dead.* Englewood Cliffs, NJ: Prentice-Hall.

Rojcewicz, P.M. (1986). The extraordinary encounter continuum hypothesis and its implications for the study of belief materials. *Folklore Forum, 19*, 131-152.

Roll, W. (1975). *Theory and Experiment in Psychical Research*. New York: Arno Press.

Roll, W.G. (1976). *The Poltergeist.* Metuchen, NJ: Scarecrow Press.

Roll, W.G. (1981). A majority vote test to open the Pratt lock. In W.G. Roll and J. Beloff (Eds.), *Research in Parapsychology, 1980.* Metuchen, NJ: Scarecrow Press.

Roll, W.G. (1982). The changing perspective on life after death. In S. Krippner (Ed.), *Advances in Parapsychological Research*, Vol. 3. New York and London: Plenum Press, 147-291.

Roll, W.G. (1985). Will personality and consciousness survive the death of the body? An examination of parapsychological findings suggestive of survival. Ph.D. dissertation, University of Utrecht.

Roll, W.G. (1989). *This World or That.* Sweden: Lund.

Roll, W.G., & Harary, K. (1976). Target responses during out-of-body experiences. *Journal of Parapsychology, 40*, 53.

Roll, W.G., & Lagle, J. (1987). *The Case of Georgia Rudolph.* Unpublished manuscript.

Roll, W.G., & Braun, B.A. (1995). Psychomanteum research: A Pilot Study. *Proceedings of Presented Papers: 38th Annual Convention of the Parapsychological Assoication*, pp. 438-443.

Rucker, R. (1984). *The Fourth Dimension: Toward a Geometry of Higher Reality.* Boston: Houghton Mifflin Company.

Salter, W.H. (1958). F.W.H. Myers's posthumous message. *Proceedings of the Society for Psychical Research, 52*, 1-32.

Saltmarsh, H.F. (1929). A report on the investigation of some sittings with Mrs. Warren Elliott. *Proceedings of the Society for Psychical Research, 39*, 47-184.

Schmidt, H. (1974). Psychokinesis. In E.D. Mitchell & J. White (Eds.), *Psychic Exploration: A Challenge for Science.* New York: Putnam, 179-193.

Shannon, W.H. (1992). *Silent Lamp: The Thomas Merton Story.* New York: Crossroads.

Sheilds, E. (1976). Severely mentally retarded children's psi ability [Summary]. In W.G. Roll (Ed.), *Research in Parapsychology 1976.* Metuchen, NJ: Scarecrow Press.

Sidgwick, E.M. (1915). A contribution to the study of the psychology of Mrs. Piper's trance phenomena. *Proceedings of the Society for Psychical Research, 28*, 1-657.

Sidgwick, E.M. (Mrs. H.) (1885). Notes on the evidence, collected by the Society, for phantasms of the dead. *Proceedings of the Society for Psychical Research, 3*, 69-150.

Siegel, R.K. (1980). The psychology of life after death. *American Psychologist, 35,* 911-931.

Simon, N. (1989). Making management decisions: The role of intuition and emotions. In W. Agor (Ed.), *Intuition in Organizations.* Newbury Park, CA: Sage Publications.

Sirag, S.P. (1993). Consciousness: A Hyperspace View. In J. Mishlove, *The Roots of Consciousness*, 2nd ed. Tulsa, OK: Council Oak, 1993, appendix.

Smith, A.J. (1951). *Religion and the New Psychology.* New York: Doubleday.

Smith, E.L. (1982). *Occult Chemistry Re-evaluated.* Wheaton, IL: Theosophical Publishing House.

Smith, H. (1992). *Beyond the Post-modern Mind.* Wheaton, IL: Theosophical Publishing House.

Solfvin, J. (1984). Mental healing. In S. Krippner (Ed.), *Advances in Parapsychological Research*, Vol. 4. Jefferson, NC: McFarland, 31-63.

Stanford, R.G. (1977). Experimental psychokinesis: A review from diverse perspectives. In B.B. Wolman et al. (Eds.), *Handbook of Parapsychology.* New York: Van Nostrand Reinhold, 324-381.

Stanford, R.G. (1987). Ganzfeld and hypnotic-induction procedures in ESP research: Toward understanding their success. In S. Krippner (Ed.), *Advances in Parapsychological Research*, Vol. 5. Jefferson, NC: McFarland, 39-76.

Stevenson, I. (1973a). Carington's psychon theory as applied to cases of the reincarnation type: A reply to Gardner Murphy. *Journal of the American Society for Psychical Research*, *67*, 130-146.

Stevenson, I. (1973b). A communicator of the "drop-in" type in France: The case of Robert Marie. *Journal of the American Society for Psychical Research, 67,* 47-76.

Stevenson, I. (1974). *Twenty Cases Suggestive of Reincarnation*, 2nd ed. Charlottesville: University Press of Virginia.

Stevenson, I. (1975-1983). *Cases of the Reincarnation Type*. 4 vols. Charlottesville: University Press of Virginia.

Stevenson, I. (1975). *Cases of the Reincarnation Type*, Vol. 1: *Ten Cases in India.* Charlottesville: University Press of Virginia.

Stevenson, I. (1977). *Cases of the Reincarnation Type*, Vol. 2: *Ten Cases of Sri Lanka.*

Reincarnation: Field studies and theoretical issues. In B.B. Wolman et al. (Eds.), *Handbook of Parapsychology.* New York: Van Nostrand Reinhold, 631-663.

Stevenson, I. (1980). *Cases of the Reincarnation Type*, Vol. 3: *Twelve cases in Lebanon and Turkey.* Charlottesville: University Press of Virginia.

Stevenson, I. (1987). *Children Who Remember Previous Lives*. Charlottesville: University Press of Virginia.

Stevenson, I. & Samararatne, G. (1988). Three new cases of the reincarnation type in Sri Lanka with written records made before verifications. *Journal of Scientific Exploration*, 2(2), 217-238.

Stillings, D. (1989a). *Cyberbiological Studies of the Imaginal Component in the UFO Contact Experience.* St. Paul, MN: Archaeus Project.

Stillings, D. (1989b). Helicopters, UFOs, and the psyche. *ReVision*, *11*(4), 25-32.

Stockton, B. (1989). *Catapult: The Biography of Robert A. Monroe.* Norfolk, VA: Donning.

Swann, I. (1993). Unpublished report. SRI International.

Taimni, I.K. (1961). *The Science of Yoga.* Wheaton, IL: Theosophical Publishing House.

Targ, R. & Harary, K. (1984). *The Mind Race: Understanding and Using Psychic Abilities.* New York: Villard Books.

Targ, R., & Puthoff, H.E. (1977). *Mind Reach: Scientists Look at Psychic Ability.* New York: Delacorte.

Tart, C. (1967). A second psychophysiological study of out-of-the-body experiences in a gifted subject. *International Journal of Parapsychology, 9,* 251-258.

Tart, C. (1968). A psychophysiological study of out-of-the-body experiences in a selected subject. *Journal of the American Society for Psychical Research, 62,* 3-27.

Tart, C. (1972). States of consciousness and state-specific sciences. *Science, 176,* 1203-1210.

Tart, C. (Ed.)(1975). *Transpersonal Psychologies.* New York: Harper & Row.

Tart, C. (1976). *Learning to Use Extrasensory Perception.* Chicago: University of Chicago Press.

Tart, C. (1977). *Psi: Scientific Studies of the Psychic Realm.* New York: E.P. Dutton.

Tart, C. (1979). An emergent-interactionist understanding of human consciousness. In B. Shapin & L. Coly (Eds.), *Brain/Mind and Parapsychology.* New York: Parapsychology Foundation, 177-200.

Tart, C. (1979). Science and the sources of value. *Phoenix: New Directions in the Study of Man, 3,* 25-29.

Tart, C. (1981). Transpersonal realities or neurophysiological illusions? Toward a dualistic theory of consciousness. In R. Valle & R. von Eckartsberg (Eds.), *The Metaphors of Consciousness.* New York: Plenum, 199-222.

Tart, C. (1982). The controversy about psi: Two psychological theories. *Journal of Parapsychology, 46,* 313-320.

Tart, C. (1984). Acknowledging and dealing with the fear of psi. *Journal of the American Society for Psychical Research, 78,* 133-143.

Tart, C. (1986a). Psychics' fear of psychic powers. *Journal of the American Society for Psychical Research, 80,* 279-292.

Tart, C. (1986b). *Waking Up: Overcoming the Obstacles to Human Potential.* Boston: New Science Library.

Tart, C. (1987). On the scientific study of other worlds. In D. Weiner & R. Nelson (Eds.), *Research in Parapsychology 1986.* Metuchen, NJ: Scarecrow Press, 145.

Tart, C. (1988). Is searching for a soul inherently unscientific? *Behavioral and Brain Sciences, 10*(4) 612-613.

Tart, C. (1991). Adapting Eastern teachings to Western Culture: A discussion with Shinzen Young. *Journal of Transpersonal Psychology, 22,* 149-165.

Tart, C. (1994). *Living the Mindful Life.* Boston: Shambhala.

Tart, C. & Deikman, A. (1991). Mindfulness, spiritual seeking and psychotherapy. *Journal of Transpersonal Psychology, 23,* 29-52.

Tart, C. & LaBore, C. (1986). Attitudes toward strongly functioning psi: A preliminary study. *Journal of the American Society for Psychical Research, 80,* 163-173.

Thalbourne, M. (1982). *A Glossary of Terms Used in Parapsychology.* London: William Heinemann Ltd.

Thomas, C.D. (1928-29). The modus operandi of trance-communication according to descriptions received through Mrs. Osborne Leonard. *Proceedings of the Society for Psychical Research, 38,* 49-100.

Thouless, R.H. (1984). Do we survive bodily death? *Proceedings of the Society for Psychical Research, 57,* 1-52.

Toynbee, A. (1956). *An American's Approach to Religion.* London: Oxford University Press.

Twigg, E., with Brod, R.H. (1972). *Ena Twigg: Medium.* New York: Hawthorn.

Tyrrell, G.N.M. (1938/1961). *Science and Psychical Phenomena.* New York: University Books.

Tyrrell, G.N.M. (1942/1961). *Apparitions.* New York: University Books.

Tyrrell, G.N.M. (1947). The modus operandi of paranormal cognition. *Proceedings of the Society for Psychical Research*, 48, 65-120.

Underhill, E. (1969). *Mysticism: A Study in the Nature and Development of Man's Spiritual Consciousness.* Cleveland, OH: World Publishing Company. (Original work published 1911.)

Vaughan, F. (1991). Spiritual issues in psychotherapy. *Journal of Transpersonal Psychology, 23*, 105-120.

Verrall, A.W. (1901-03). Notes on the trance phenomena of Mrs. Thompson. *Proceedings of the Society for Psychical Research, 17*, 164-244.

Vigne, J. (1991). Guru and psychotherapist: Comparisons from the Hindu tradition. *Journal of Transpersonal Psychology, 23*, 121-138.

Vivekananda, S. (1955). *Raja Yoga.* New York: Ramakrishna-Vivekananda Center.

Walker, E.W. (1975). Foundations of paraphysical and parapsychological phenomena. In L. Oteri (Ed.), *Quantum Physics and Parapsychology* (pp. 1-53). New York: Parapsychology Foundation.

Walsh, R. & Vaughan, F. (1993). The art of transcendence: An introduction to common elements of transpersonal practices. *Journal of Transpersonal Psychology, 25*, 1-10.

Weinberg, S. (1974). Reflections of a working scientist. *Daedalus, 103*(3), 42.

Weinberg, S. (1977). *The First Three Minutes: A Modern View of the Origin of the Universe.* New York: Basic Books.

Wheatley, J.M.O. & Edge, H.L. (Eds.) (1976). *Philosophical Dimensions of Parapsychology.* Springfield, IL: Charles C. Thomas.

White, F.D. (1987). *The Overview Effect: Space Exploration and Human Evolution.* Boston: Houghton Mifflin.

White, R.A. (1982) An analysis of ESP phenomena in the saints. *Parapsychology Review, 13* (1), 15-18.

White, R.A. (1992). *The Sacralization of Everyday Life: Projects of Transcendence.* Unpublished manuscript, SUNY Stony Brook, Department of Sociology.

White, R.A. (1993a). A dynamic view of psi experience: By their fruits ye shall know them. *Proceedings of Presented Papers: The 36th Annual Convention of the Parapsychological Association*, 285-297.

White, R.A. (1993b, January). The inward Olympics: On finding ways to deepen consciousness to touch the self we all are. Paper given at the III International Symposium on Science and Consciousness, Olympia, Greece.

White, R.A. (1993c). Review essay 2: Acts of Meaning by Jerome Bruner: A call to psychology and parapsychology. *Exceptional Human Experience, 11*, 5-13.

White, R.A. (1994). Exceptional human experiences: The generic connection. *ASPR Newsletter*, *18*(3), 1-6.

Wilber, K. (1990). *Eye to Eye: The Quest for the New Paradigm.* Boston: Shambhala.

Wirz, P. (1966). Katagarama: The Holiest Place in Ceylon (D.B. Pralle, Trans.). Colombo: Lake House Publishers.

Wittgenstein, L. (1961). *Tractatus Logico-philosophicus.* London: Routledge & Kegan Paul.

Wolman, B. (1977). *Handbook of Parapsychology.* New York: Van Nostrand Reinhold.

Index

Hampton Roads Publishing Company
publishes and distributes books on a variety of subjects,
including metaphysics, health, complementary medicine,
visionary fiction, and other related topics.

To order or receive a copy of our latest catalog, call toll-free,
(800) 766-8009, or send your name and address to:

Hampton Roads Publishing Company, Inc.
134 Burgess Lane
Charlottesville, VA 22902